Research
Methodology

Research
Methodology
A STEP-BY-STEP GUIDE FOR BEGINNERS

Ranjit Kumar

SAGE Publications
London • Thousand Oaks • New Delhi

First published 1996
by Addison Wesley Longman Australia Pty Limited

Sage Publications edition 1999

 SAGE Publications Ltd
6 Bonhill Street
London EC2A 4PU

SAGE Publications Inc
2455 Teller Road
Thousand Oaks, California 91320

SAGE Publications India Pvt Ltd
32, M-Block Market
Greater Kailash - I
New Delhi 110 048

British Library Cataloguing in Publication data

A catalogue record for this book is available from the British Library

ISBN 0 7619 6213 1
ISBN 0 7619 6214 X (pbk)

Library of Congress catalog record available

Designed by Melissa Fraser
Typeset in 10.5pt Plantin
Printed in Malaysia

Contents

Preface

This book is based upon my experiences as a research student, practitioner, and teacher. The difficulties I faced in understanding research as a student, my discoveries about what was applicable and inapplicable in the field as a practitioner, and my development of the ability to communicate difficult concepts in simple language without sacrificing technicality and accuracy as a teacher, have become the basis of this book.

Research methodology is taught as a supporting subject in several ways in many academic disciplines such as health, education, psychology, social work, nursing, public health, library studies and marketing research. The core philosophical base for this book comes from my conviction that although these disciplines vary in content, their broad approach to a research inquiry is similar. This book, therefore, is addressed to these academic disciplines.

It is true that some disciplines place greater emphasis on quantitative research and some, on qualitative. My own approach to research is a combination of both. Firstly, the objective decides whether a study should be carried out adopting a qualitative or a quantitative approach. Secondly, in real life most research is a combination of both methods. In a study, some aspects may be qualitative, and others, quantitative. This book, therefore, has been written to provide information in a systematic way about methods, procedures, and techniques that are applicable to both approaches, though heavily slanted towards quantitative research.

Research as a subject is taught at different levels. The book is designed specifically for students who are newcomers to research, and who may have a psychological barrier with regard to the subject. I have therefore not assumed any knowledge on the part of the reader; I have omitted detailed discussion of aspects that may be inappropriate for beginners; I have used many flow charts and examples to communicate concepts; and areas covered in the book follow a 'simple to complex' approach in terms of their discussion.

The structure of this book, which is based on the teaching model developed during my teaching career, is designed to be practical. The text of the book is therefore organised around the operational steps in the research process. All the information needed to take a particular step is provided in one place. Each chapter is devoted to a particular aspect of that step. For example, 'formulating a research problem' is the first operational step in the research process. For this you need to know about reviewing literature, formulating a research problem, identifying variables, and constructing hypotheses. Hence, under this step, the four chapters are: 'Reviewing literature', 'Formulating a research problem', 'Identifying variables', and 'Constructing hypotheses'. At each step, a smorgasbord of methods, models, and procedures is provided so the most appropriate one can be selected.

It is my belief that a sound knowledge of research methodology is essential for undertaking a study. Up to the process of data collection, a knowledge of research methods is crucial. Statistics and computers play a significant role in research but their application is mainly after the data has been collected. To me, statistics are useful in confirming or contradicting conclusions drawn from analysed data, in providing an indication of the magnitude of the relationship between two or more variables under study, in helping to establish causality, and in ascertaining the level of confidence that can be placed in your findings. A computer's application is primarily in data analysis, the calculation of statistics, word processing, and the graphic presentation of data, where it saves time and makes it easier for you. This book does not include statistics or information about computers.

I am grateful to a number of people who have helped me in the writing of this book. I am immensely thankful to Dr Norma Watson, who has put enormous effort into editing this book and in providing valuable comments on its contents. I would not have been able to complete the task without her unqualified help. I dedicate this book to her as a token of my gratitude.

My students have taught me how to teach research. This book is an outcome of the feedback I have received from them over the years. How, and at what stage, a concept should be taught, I have learnt from my students. I thankfully acknowledge their contribution to this book.

I will fail in expressing my thanks if I do not mention Ron Harper and Carmen Riordan of Addison Wesley Longman. Ron for his encouragement and support in the publication of this book and Carmen for her efforts, care and co-operation in editing.

I also thank Dr Denis Ladbrook, who has reviewed some of the chapters and given valuable suggestions. My thanks also to Mrs Anne Blanchard who, as Head of School, provided every facility and encouragement to complete this book.

Ranjit Kumar

Tables

Figures

1

Research: a way of thinking

Research: a way of thinking

Research is undertaken within most professions. More than a set of skills, research is a way of thinking: examining critically the various aspects of your profession; understanding and formulating guiding principles that govern a particular procedure; and developing and testing new theories for the enhancement of your profession. It is a habit of questioning about what you do, and empirical examination to find answers, with a view to instituting appropriate changes for a more effective professional service. Let us take some disciplines as examples.

Suppose you are working in the field of health. You might be a front-line service provider, supervisor, or health administrator/planner. You may be in a hospital or working as an out-reach community health worker. You may be a nurse, doctor, occupational therapist, physiotherapist, social worker or other paramedic. In any of these positions, some of the following questions may come to mind:

- How many patients do I see every day?
- What are some of the most common conditions prevalent among my patients?
- What are the causes of these conditions?
- Why do some people have a particular condition whereas others do not?
- What are the health needs of the community?
- Why do some people use the service while others do not?
- What do people think about the service?
- How satisfied are patients with the service?
- How effective is the service?
- How can the service be improved?

You can add many other questions to this list. At times it may be possible to ignore these questions because of the level at which you work, at other times you may make an effort to find answers on your own initiative, or sometimes, you may be required to obtain answers for effective administration and planning.

Let us take another discipline: business studies. Assume you work in the area of marketing. Again, you can work at different levels: as a salesperson, sales manager or sales promotion executive. The list of questions that may come to mind is endless. The types of question and the need to find answers to them will vary with the level at which you work in the organisation. You may just want to find out the monthly fluctuation in the sale of a particular product, or you may be asked to develop a R & D strategic plan to compete for a greater share of the market for the products produced by your company. Besides these, there could be many other questions for which you require answers. For example:

- What is the best strategy to promote the sale of a particular product?
- How many salespersons do I need?
- What is the effect of a particular advertising campaign on the sale of this product?
- How satisfied are the consumers with this product?

- How much are consumers prepared to spend on this item?
- What do consumers like or dislike about this product?
- What type of packaging do consumers prefer for this product?
- What training do the salespersons need to promote the sale of this product?
- What are the attributes of a good salesperson?

To take a different example, let us assume that you work as a psychologist, counsellor or social worker. While engaging in the helping process you may ask yourself the following questions:

- What are my clients' most common presenting problems?
- What are their most common underlying problems?
- What is the socio-economic background of my clients?
- Why am I successful in certain cases and not in others?
- What resources are available in the community to help a client with a particular need?
- What intervention strategies are appropriate for this problem?
- How satisfied are my clients with my services?

As a supervisor, administrator or manager of an agency, again, different questions may come to mind. For example:

- How many people are coming to my agency?
- What are the socio-economic-demographic characteristics of my clients?
- How many cases in a day can a worker handle?
- Why do some people use the service while others do not?
- How effective is the service?
- What are the most common needs of clients who come to this agency?
- What are the strengths and weaknesses of the service?
- How satisfied are the clients with the service?
- How can I improve this service for my clients?

As a professional you might be interested in finding answers to theoretical questions, such as:

- Which is the most effective intervention for a particular problem?
- What causes X or what are the effects of Y?
- What is the relationship between two phenomena?
- How do I measure the self-esteem of my clients?
- How do I ascertain the validity of my questionnaire?
- What is the pattern of program adoption in the community?
- Which is the best way of finding out community attitudes towards an issue?
- Which is the best way to find out the effectiveness of a particular treatment?
- How can I select an unbiased sample?

In this age of consumerism you cannot afford to ignore the consumers of a service. Consumers have the right to ask questions about the quality and effectiveness of the service they are receiving and you, as a service provider, have an obligation to answer their questions. Some of the questions that a consumer may ask are:

- How effective is the service that I am receiving?
- Am I getting value for money?
- How well-trained are the service providers?

Most disciplines in the humanities would lend themselves to the questions raised above.

Applications of research

As we have just seen, the questions that can be raised about any profession where you directly or indirectly provide a service—health (nursing, occupational therapy, physiotherapy, community health, health promotion, public health), education, town planning, library studies, psychology, business studies, social work—can be looked at from the perspective of:

- the service provider;
- the service consumer;
- the service administrator, manager or planner; and
- the professional.

These perspectives are summarised in Figure 1.1. It is impossible to list all of the issues in every discipline but this framework can be applied to most disciplines and situations in the humanities and the social sciences to identify, from the viewpoint of the above perspectives, the possible issues in one's own academic field.

Definitions of research

There are several ways of obtaining answers to the above types of question. These methods range from the fairly informal, based upon clinical impressions, to the strictly scientific, adhering to the conventional expectations of scientific procedures. *Research* is one of these ways. When you say that you are undertaking a research study to find out answers to a question, you are implying that the process:

1 is being undertaken within a framework of a set of philosophies;
2 uses procedures, methods and techniques that have been tested for their validity and reliability; and
3 is designed to be unbiased and objective.

Your philosophical orientation may stem from one of the two paradigms in research—positivism and naturalism—and the academic discipline in which you have been trained. The concept of validity can be applied to any aspect of the research process. It ensures that in a research study correct procedures have been applied to find answers to a question. 'Reliability' refers to the quality of a measurement procedure. 'Unbiased and objective' means that you have taken each step and drawn each conclusion to the best of your ability and without introducing your own vested interest. The author would like to make a distinction between bias and subjectivity.

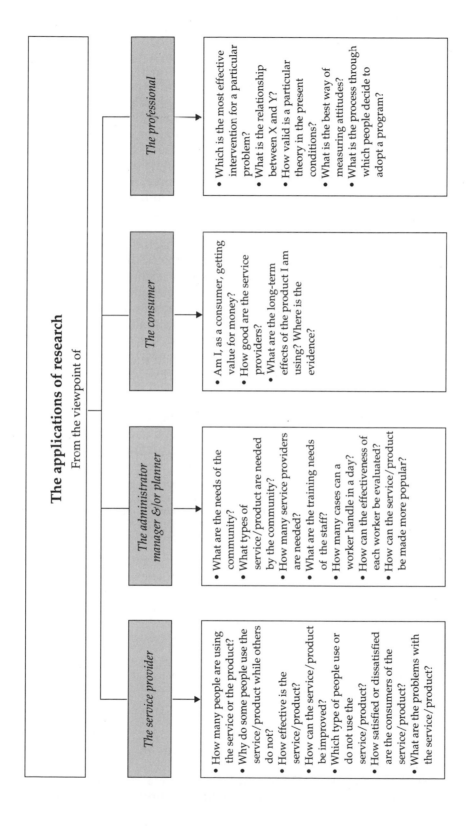

The applications of research
From the viewpoint of

The service provider

- How many people are using the service or the product?
- Why do some people use the service/product while others do not?
- How effective is the service/product?
- How can the service/product be improved?
- Which type of people use or do not use the service/product?
- How satisfied or dissatisfied are the consumers of the service/product?
- What are the problems with the service/product?

The administrator manager &/or planner

- What are the needs of the community?
- What types of service/product are needed by the community?
- How many service providers are needed?
- What are the training needs of the staff?
- How many cases can a worker handle in a day?
- How can the effectiveness of each worker be evaluated?
- How can the service/product be made more popular?

The consumer

- Am I, as a consumer, getting value for money?
- How good are the service providers?
- What are the long-term effects of the product I am using? Where is the evidence?

The professional

- Which is the most effective intervention for a particular problem?
- What is the relationship between X and Y?
- How valid is a particular theory in the present conditions?
- What is the best way of measuring attitudes?
- What is the process through which people decide to adopt a program?

Figure 1.1   Applications of research

Subjectivity is an integral part of your way of thinking that is conditioned by your educational background, discipline, philosophy, experience and skills. Bias, on the other hand, is a deliberate attempt to either conceal or highlight something. For example, a psychologist may look at a piece of information differently from the way an anthropologist or a historian looks at it.

Adherence to the three criteria enables the process to be called 'research'. Therefore, when you say you are undertaking a research study to find out the answer to a question, this implies that the method you are adopting fulfils these expectations (discussed later in the chapter).

However, the degree to which these criteria are expected to be fulfilled varies from discipline to discipline and so the meaning of 'research' differs from one academic discipline to another. For example, the expectations of the research process are markedly different between the physical and the social sciences. In the physical sciences a research endeavour is expected to be strictly controlled at each step, whereas in the social sciences rigid control cannot be enforced and sometimes is not even demanded.

Within the social sciences the level of control required also varies markedly from one discipline to another, as social scientists differ over the need for the research process to meet the above expectations. Despite these differences among disciplines, their broad approach to inquiry is similar. The research model in this book is based upon this philosophy.

As beginners in research you should understand that research is not all technical, complex, statistics and computers. It can be a very simple activity designed to provide answers to very simple questions relating to day-to-day activities. On the other hand, research procedures can also be employed to formulate intricate theories or laws that govern our lives. The difference between research and non-research activity is, as mentioned, in the way we find answers: the process must meet certain requirements to be called research. To identify these requirements let us examine some definitions of research.

> The word *research* is composed of two syllables, *re* and *search*. The dictionary defines the former as a prefix meaning again, anew or over again and the latter as a verb meaning to examine closely and carefully, to test and try, or to probe. Together they form a noun describing a careful, systematic, patient study and investigation in some field of knowledge, undertaken to establish facts or principles (Grinnell 1993: 4).

Grinnell further adds: 'research is a structured inquiry that utilises acceptable scientific methodology to solve problems and creates new knowledge that is generally applicable.' (1993: 4)

Lundberg (1942) draws a parallel between the social research process, which is considered scientific, and the process that we use in our daily lives. According to him:

> Scientific methods consist of systematic observation, classification and interpretation of data. Now, obviously, this process is one in which nearly all people engage in the course of their daily lives. The main difference between our day-to-day generalisations and the conclusions usually recognised as scientific method lies in the degree of formality, rigorousness, verifiability and general validity of the latter (Lundberg 1942: 5).

Burns (1994: 2) defines research as 'a systematic investigation to find answers to a problem.'

According to Kerlinger (1986: 10), 'scientific research is a systematic, controlled empirical and critical investigation of propositions about the presumed relationships about various phenomena.' Bulmer (1977: 5) states: 'Nevertheless sociological research, as research, is primarily committed to establishing systematic, reliable and valid knowledge about the social world.'

Characteristics of research

From these definitions it is clear that research is a process for collecting, analysing and interpreting information to answer questions. But to qualify as research, the process must have certain characteristics: it must, as far as possible, be controlled, rigorous, systematic, valid and verifiable, empirical, and critical.

Let us briefly examine these characteristics to understand what they mean.

- **Controlled**—in real life there are many factors that affect an outcome. A particular event is seldom the result of a one-to-one relationship. Some relationships are more complex than others. Most outcomes are a sequel to the interplay of a multiplicity of relationships and interacting factors. In a study of cause and effect relationships it is important to be able to link the effect(s) with the cause(s) and vice versa. Though, in the study of causation, the establishment of this linkage is essential, in practice, particularly in the social sciences, it is extremely difficult—and often impossible—to make the link.

  The concept of control implies that, in exploring causality in relation to two variables, you set up your study in a way that minimises the effects of other factors affecting the relationship. This can be achieved to a large extent in the physical sciences, as most of the research is done in a laboratory. However, in the social sciences it is extremely difficult as research is carried out on issues relating to human beings living in society, where such controls are impossible. Therefore, in the social sciences, as you cannot control external factors, you attempt to quantify their impact.
- **Rigorous**—you must be scrupulous in ensuring that the procedures followed to find answers to questions are relevant, appropriate, and justified. Again, the degree of rigour varies markedly between the physical and the social sciences and within the social sciences.
- **Systematic**—this implies that the procedures adopted to undertake an investigation follow a certain logical sequence. The different steps cannot be taken in a haphazard way. Some procedures must follow others.
- **Valid and verifiable**—this concept implies that whatever you conclude on the basis of your findings is correct and can be verified by you and others.
- **Empirical**—this means that any conclusions drawn are based upon hard evidence gathered from information collected from real life experiences or observations.
- **Critical**—critical scrutiny of the procedures used and the methods employed is crucial to a research inquiry. The process of investigation must be foolproof and free from any drawbacks. The process adopted and the procedures used must be able to withstand critical scrutiny.

Types of research

Research can be classified from three perspectives (Figure 1.2):

1 The *application* of the research study;
2 The *objectives in undertaking* the research; and
3 The *type of information* sought.

These three classifications are not mutually exclusive—that is, a research study classified from the viewpoint of 'application' can also be classified from the perspectives of 'objectives' and 'type of information sought'. For example, a research project may be classified as pure or applied research (from the perspective of application), as descriptive, correlational, explanatory or exploratory (from the perspective of objectives) and as qualitative or quantitative (from the perspective of the type of information sought).

Figure 1.2   Types of research

Application

If you examine a research endeavour from the perspective of its application, there are two broad categories: pure research and applied research. In the social sciences, according to Bailey (1978: 17):

> Pure research involves developing and testing theories and hypotheses that are intellectually challenging to the researcher but may or may not have practical application at the present time or in the future. Thus such work often involves the testing of hypotheses containing very abstract and specialised concepts.

Pure research is also concerned with the development, examination, verification, and refinement of research methods, procedures, techniques and tools that form the body of research methodology. Examples of pure research include: developing a sampling technique that can be applied to a particular situation; developing a methodology to assess the validity of a procedure; developing an instrument, say, to measure the stress level in people; and finding the best way of measuring people's attitudes. The knowledge produced through pure research is sought in order to add to the existing body of knowledge of research methods.

Most of the research in the social sciences is applied. In other words the research techniques, procedures, and methods that form the body of research methodology are applied to the collection of information about various aspects of a situation, issue, problem or phenomenon so that information gathered can be used in other ways—such as for policy formulation, administration, and the enhancement of understanding of a phenomenon.

Objectives

If you examine a research study from the perspective of its objectives, broadly, a research endeavour can be classified as: descriptive, correlational, explanatory or exploratory.

A study classified as *descriptive research* attempts to describe systematically a situation, problem, phenomenon, service or program, or provides information about, say, the living conditions of a community, or describes attitudes towards an issue. For example, it may attempt to describe the types of service provided by an organisation, the administrative structure of an organisation, the living conditions of Aboriginal people in the outback, the needs of a community, what it means to go through a divorce, how a child feels living in a house with domestic violence, or the attitudes of employees towards management.

The main emphasis in a *correlational research* study is to discover or establish the existence of a relationship/association/interdependence between two or more aspects of a situation. What is the impact of an advertising campaign on the sale of a product? What is the relationship between stressful living and the incidence of heart attacks? What is the relationship between fertility and mortality? What is the relationship between technology and employment? What is the effect of a health service on the control of a disease, or the home environment on educational achievement? These studies examine whether there is a relationship between two or more aspects of a situation or phenomenon.

Explanatory research attempts to clarify why and how there is a relationship between two aspects of a situation or phenomenon. This type of research attempts to explain, for example, why stressful living results in heart attacks; why a decline in mortality is followed by fertility decline; or how the home environment affects children's level of academic achievement.

The fourth type of research, from the viewpoint of the objectives of a study, is called *exploratory research*. This is carried out to investigate the possibilities of undertaking a particular research study. This type of research study is also called a 'feasibility study' or a 'pilot study'. It is usually carried out when a researcher wants to explore areas about which s/he has little or no knowledge. A small-scale study is undertaken to decide if it is worth carrying out a detailed investigation. On the basis of the assessment made during the exploratory study, a full study may eventuate. Exploratory studies are also conducted to develop, refine and/or test measurement tools and procedures. Figures 1.3 shows types of research study from the viewpoint of objectives.

Although, theoretically, a research study can be classified in one of the above perspectives, in practice, most studies are a combination of the first three categories, that is, they contain elements of descriptive, correlational and explanatory research. In this book the guidelines suggested for writing a research report encourage you to integrate these aspects.

Type of information sought

The third perspective in our typology of research is the type of information sought through research activity. From this perspective, research can be classified as *qualitative* or *quantitative*. The quantitative–qualitative classification is dependent on three criteria:

1 the purpose of the study;
2 how the variables are measured; and
3 how the information is analysed.

The study is classified as qualitative if: the purpose of the study is primarily to describe a situation, phenomenon, problem or event; the information is gathered through the use of variables measured on nominal or ordinal scales (qualitative measurement scales); and if analysis is done *to establish the variation* in the situation, phenomenon or problem *without quantifying it*. The description of an observed situation, the historical enumeration of events, an account of the different opinions people have about an issue, and a description of the living conditions of a community, are examples of qualitative research.

On the other hand, if you want to *quantify the variation* in a phenomenon, situation, problem or issue, if information is gathered using predominantly quantitative variables, and if the analysis is geared to ascertain the *magnitude of the variation*, the study is classified as a quantitative study. Examples of quantitative aspects of a research study are: How many people have a particular problem? How many people hold a particular attitude?

The use of statistics is *not* an integral part of a quantitative study. The main function of statistics is to act as a test to confirm or contradict the conclusions that you have drawn on the basis of your understanding of analysed data. Statistics, among other things, help you to quantify the magnitude of an association or relationship, provide an indication of the confidence you can place in your findings and help you to isolate the effect of different variables.

It is strongly recommended that you do not lock yourself into becoming either solely a quantitative or solely a qualitative researcher. It is true that there are disciplines that lend themselves predominantly either to qualitative or to quantitative research. For example, disciplines like anthropology, history, and sociology are more inclined towards qualitative research,

Examples	Aim	Main theme	Type of research
• Socio-economic characteristics of residents of a community • Attitudes of students towards quality of teaching • Types of service provided by an agency • Needs of a community • Sale of a product • Attitudes of nurses towards death and dying • Attitudes of workers towards management • Number of people living in a community • Problems faced by new immigrants • Extent of occupational mobility among immigrants • Consumers' likes and dislikes with regard to a product • Effects of living in a house with domestic violence. • Strategies put in place by a company to increase productivity of workers	**To describe what is prevalent regarding:** • a group of people • a community • a phenomenon • a situation • a program • an outcome	**To describe what is prevalent**	**Descriptive research**
• Impact of a program • Relationship between stressful living and incidence of heart attacks • Impact of technology on employment • Impact of maternal and child health services on infant mortality • Effectiveness of a marriage counselling service on extent of marital problems • Impact of an advertising campaign on sale of a product • Impact of incentives on productivity of workers • Effectiveness of an immunisation program in controlling infectious disease	**To establish or explore:** • a relationship • an association • an interdependence	**To ascertain if there is a relationship**	**Correlational research**
• Why does stressful living result in heart attacks? • How does technology create unemployment/employment? • How do maternal and child health services affect infant mortality? • Why do some people have a positive attitude towards an issue while others do not? • Why does a particular intervention work for some and not for others? • Why do some people use a product while others do not? • Why do some people migrate to another country while others do not? • Why do some people adopt a program while others do not?	**To explain:** • *Why* a relationship, association or interdependence exists. • *Why* a particular event occurs.	**To explain why the relationship is formed.**	**Explanatory research**

Figure 1.3 Types of research studies from the viewpoint of objectives

whereas psychology, epidemiology, education, economics, public health, and marketing are more inclined towards quantitative research. However, this does not mean that an economist or a psychologist never uses the qualitative approach, or that an anthropologist never uses quantitative information. There is increasing recognition by most disciplines in the social sciences that both types of research are important for a good research study. The research problem itself should determine whether the study is classified as qualitative or quantitative.

Both qualitative and quantitative approaches have their strengths and weaknesses, and advantages and disadvantages. 'Neither one is markedly superior to the other in all respects' (Ackroyd and Hughes 1992: 30). The measurement and analysis of the variables about which information is obtained in a research study are dependent upon the purpose of the study. In many studies you need to combine both qualitative and quantitative approaches. For example, suppose you want to find out the types of service available to victims of domestic violence in a city and the extent of their utilisation. Types of service is the qualitative aspect of the study as finding out about them entails description of the services. The extent of utilisation of the services is the quantitative aspect as it involves estimating the number of people who use the services and calculating other indicators that reflect the extent of utilisation.

Paradigms of research

There are two main paradigms that form the basis of research in the social sciences. It is beyond the scope of this book to go into any detail about these. The crucial question that divides the two is whether the methodology of the physical sciences can be applied to the study of social phenomena. The paradigm that is rooted in the physical sciences is called the systematic, scientific or positivist approach. The opposite paradigm has come to be known as the qualitative, ethnographic, ecological or naturalistic approach. The advocates of the two opposing sides have developed their own values, terminology, methods and techniques to understand social phenomena. However, since the mid-1960s there has been a growing recognition that both paradigms have their place. The research purpose should determine the mode of inquiry, hence the paradigm. To indiscriminately apply one approach to all the research problems can be misleading and inappropriate.

A positivist paradigm lends itself to both quantitative and qualitative research. You can conduct qualitative research within the positivist paradigm. However, the author makes a distinction between qualitative research on the one hand and naturalistic and ethnographic research on the other as they follow different value systems and to some extent different methodologies.

The author believes that no matter what paradigm the researcher works within, s/he should adhere to certain values regarding the control of bias, and the maintenance of objectivity in terms of both the research process itself and the conclusions drawn. It is the application of these values to the process of information gathering, analysis and interpretation that enables it to be called a research process.

Summary

There are several ways of collecting and understanding information and finding answers to your questions—research is one way. The difference between research and other ways of obtaining answers to your questions is that in a process that is classified as research, you work within a framework of a set of philosophies, use methods that have been tested for validity and reliability, and attempt to be unbiased and objective.

Research has many applications. You need to have research skills to be an effective service provider, administrator/manager or planner. As a professional who has a responsibility to enhance professional knowledge, research skills are essential.

The typology of research can be looked at from three perspectives: application, objectives and the type of information sought. From the point of view of the application of research, there is applied and pure research. Most of the research undertaken in the social sciences is applied, the findings being designed either for use in understanding a phenomenon/issue or to bring change in a program/situation. Pure research is academic in nature and is undertaken in order to gain knowledge about phenomena that may or may not have application in the near future, and to develop new techniques and procedures that form the body of research methodology. A research study can be carried out with four objectives: to describe a situation, phenomenon, problem or issue (descriptive research); to establish or explore a relationship between two or more variables (correlational research); to explain why certain things happen the way they do (explanatory research); and to examine the feasibility of conducting a study (exploratory research). From the point of view of the type of information sought, there are two types of research: quantitative and qualitative. The main objective of a qualitative study is to describe the variation in a phenomenon, situation or attitude, whereas quantitative research, in addition, helps you to quantify the variation.

There are two main paradigms that form the basis of social science research: positivist and naturalist. The crucial question that divides the two is whether the methodology of research in the physical sciences can be applied to research in the social sciences.

2

The research process: a quick glance

The research process: an eight-step model
- Step I: formulating a research problem
- Step II: conceptualising a research design
- Step III: constructing an instrument for data collection
- Step IV: selecting a sample
- Step V: writing a research proposal
- Step VI: collecting data
- Step VII: processing data
- Step VIII: writing a research report

Summary

But much advantage will occur if men of science become their own epistemologists, and show to the world by critical exposition in non-technical terms the results and methods of their constructive work, that more than mere instinct is involved in it: the community has indeed a right to expect as much as this (Poincaré 1952: xii).

The research process: an eight-step model

Research methodology is taught as a supporting subject in several ways in many academic disciplines at various levels by people committed to a variety of research paradigms. Though paradigms vary in their contents and substance, their broad approach to inquiry, in the author's opinion, is similar. Such ideas have also been expressed by Festinger and Katz, who in the foreword of their book, *Research Methods in Behavioral Sciences*, say that, 'Although the basic logic of scientific methodology is the same in all fields, its specific techniques and approaches will vary, depending upon the subject matter' (1966: vi). Therefore, the model developed here is generic in nature and can be applied to a number of disciplines in the social sciences (Figure 2.1). It is based upon a practical and step-by-step approach to a research inquiry and each step provides a smorgasbord of methods, models and procedures.

The tasks identified in **arrows** are the operational steps you need to follow in order to conduct a study. Topics identified in **rectangles** are the required theoretical knowledge needed to carry out these steps. The tasks identified in **circles** are the intermediary steps that you need to complete to go from one step to another. It is important for a beginner to work through these steps in the proposed sequence, though with experience you can change it.

This book is written around the theoretical knowledge required to undertake each operational step and follows the same sequential progression as is needed to undertake a research investigation. For each operational step, the required theoretical knowledge is further organised, in different chapters, around the operational step to which it is most logically related (Figure 2.2). Again, for a beginner, it is important to study this diagram to relate the theoretical knowledge to the operational steps.

The following sections of this chapter provide a quick glance at the whole process to acquaint you with the various tasks you need to undertake to carry out your study.

Step I: formulating a research problem

Formulating a research problem is the first and most important step in the research process. A research problem identifies your destination: it should tell you, your research supervisor and your readers *what* you intend to research. The more specific and clear you are the better, as everything that follows in the research process—study design, measurement procedures, sampling strategy, frame of analysis and the style of writing of your dissertation or report—is greatly influenced by the way in which you formulate your research problem. Hence, you should give it considerable and careful thought at this stage. Chapter 4 deals in detail with various aspects of formulating a research problem.

It is extremely important to evaluate the research problem in the light of the financial resources at your disposal, the time available, and your own and your research supervisor's expertise and knowledge in the field of study. It is equally important to identify any gaps in your knowledge of relevant disciplines, such as statistics, required for analysis. Also, ask yourself whether you have sufficient knowledge about computers and software if you plan to use them.

Step II: conceptualising a research design

An extremely important feature of research is the use of scientific methods. Research involves systematic, controlled, valid and rigorous establishment of associations and causation that permit the accurate prediction of outcomes under a given set of conditions. It also involves identifying gaps in knowledge, verification of what is already known and identification of past errors and limitations. The validity of *what* you find largely rests on *how* it was found. The main function of a research design is to explain how you will find answers to your research questions. The research design sets out the logic of your inquiry. A research design should include the following: the study design *per se* and the logistical arrangements that you propose to undertake, the measurement procedures, the sampling strategy, the frame of analysis and the time-frame. For any investigation, the selection of an appropriate research design is crucial in enabling you to arrive at valid findings, comparisons and conclusions. A faulty design results in misleading findings and is therefore tantamount to wasting human and financial resources. In scientific circles, the strength of an empirical investigation is primarily evaluated in the light of the research design adopted. When selecting a research design it is important to ensure that it is *valid, workable* and *manageable*. Chapter 7 provides details about research design.

There is an enormous variety of study designs and you need to be acquainted with some of the most common ones. Chapter 8 explains some of these designs. Select or develop the design that is most suited to your study. You must have strong reasons for selecting a particular design; you must be able to justify your selection; and you should be aware of its strengths, weaknesses and limitations. In addition, you will need to explain the logistical details needed to implement the suggested design.

Step III: constructing an instrument for data collection

Anything that becomes a means of collecting information for your study is called a 'research tool' or a 'research instrument'. For example, observation forms, interview schedules, questionnaires, and interview guides are all classified as research tools.

The construction of a research tool is the first 'practical' step in carrying out a study. You will need to decide how you are going to collect data for

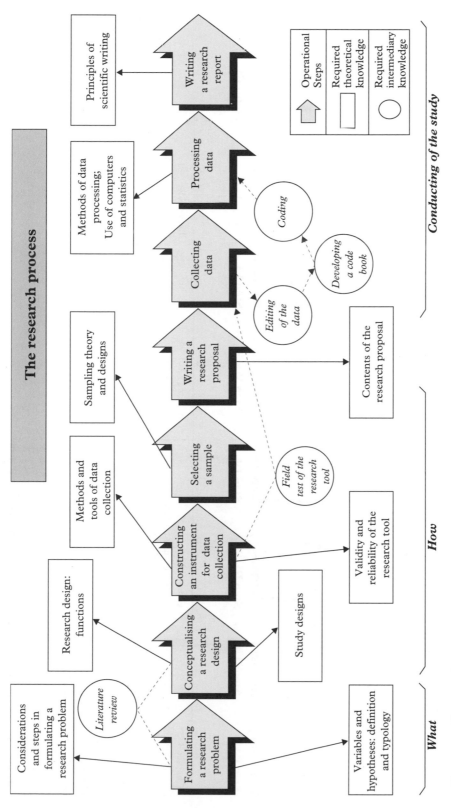

Figure 2.1 The research process

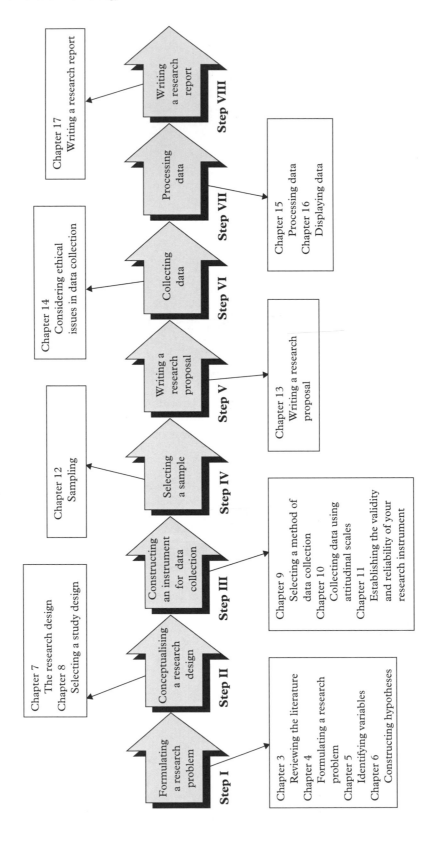

Figure 2.2   The chapters in the book in relation to the operational steps

the proposed study and then construct a research instrument for data collection. Chapter 9 details the various methods of data collection and Chapter 10 deals with methods for collecting data using attitudinal scales.

If you are planning to collect data specifically for your study (primary data), you need to either construct a research instrument or select an already constructed one. The process of developing a research instrument is also discussed in Chapter 9. The concepts of validity and reliability in relation to a research instrument are discussed in Chapter 11.

If you are using secondary data (information already collected for other purposes), develop a form to extract the required data. In order to determine what information is required, go through the same process as described for primary data above.

Field testing a research tool is an integral part of instrument construction. As a rule, the field test should not be carried out on the sample of your study but on a similar population.

If you are planning to use a computer for data analysis, you may wish to provide space for coding the data on the research instrument.

Step IV: selecting a sample

The accuracy of your estimates largely depends upon the way you select your sample. The basic objective of any sampling design is to minimise, within the limitation of cost, the gap between the values obtained from your sample and those prevalent in the population.

The underlying premise in sampling is that, if a relatively small number of units is scientifically selected, it can provide—with a sufficiently high degree of probability—a fairly true reflection of the sampling population that is being studied.

Sampling theory is guided by two principles:

1 the avoidance of bias in the selection of a sample; and
2 the attainment of maximum precision for a given outlay of resources.

There are three categories of sampling design (Chapter 12):

1 Random/probability sampling designs;
2 Non-random/probability sampling designs; and
3 'Mixed' sampling design.

There are several sampling strategies within the first two categories. You need to be acquainted with these sampling designs to select the one most appropriate for your study. You need to know the strengths and weaknesses of each and the situations in which they can or cannot be applied in order to select the most appropriate design. The type of sampling strategy you use also determines your ability to generalise from the sample to the total population and the type of statistical tests you can perform on the data.

Step V: writing a research proposal

Now, step-by-step, you have done all the preparatory work. Next put everything together in a way that provides adequate information, for your research supervisor and others, about your research study. This overall plan tells a reader about your research problem and how you are planning to investigate, and is called a *research proposal*. Broadly, a research proposal's main function is to detail the operational plan for obtaining answers to your research questions. In doing so it ensures—and reassures the readers of—the validity of the methodology to obtain answers accurately and objectively.

Universities and other institutions may have differing requirements regarding the style and content of a research proposal, but the majority of institutions would require most of what is set out here. Requirements may also vary within an institution, from discipline to discipline or from supervisor to supervisor. However, the guidelines set out in Chapter 13 provide a framework, which will be acceptable to most.

A research proposal must tell you, your research supervisor and a reviewer the following information about your study:

- *What* you are proposing to do;
- *How* you plan to proceed; and
- *Why* you selected the proposed strategy.

Therefore it should contain the following information about your study (Chapter 13):

- a statement of the *objectives* of the study;
- a list of *hypotheses*, if you are testing any;
- the *study design* you are proposing to use;
- the *setting* for your study;
- the research *instrument(s)* you are planning to use;
- information on *sample size* and *sampling design*;
- information on *data processing* procedures;
- an outline of the proposed *chapters* for the report;
- the study's *problems* and *limitations*; and
- the proposed *time-frame*.

Step VI: collecting data

Having formulated a research problem, developed a study design, constructed a research instrument and selected a sample, you then collect the data from which you will draw inferences and conclusions for your study.

Many methods could be used to gather the required information. As a part of the research design, you decided upon the procedure you wanted to adopt to collect your data. *At this stage you actually collect the data.* For example, depending upon your plans, you might commence interviews, mail out a questionnaire, conduct nominal/focused group discussions, or make observations. Collecting data through any one of the methods may involve some ethical issues which are discussed in Chapter 14.

Step VII: processing data

The way you analyse the information you collected largely depends upon two things:

1 the type of information—descriptive, quantitative, qualitative or attitudinal; and
2 the way you want to write your dissertation/report.

There are two broad categories of report: quantitative and qualitative. As mentioned earlier, the distinction is more academic than real as in most studies you need to combine quantitative and qualitative skills. Nevertheless, there are some solely qualitative and some solely quantitative studies. Chapter 15 describes different ways of analysing quantitative data and Chapter 16 details various methods of displaying analysed data.

In addition to the qualitative–quantitative distinction, it is equally important for data analysis that you consider whether the data is to be analysed manually or by a computer.

If your study is purely descriptive, you can write your dissertation/report on the basis of your field notes, manually analyse the contents of your notes (content analysis), or use a computer program such as Nudist or Ethnograph for this purpose.

If you want quantitative analysis, it is also necessary to decide upon the type of analysis required (i.e., frequency distribution, cross-tabulations, or other statistical procedures, such as regression analysis, factor analysis, analysis of variance) and how it should be presented. Also identify the variables to be subjected to these statistical procedures.

Step VIII: writing a research report

Writing the report is the last and, for many, the most difficult step of the research process. This report informs the world of what you have done, what have you discovered and what conclusions you have drawn from your findings. If you are clear about the whole process, you will also be clear about the way you want to write your report. Your report should be written in an academic style and be divided into different chapters and/or sections based upon the main themes of your study. Chapter 17 suggests some of the ways of writing a research report.

Summary

This chapter has provided an overview of the research process, which has been broken into eight steps, the details of which are covered in the remainder of this book. At each step the model provides a smorgasbord of methods, models, techniques and procedures so you can select the one most appropriate for your study. It is like a buffet party with eight tables, each with different dishes, but the dishes are made out of similar ingredients. You go to all eight tables and select the dish that you like most from each table. The main difference between the model and the example given is that in the model you select what is most appropriate for your study and not what you like the most, as in a buffet. For a beginner it is important to go through all the steps, although perhaps not in the same sequence. With experience you can take a number of short cuts.

The eight steps cover the total spectrum of a research endeavour, starting from problem formulation through to writing a research report. The steps are operational in nature, following a logical sequence, and detailing the various methods and procedures in a simple step-by-step manner.

Step 1

Formulating a
research problem

3

Reviewing the literature

Reasons for reviewing the literature
- Bring clarity and focus to your research problem
- Improve your methodology
- Broaden your knowledge base in your research area

Procedure for reviewing the literature
- Search for existing literature
- Review the literature selected
- Develop a theoretical framework
- Develop a conceptual framework

Writing up the literature reviewed

Summary

Reasons for reviewing the literature

One of the essential preliminary tasks when you undertake a research study is to go through the existing literature in order to acquaint yourself with the available body of knowledge in your area of interest. Reviewing this literature is time-consuming and, sometimes, daunting and frustrating, but you should not become discouraged because you will also find it rewarding. A literature review has three functions. It helps you to:

1 bring clarity and focus to your research problem;
2 improve your methodology; and
3 broaden your knowledge base in your research area.

Bring clarity and focus to your research problem

The literature review involves a paradox. On the one hand, you cannot effectively undertake a literature search without some idea of the problem you wish to investigate. On the other, the literature review can play an extremely important role in shaping your research problem because the process of reviewing the literature helps you to understand the subject area better and thus helps you to conceptualise your research problem clearly and precisely. It also helps you to understand the relationship between your research problem and the body of knowledge in the area.

Improve your methodology

Going through the literature acquaints you with the methodologies that have been used by others to find answers to research questions similar to the one you are investigating. A literature review tells you if others have used procedures and methods similar to the ones that you are proposing, which procedures and methods have worked well for them, and what problems they have faced with them. By becoming aware of any problems and pitfalls, you will be better positioned to select a methodology that is capable of providing valid answers to your research questions. This will increase your confidence in the methodology you plan to use and will equip you to defend its use.

Broaden your knowledge base in your research area

The most important function of the literature review is to ensure you read widely around the subject area in which you intend to conduct your research study. It is important that you know what other researchers have found in regard to the same or similar questions, what theories have been put forward and what gaps exist in the relevant body of knowledge. When you undertake a research project for a higher degree, that is, an MA or a PhD, you are expected to be an expert in your area of study. A thorough literature review helps to ensure that you fulfil this expectation. Another important reason for doing a literature review is that it helps you to understand how the findings of your study fit into the existing body of knowledge (Martin 1985: 30).

Procedure for reviewing the literature

If you do not have a specific research problem, you should review the literature in your broad area of interest with the aim of gradually narrowing down to what you want to find out about. After that the literature review should be focused around your research problem. There is a danger in reviewing the literature without having a reasonably specific idea of what you want to study. It can condition your thinking about your study and the methodology you might use, resulting in a less innovative choice of research problem and methodology than otherwise would have been the case. Hence, you should try to conceptualise your research problem before undertaking your major literature review.

Reviewing the literature is a continuous process. Often it begins before a specific research problem has been formulated and continues until the report is finished. Although you need to complete most of the literature review before you undertake your study, you continue it until you have written your report as you need to integrate the findings from your study with those from others, stating whether your findings support or contradict other studies. This comparison is an integral part of your report.

There are four steps involved in conducting a literature review:

1 search for existing literature in your area of study;
2 review the literature selected;
3 develop a theoretical framework; and
4 develop a conceptual framework.

The skills required for these tasks are different. Developing theoretical and conceptual frameworks are more difficult than the other tasks.

Search for existing literature

To effectively search for literature in your field of inquiry, it is imperative that you have in mind at least some idea of the broad subject area and of the problem you wish to investigate, in order to set parameters for your search. Next compile a bibliography for this broad area. There are two sources that you can use to prepare a bibliography:

1 books; and
2 journals.

The best way to search for a book is to look at your library catalogues. When librarians catalogue a book they also assign to it subject headings that usually are based on *Library of Congress Subject Headings*. If you are not sure, ask your librarian to help you to find the best subject heading for your area. This can save you a lot of time. Publications such as *Book Review Index* can help you to locate books of interest.

There are several sources designed to make your search for journals easier and these can save you enormous time. They are:

1 Indices of journals, e.g., *Humanities Index*;
2 Abstracts of articles, e.g., *ERIC*; and
3 Citation indices, e.g., *Social Sciences Citation Index*.

All the above indexing, abstracting and citation services are available in print, on CD-ROM or are stored on a mainframe computer accessible through the Internet, a world-wide electronic communication system.

In most libraries, information on books, journals, abstracts, etc. is stored on computers, microfiche and CD-ROMs (catalogue cards are now outdated). In each case the information is classified by subject, author, and title. If your library catalogue is computerised, you may also have the keywords option (author/keyword; title/keyword; subject/keyword; expert/keyword; or just keywords). What system you use depends upon what is available in your library and what you are familiar with.

There are specially prepared electronic databases in a number of disciplines. These can also be helpful in preparing a bibliography. For example, most libraries carry the electronic databases shown in table 3.1.

Table 3.1: Some commonly used electronic databases in public health, sociology, education and business studies

Electronic Database	Description	Printed Equivalent
ABI/INFORM	Abstracted Business Information contains references to business information worldwide. It covers subjects such as accounting, banking, data processing, economics, finance, health care, insurance, law, management, marketing, personnel, product development, public administration, real estate, taxation and telecommunications.	none
ERIC	ERIC is a database of educational material collected by the Education Resources Information Centre of the US Department of Education. It covers subjects such as adult career or vocational education, counselling and personnel services, educational management, primary and early childhood education, handicapped and gifted children, higher education, information resources, language and linguistics, reading and communication, rural education, science, mathematics and environment education, social science education, teacher education, secondary education, evaluation and urban education.	*CIJE: Current Index to Journals in Education*
HEALTHROM	HEALTHROM provides references and some full-text publications on environment, health, HIV/AIDS and communicable diseases, Aboriginal health, clinical medicine, nutrition, alcohol and drug addiction.	none
MEDLINE	MEDLINE contains references to material in the biomedical sciences, including medicine, pharmacology, nursing, dentistry, allied health professions, public health, behavioural sciences, physiotherapy, occupational therapy, medical technology, hospital administration, and basic sciences such as anatomy and physiology.	*Index Medicus*
CINAHL	CINAHL (Cumulative Indices to Nursing and Allied Health Literature) provides access to virtually all English-language nursing journals and primary journals from 13 allied health disciplines including health education, medical records, occupational therapy, physical therapy and radiologic technology.	Cumulative indices to nursing and allied health literature

Select the database most appropriate to your area of study to see if there are any useful references. Of course, any computer database search is restricted to those journals and articles that are already on the database. You should also talk to your research supervisor and other available experts to find out about any additional relevant literature to include in your reading list.

Books

Books, though a central part of any bibliography, have their advantages as well as disadvantages. The main advantage is that the material published in books is usually important and of good quality, and the findings are 'integrated with other research to form a coherent body of knowledge' (Martin 1985: 33). The main disadvantage is that the material is not completely up-to-date, as it can take a few years between the completion of a work and its publication in the form of a book.

The best way to identify books is to use a computer catalogue or microfiche. Use the *subject catalogue* or *keywords* option to search for books in your area of interest. Narrow the subject area searched by selecting the appropriate key words. Look through these titles carefully and identify the books you think are likely to be of interest to you. If you think the titles seem appropriate to your topic, print them out if this facility is available (this will save you time) or note them down on a piece of paper. Be aware that sometimes a title does not provide enough information to decide if a book is going to be of use. To make this decision you may have to search for such books in the library and examine their contents.

When you have selected ten to fifteen books that you think are appropriate for your topic, examine the bibliography of each. It will save time to photocopy their bibliographies. Go through these bibliographies carefully to identify the books common to several of them. If a book has been referenced by a number of authors, you should include it in your reading list. Prepare a final list of books that you consider essential reading.

Having prepared your reading list, locate these books in your library or borrow them from other sources. Examine their contents to double check that they really are relevant to your topic. If you find that a book is not relevant to your research, delete it from your reading list. If you find that something in a book's contents is relevant to your topic, make an annotated bibliography. An annotated bibliography contains a brief abstract of the aspects covered in a book and your own notes of its relevance. Be careful to keep track of your references. To do this you can prepare your own card index or use a computer program such as *Endnotes* or *Pro-Cite*.

Journals

In the same way, you need to go through the journals in your research area. Journals provide you with the most up-to-date information, even though there is often a gap of between two and three years between the completion of a research project and its publication in a journal. You should select as many journals as you possibly can, though the number of journals available depends upon the field of study—certain fields have more journals than others. As with books, you need to prepare a list of the journals you want to examine for identifying literature relevant to your study. This can be done in a number of ways. You can:

- locate the hard copies of the journals that are appropriate to your study;
- look at citation or abstract indices to identify and/or read the abstracts of such articles;
- search electronic databases; and
- use the Internet.

Whichever method you choose, first identify the journals that you want to look at in more detail for your review of the literature. The next step is to make preparations to go through them.

If you have been able to identify any useful journals and articles, prepare a list of those you want to examine, by journal. Select one of these journals and, starting with the latest issue, examine its contents page to see if there is an article of relevance to your research topic. If you feel that a particular article is of interest to you, read its abstract. If you think you are likely to use it, depending upon your financial resources, either photocopy it, or prepare a summary and record its reference for later use.

Review the literature selected

Now that you have identified several books and articles as useful, the next step is to start reading them critically to pull together themes and issues that belong together. If you do not have a theoretical framework in mind, to start with, use separate sheets of paper for each article or book. Once you develop a rough framework, slot the findings from the material so far reviewed into that framework, using a separate sheet of paper for each heading of that framework. As you read further, go on slotting the information where it logically belongs under the headings so far developed. You may need to add more headings as you go. In doing so, read critically with particular reference to the following aspects:

- note whether the knowledge relevant to your theoretical framework has been confirmed beyond doubt;
- note the theories put forward, the criticisms of these and their basis, the methodologies adopted (study design, sample size and its characteristics, measurement procedures, etc.) and the criticisms of them;
- examine to what extent the findings can be generalised to other situations;
- notice where there are significant differences of opinion among researchers and give your opinion about the validity of these differences;
- ascertain the areas in which little or nothing is known—the gaps that exist in the body of knowledge.

Develop a theoretical framework

Examining the literature can be a never-ending task but as you have limited time, it is important to set parameters by reviewing the literature in relation to some main themes pertinent to your research topic. As you start reading the literature, you will soon discover that the problem you wish to investigate has its roots in a number of theories that have been developed from different perspectives. The information obtained from different books and journals now needs to be sorted under the main themes and theories, highlighting agreements and disagreements among the authors and identifying the unanswered questions or gaps. You will also realise that the literature deals with a number of aspects that have a direct or indirect bearing on your research topic. Use these aspects as a basis for developing your theoretical framework. Your review of the literature should sort out the information, as mentioned earlier, within this framework. Unless you review the literature in relation to this framework, you will not be able to develop a focus in your literature search: i.e., your theoretical framework provides you with a guide as you read. This brings us to the paradox mentioned previously: until you go through the literature you cannot develop a theoretical framework and until you have developed a theoretical framework, you cannot effectively review the literature. The solution is to read some of the literature, then attempt to develop a framework, even a loose one, within which you can organise the rest of the literature you read. As you read more about the area, you are likely to change the framework. However, without it, you will get bogged down in a great deal of unnecessary reading and note-taking that may not be relevant to your study.

If you want to study the relationship between mortality and fertility, you should review literature about:

- *fertility*—trends, theories, some of the indices and critiques of them, factors affecting fertility, methods of controlling fertility, factors affecting acceptance of contraceptives, etc.;
- *mortality*—factors affecting mortality, mortality indices and their sensitivity in measuring change in mortality levels of a population, trends in mortality, etc.; and, most importantly
- *the relationship between fertility and mortality*—theories that have been put forward to explain the relationship, implications of the relationship.

Out of this literature review you need to develop the theoretical framework for your study. Primarily this should revolve around theories that have been put forward about the relationship between mortality and fertility. You will discover that a number of theories has been proposed to explain this relationship. For example, it has been explained from economic, religious, medical, and psychological perspectives. Within each perspective several theories have been put forward: 'insurance theory', 'fear of non-survival', 'replacement theory', 'price theory', 'utility theory', 'extra' or 'hoarding theory' and 'risk theory'.

Your literature review should be written under the following headings, with most of the review involving examining the relationships between fertility and mortality:

- fertility theories;
- the theory of demographic transition;
- trends in fertility (global, then narrow it to national and local levels);
- methods of contraception (their acceptance and effectiveness);
- factors affecting mortality;
- trends in mortality (and their implications);
- measurement of mortality indices (their sensitivity), and
- *relationships between fertility and mortality* (different theories such as 'insurance', 'fear of non-survival', 'replacement', 'price', 'utility', 'risk', 'hoarding').

Figure 3.1   Developing a theoretical framework—the relationship between mortality and fertility

Literature pertinent to your study may deal with two types of information:

1 universal; and
2 more specific, i.e., local trends, or a specific program.

In writing about such information you should start with the general information, gradually narrowing it down to the specific.

Look at the example in Figure 3.1

Develop a conceptual framework

The conceptual framework stems from the theoretical framework and concentrates, usually, on one section of that theoretical framework. The latter consists of the theories or issues in which your study is embedded whereas the former describes the aspects you selected from the theoretical framework to become the basis of your study. The conceptual framework is the basis of your research problem. For instance, in the example cited in Figure 3.1, the theoretical framework includes all the theories that have been put forward to explain the relationship between fertility and mortality. However, out of these, you may be planning to test only one, say, the fear of non-survival. Hence the conceptual framework grows out of the theoretical framework and relates to the specific research problem, concerning the fear of non-survival theory.

Writing up the literature reviewed

Now, all that remains to be done is to write about the literature you have reviewed. Some people write about it under one heading: 'Review of the literature' or 'Literature review'. The author strongly suggests that you do not follow this convention. The literature review should be written around themes that have emerged from reading the literature. The headings displaying themes should be precise, descriptive of the contents, and should follow a logical progression. Findings from the literature should be organised under these themes, providing references for substantiations or contradictions. Your arguments should be conceptually clear, highlighting the reasons for and against, and referring to the main findings, gaps, and issues.

Summary

Reviewing the literature is a continuous process. It begins before a research problem is finalised and continues until the report is finished. There is a paradox in literature review: you cannot undertake an effective literature review unless you have formulated a research problem yet your literature search plays an extremely important role in helping you to formulate your research problem. The literature review brings clarity and focus to your research problem, improves your methodology, and broadens your knowledge base.

Reviewing the literature involves a number of steps: searching for existing literature in your area of study, reviewing the selected literature, using it to develop a theoretical framework from which your study emerges, and to develop a conceptual framework which will become the basis of your investigation. The main sources for identifying literature are books and journals. There are several sources which can provide information about locating relevant journals.

4

Formulating a research problem

The central aim of this chapter is to detail the process of problem formulation. However, the specific contents of this process depend upon:

- your expertise in research methodology;
- your knowledge of the subject area;
- your understanding of the issues to be examined; and
- the extent to which the focus of your study is pre-determined.

If you are not very familiar with the research process and/or do not have a very specific idea about what is to be researched, you need to follow every step detailed in this chapter. However, more experienced researchers can take a number of short cuts. The process of formulating a research problem outlined here assumes that you have neither the required knowledge in research methodology nor a specific idea about what is to be researched.

The research problem

Broadly speaking, any question that you want answered and any assumption or assertion that you want to challenge or investigate can become a research problem or a research topic for your study. However, it is important to remember that not all questions can be transformed into research problems and some may prove to be extremely difficult to study. According to Powers et al. (1985: 38), 'Potential research questions may occur to us on a regular basis, but the process of formulating them in a meaningful way is not at all an easy task'. As a newcomer it might seem easy to formulate a problem but it requires a considerable knowledge of both the subject area and research methodology. Once you examine a question more closely you will soon realise the complexity of formulating an idea into a problem which is researchable. 'First identifying and then specifying a research problem might seem like research tasks that ought to be easy and quickly accomplished. However, such is often not the case' (Yegidis and Weinback 1991: 35).

It is essential for the problem you formulate to be able to withstand scientific scrutiny in terms of the procedures required to be undertaken. Hence you should spend considerable time in thinking it through.

The importance of formulating a research problem

The formulation of a research problem is the first and most important step of the research process. It is like the identification of a destination before undertaking a journey. As in the absence of a destination, it is impossible to identify the shortest—or indeed any—route, in the absence of a clear research problem, a clear and economical plan is impossible. A research problem is like the foundation of a building. The type and design of the building is dependent upon the foundation. If the foundation is well-designed and strong you can expect the building to be also. The research problem serves as the foundation of a research study: if it is well formulated, you can expect a good study to follow. According to Kerlinger,

If one wants to solve a problem, one must generally know what the problem is. It can be said that a large part of the problem lies in knowing what one is trying to do (1986: 17).

You must have a clear idea with regard to what it is that you want to find out *about* and not what you think you must find.

A research problem may take a number of forms, from the very simple to the very complex. The way you formulate a problem determines almost every step that follows: the type of study design that can be used; the type of sampling strategy that can be employed; the research instrument that can be used or developed; and the type of analysis that can be undertaken. The formulation of a problem is like the 'input' into a study, and the 'output'—the quality of the contents of the research report and the validity of the associations or causation established—is entirely dependent upon it. Hence the famous saying about computers—'garbage in, garbage out'—is equally applicable to a research problem.

In the beginning you may become more confused but this is normal and a sign of progression. *Remember: confusion is often but a first step towards clarity.* Take time over formulating your problem, for the clearer you are about your research problem, the easier it will be for you later on. *Remember, this is the most crucial step.*

Sources of research problems

This section is of particular relevance if you have not yet selected a research topic and do not know where to start. If you have already selected your topic, go to the next section.

Most research in the humanities revolves around four 'P's:

- People;
- Problems;
- Programs; and
- Phenomena.

The emphasis on a particular 'P' may vary from study to study but generally, in practice, most research studies are based upon at least a combination of two 'P's. You may select a group of individuals (a group or a community as such), either to examine the existence of certain issues or problems to ascertain the attitudes towards different aspects of their lives, or to establish the prevalence of a phenomenon. Your focus may be the study of an issue, an association or a phenomenon *per se*. For example, the relationship between unemployment and street crime, smoking and cancer or fertility and mortality, which is done on the basis of information collected from individuals, groups, communities or organisations. The emphasis in these studies is on exploring, discovering or establishing associations or causation. Similarly, you can study different aspects of a program: its effectiveness, its structure, the need for it, consumers' satisfaction with it, and so on. In order to ascertain these you collect information from people. The 'people' provide you with the 'study population' whereas the other three 'P's furnish the 'subject areas'. Your study population—individuals, groups and communities—is the people from whom the information is collected. Your subject area is a 'problem', 'program' or 'phenomenon' about which the information is collected. A closer look at any academic discipline or occupational field will show that most research revolves around the four 'P's. The different sources of a research problem are listed in table 4.1.

Table 4.1: Sources of a research problem

Aspects of a study	*About*	*Study of*
Study population	People	Individuals, organisations, groups, communities.
Subject area	Problem	Issues, situations, associations, needs, population composition, profiles, etc.
	Program	Contents, structure, outcomes, attributes, satisfaction, consumers, service providers, etc.
	Phenomenon	Cause and effect relationships, the study of a phenomenon itself, etc.

The study of an aspect of a program can be carried out in any academic/ professional field. For example, you can measure the effectiveness of a program in the field of health, education, social work, industrial management, public health, nursing, health promotion or a welfare program. Similarly you can gauge consumers' opinions about any aspect of a program in the above fields.

Examine your own academic discipline or professional field in the context of the four 'P's in order to identify anything that looks interesting. Consider some of the aspects identified under 'study of' against problem, program or phenomenon for a possible research topic. For example, if you are a student in the health field there is an enormous number of issues, situations, and associations within each sub-field of health that you could examine. Issues relating to the spread of a disease, drug rehabilitation, an immunisation program, the effectiveness of a treatment, the extent of consumers' satisfaction, or issues concerning a particular health program, can all provide you with a range of research problems. Similarly, in education there are several issues: students' satisfaction with a teacher, attributes of a good teacher, the impact of the home environment on the educational achievement of students, and supervisory needs of postgraduate students in higher education. Any other academic or occupational field can similarly be dissected into sub-fields and examined for a potential research problem. Most fields lend themselves to the above categorisation even though specific problems and programs vary markedly from field to field.

Considerations in selecting a research problem

When selecting a research problem/topic there is a number of considerations to keep in mind. These help to ensure that your study will be manageable and that you will remain motivated. These considerations are: interest, magnitude, measurement of concepts, level of expertise, relevance, availability of data and ethical issues.

- **Interest**—select a topic that really interests you: this is one of the most important considerations. A research endeavour is usually time-consuming, and involves hard work and possibly unforeseen problems. If you select a topic which does not greatly interest you, it could become extremely difficult to sustain the required motivation, and hence the completion time could be affected.
- **Magnitude**—you should have sufficient knowledge about the research process to be able to visualise the work involved in completing the proposed study. Narrow the topic down to something manageable, specific and clear. It is extremely important to select a topic that you can manage within the time and resources at your disposal.
- **Measurement of concepts**—if you are using a concept in your study, make sure you are clear about its indicators and their measurement. For example, if you plan to measure the effectiveness of a health promotion program, you must be clear as to what determines effectiveness and how it will be measured. Do not use concepts in your research problem that you are not sure how to measure. This does not mean you cannot develop a measurement procedure as the study progresses. While most of the developmental work will be done during your study, it is imperative that you are reasonably clear about the measurement of these concepts at this stage.
- **Level of expertise**—make sure you have an adequate level of expertise for the task you are proposing. Allow for the fact that you will learn during the study and may receive help from your research supervisors and others, but remember you need to do most of the work yourself.
- **Relevance**—select a topic that is of relevance to you as a professional. Ensure that your study adds to the existing body of knowledge, bridges current gaps or is useful in policy formulation. This will help you to sustain interest in the study.
- **Availability of data**—if your topic entails collection of information from secondary sources (office records, client records, census or other already-published reports, etc.), before finalising your topic, make sure that these data are available and in the format you want.
- **Ethical issues**—another important consideration in formulating a research problem is the ethical issues involved. In the course of conducting a research study, the study population may be: adversely affected by some of the questions (directly or indirectly); deprived of an intervention; expected to share sensitive and private information; or expected to be simply experimental 'guinea pigs'. How ethical issues can affect the study population and how ethical problems can be overcome should be thoroughly examined at the problem formulation stage.

Steps in the formulation of a research problem

Though the formulation of a research problem is the most important aspect of a research study, there are few manuals detailing the specific guiding principles. This task is largely left either to the teachers of research methodology or to the students. However, it is possible to offer some broad guidelines for developing a research problem that would be of immense help to a beginner.

The process of formulating a research problem consists of a number of steps. Working through these steps presupposes a reasonable degree of knowledge in the broad area within which the study is being carried out. A review of the relevant literature helps enormously in widening the knowledge base you must build before formulating a problem. A lack of such knowledge may stand in the way of clearly 'dissecting' a problem.

If you do not have a specific research topic, one approach is to first identify a broad field of interest to you. Then, have a brain-storming session with yourself to dissect it into sub-fields or areas: write down on a piece of paper whatever comes to your mind. Go through the same process with your peers. From the list generated through the two sessions, prepare a common list and supplement it with ideas from literature and/or experts. After preparing such a list begin eliminating from the list what is of least interest to you until you arrive at aspects you are really interested in. Towards the end it may become difficult for you to choose but continue until you reach a stage where you think the study is manageable. In choosing a research problem, the two crucial determinants to keep in mind are:

- your *interest in the subject area*; and
- *manageability* of the study within your own constraints.

The following steps, based upon the principle of 'narrowing the problem' or 'zeroing in on the problem', can be of help to you in formulating a research problem. If you have already identified a sub-area, you do not need to go through steps 1 and 2. These steps are:

1 **Identify** a broad area of interest in your academic/professional field.
2 **Dissect** the broad area into sub-areas (hold a brain-storming session with yourself, peers, professionals and others to identify the sub-areas).
3 **Select** a sub-area or areas in which you would like to conduct your research. Start with a process of elimination.
4 **Raise research questions** that you would like to answer through your study.
5 **Formulate objectives**, main and sub-, for your study (see the following section on formulation of objectives).
6 **Assess** these objectives to ascertain the feasibility of attaining them in the light of the time, resources (financial and human) and technical expertise at your disposal.
7 **Double check** that you are sufficiently interested in the study and have adequate resources for undertaking it. Ask yourself: am I really enthusiastic about this study and do I really have enough resources for it?

Answer these questions with considerable thought. If your answer to any one of the questions is 'no', re-assess your objectives.

Figures 4.1 to 4.3 operationalise these steps with examples from different academic disciplines (health/population, social work/social sciences and health/sociology). Every study in the social sciences has two aspects:

- the research problem, which is the basis of your inquiry; and
- the study population—the source of information.

As you narrow the research problem, similarly, you need to be extremely specific in identifying the study population   the source of your information in order to select the appropriate respondents.

The formulation of objectives

Objectives are the goals you set out to attain in your study. Since these objectives inform a reader of what you want to achieve through the study, it is extremely important to word them clearly and specifically.

Objectives should be listed under two headings:

- main objectives; and
- sub-objectives.

The main objective is an overall statement of the thrust of your study. It is also a statement of the main associations and relationships that you seek to discover or establish. The sub-objectives are the specific aspects of the topic that you want to investigate within the main framework of your study.

Sub-objectives should be numerically listed. They should be worded clearly and unambiguously. Make sure that each objective contains only one aspect of the study. Use action-oriented words or verbs when writing your objectives. The objectives should start with words such as 'to determine', 'to find out', 'to ascertain', 'to measure', 'to explore'.

The way the main and sub-objectives are worded determines how your research is classified (e.g., descriptive, correlational or experimental). In other words, the wording of your objectives determines the type of research design you need to adopt to achieve them. Hence, be careful about the way you word your objectives.

Irrespective of the type of research, the objectives should be worded in such a way that the wording clearly, completely and specifically communicates to your readers your intention. There is no place for ambiguity, non-specificity or incompleteness, either in the wording of your objectives or in the ideas they communicate. Figure 4.1 displays the characteristics of the wording of objectives in relation to the type of research study.

Figure 4.1   Characteristics of objectives

If your study is primarily descriptive, your main objective should clearly describe the major focus of your study, even mentioning the organisation and its location unless these are to be kept confidential (e.g., to describe the types of treatment program provided by … [name of the organisation] to alcoholics in … [name of the place] … *or* to find out the opinion of the community about the health services provided by … [name of the health centre/department] in … [name of the place] …). Identification of the organisation and its location is important as the services may be peculiar to the place and the organisation and may not represent the services provided by others to similar populations.

If your study is correlational in nature, in addition to the above three properties, the wording of the main objective should also include the main variables being correlated (e.g., to ascertain the impact of migration on family roles *or* to compare the effectiveness of different teaching methods on the comprehension of students).

If the overall thrust of your study is to test a hypothesis, the wording of main objectives, in addition to the above, should also indicate the direction of the relationship being tested (e.g., to ascertain if an increase in youth unemployment will increase the incidence of street crime, *or* to demonstrate that the provision of maternal and child health services to Aboriginal people in rural Australia will reduce infant mortality).

Establishing operational definitions

As mentioned earlier, in every study there are two components: the subject area and the study population (discussed in 'Sources of research problems' earlier in this chapter). The main aim of formulating a research problem is to clearly and precisely define the research problem. In defining the problem you may use certain words or items that are difficult to measure and/or the understanding of which may vary from respondent to respondent. In a research study it is important to develop, define or establish a set of rules, indicators or yardsticks in order to clearly establish the meaning of such words/items. On the other hand it is sometimes also important to define clearly the study population from which you need to obtain the required information. The following studies help to explain this. The main objectives are:

- To find out the number of *children* living below the *poverty line* in Australia.
- To ascertain the impact of immigration on *family roles* among *immigrants*.
- To measure the *effectiveness* of a retraining program designed to help *young people*.

Although these objectives clearly state the main thrust of the studies, they are not specific in terms of the main variables to be studied and the study populations. You cannot count the number of children living below the poverty line until you decide what constitutes the poverty line and how to determine it; you cannot find out the impact of immigration on family roles unless you identify which roles constitute family roles; you cannot measure effectiveness until you define what effectiveness is. On the other hand, it is equally important to decide exactly what you mean by 'children', 'immigrants' or 'young'. Up to what age will you consider a person to be a child, i.e., 5, 10, 15 or 18? Who would you consider young? A person 15 years of age, 20, 25 or 30? Who would you consider to be an immigrant? A person who immigrated 40, 20 or 5 years ago? In addition, are you going to consider immigrants from every country or only a few?

Example 1: Suppose you want to conduct a study in the area of alcoholism. In formulating your research problem take the following steps.

Figure 4.2   Steps in formulating a research problem

Example 2: Suppose you want to study the relationship between fertility and mortaily. Follow these steps.

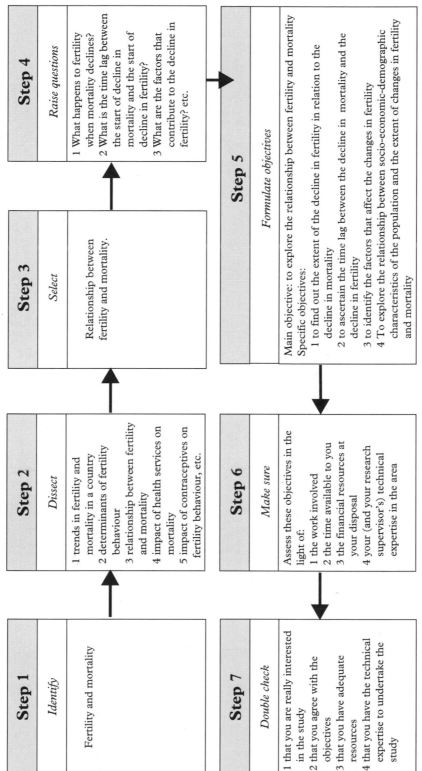

Step 1

Identify

Fertility and mortality

Step 2

Dissect

1 trends in fertility and mortality in a country
2 determinants of fertility behaviour
3 relationship between fertility and mortality
4 impact of health services on mortality
5 impact of contraceptives on fertility behaviour, etc.

Step 3

Select

Relationship between fertility and mortality.

Step 4

Raise questions

1 What happens to fertility when mortality declines?
2 What is the time lag between the start of decline in mortality and the start of decline in fertility?
3 What are the factors that contribute to the decline in fertility? etc.

Step 5

Formulate objectives

Main objective: to explore the relationship between fertility and mortality
Specific objectives:
1 to find out the extent of the decline in fertility in relation to the decline in mortality
2 to ascertain the time lag between the decline in mortality and the decline in fertility
3 to identify the factors that affect the changes in fertility
4 To explore the relationship between socio-economic-demographic characteristics of the population and the extent of changes in fertility and mortality

Step 6

Make sure

Assess these objectives in the light of:
1 the work involved
2 the time available to you
3 the financial resources at your disposal
4 your (and your research supervisor's) technical expertise in the area

Step 7

Double check

1 that you are really interested in the study
2 that you agree with the objectives
3 that you have adequate resources
4 that you have the technical expertise to undertake the study

Figure 4.3   Formulating a research problem—the relationship between fertility and mortality

Example 3: Suppose you want to conduct a study in the area of health. Follow the following steps.

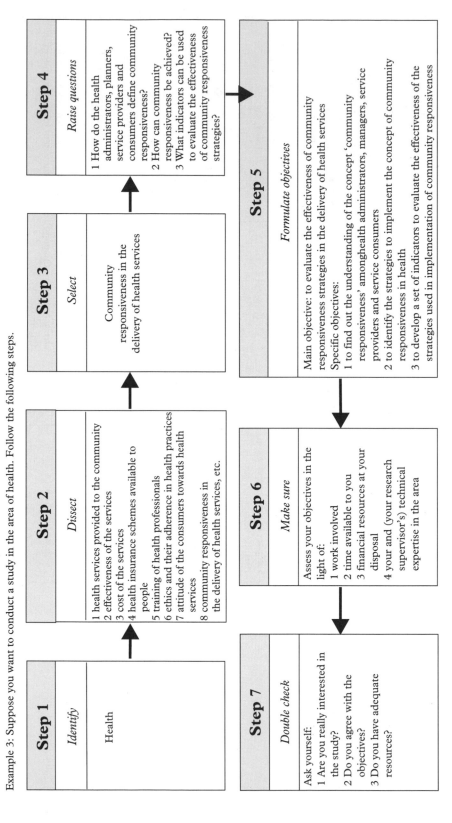

Figure 4.4   Narrowing a research problem

In many cases you need to develop operational definitions for the variable you are studying and for the population that becomes the source of the information for your study. Figure 4.5 shows the concepts and the population groups to be operationalised for the above examples.

In a research study you need to define these clearly in order to avoid ambiguity and confusion. This is achieved through the process of developing operational/working definitions. You need to develop operational definitions for the major concepts you are using in your study and to develop a framework for the study population enabling you to select appropriate respondents.

Study	Concept to be studied	Population to be studied
1	Poverty line	Children
2	Family roles	Immigrants
3	Effectiveness	The young
	Operationalise the concepts: define in practical, observable and measurable terms 'poverty line', 'family roles' and 'effectiveness'.	Operationalise the study population, define in identifiable terms children immigrants and young.

Figure 4.5   Operationalisation of concepts and the study populations.

Operational definitions may differ from dictionary definitions as well as from day-to-day meanings. These meanings may not be helpful in either identifying your study population or the concepts you are studying. Though in daily life you often use words such as children/youth/immigrant loosley, you need to be more specific when using them in a research study. You should work through your own definition.

Operational definitions give an operational meaning to the study population and the concepts used. It is only through making your procedures explicit that you can validly explain, verify and test. It is important to remember that there are no rules for deciding if an operational definition is valid. Your arguments must convince others about the appropriateness of your definitions.

Summary

The formulation of a research problem is the most important step in the research process. It is the foundation, in terms of design, on which you build the whole study. Any defects in it will adversely affect the validity and reliability of your study.

There are no specific guidelines but the model suggested in this chapter could serve as a useful framework for the beginner. The seven-step model is operational in nature and follows a logical sequence that takes the beginner through the complexities of formulating a research problem in a simple and easy-to-understand manner.

It is important to articulate the objectives of your study clearly. Objectives should be specific, free from ambiguity and each one should relate to only one aspect of the study. They should be under two headings: main objective and sub-objectives. Use action-oriented words when writing your objectives.

5

Identifying variables

The definition of a variable

The difference between a concept and a variable

Concepts, indicators and variables

Types of variable:
- From the viewpoint of causation
- From the viewpoint of the study design
- From the viewpoint of the unit of measurement

Types of measurement scales
- The nominal or classificatory scale
- The ordinal or ranking scale
- The interval scale
- The ratio scale

Summary

'If it exists, it can be measured' (Babbie 1989: 105).

In the process of formulating a research problem there are two important considerations: the use of concepts and the construction of hypotheses. Concepts are highly subjective as their understanding varies from person to person, and therefore, may not be measurable. In a research study it is important that the concepts used should be operationalised in measurable terms so that the extent of variation in respondents' understanding is reduced if not eliminated. Techniques about how to operationalise concepts, and knowledge about variables, play an important role in reducing this subjectivity. Their knowledge, therefore, is important in 'fine tuning' your research problem.

The definition of a variable

Whether we accept it or not, we all make value judgements constantly in our daily lives: 'This food is *excellent*'; 'I could not sleep *well* last night'; 'I do not *like* this'; and 'I think this is *wonderful*'. These are all judgements based upon our *own* preferences, indicators or assessment. Because these explain feelings or preferences, the basis on which they are made may vary markedly from person to person. There is no uniform yardstick with which to measure them. A particular food may be judged 'excellent' by one person but 'awful' by another and something else could be wonderful to one person but ugly to another. When people express these feelings or preferences, they do so on the basis of certain criteria in their minds. If you take the time to question them you will discover that their judgement is based upon indicators that make them conclude and express that opinion.

Let us take the same issues at another level:

- 'This program is *effective*';
- 'This program is *not effective*';
- 'We are providing a *quality* service to our clients';
- 'This is a *waste of time*';
- 'In this institution women are *discriminated* against'; and
- 'There is no *accountability* in this office'.

These are not preferences *per se*, these are judgements that require a sound basis to proclaim. For example, if you want to find out if a program is effective, if a service is of quality, or if there is discrimination, you need to be careful that such judgements have a rational and sound basis. This warrants the use of a measuring mechanism and it is in the process of measurement that knowledge about variables plays an important role.

An image, perception or concept that is capable of measurement—hence capable of taking on different values—is called a variable. In other words, a concept that can be measured is called a variable. According to Kerlinger, 'A variable is a property that takes on different values. Putting it redundantly, a variable is something that varies ... A variable is a symbol to which numerals or values are attached' (1986: 27). Black and Champion define a variable as, 'rational units of analysis that can assume any one of a number of designated sets of values' (1976: 34). A concept that can be measured on any one of the four types of measurement scale, which have varying degrees of precision in measurement, is called a variable (measurement scales are discussed later in this chapter).

However, there are some who believe that scientific methods are incapable of measuring feelings, preferences, values and sentiments. In the author's opinion most of these things can be measured, though there are situations where such feelings or judgements are incapable of direct measurement, but can be measured indirectly. These feelings and judgements are based upon observable behaviours in real life, though the extent to which the behaviours reflect their judgements may vary from person to person. Cohen and Nagel express their opinion in the following words:

> There are, indeed, a great many writers who believe that scientific method is inherently inapplicable to such judgements as estimation or value, as 'This is beautiful', 'This is good' or 'This ought to be done' ... all judgements of the latter type express nothing but feelings, tastes or individual preferences, such judgements cannot be said to be true or false (except as descriptions of the personal feelings of the one who utters them) ... Almost all human discourse would become meaningless if we took the view that every moral or aesthetic judgement is no more true or false than any other. (1966: 352)

The difference between a concept and a variable

Concepts are mental images or perceptions and therefore their meanings vary markedly from individual to individual, whereas variables are measurable, of course, with varying degrees of accuracy. Measurability is the main difference between a concept and a variable. A concept cannot be measured whereas a variable can be subjected to measurement by crude/refined or subjective/objective units of measurement. Concepts are subjective impressions—their understanding may differ from person to person—which, if measured, would cause problems in comparing responses. According to Young,

> Each collaborator must have the same understanding of the concepts if the collaborative data are to be similarly classified and the findings pooled and tested, or reproduced. Classification and comparison demand uniform and precise definitions of categories expressed in concepts (1966: 18).

It is therefore important for the concepts to be converted into variables as they can be subjected to measurement even though the degree of precision with which they can be measured varies from scale to scale. Figure 5.1 shows the difference between a concept and a variable.

Concept	Variable
• effectiveness • satisfaction • impact • excellent • high achiever • self esteem • rich • domestic violence • extent and pattern of alcohol consumption • etc.	• Gender (male/female) • attitude • age (x years, y months) • income ($ ___ per year) • weight (___ kg) • height (___ cm) • religion (Catholic, Protestant, Jew, Muslim) • etc.
Subjective impression No uniformity as to its understanding among different people As such cannot be measured	Measurable though the degree of precision varies from scale to scale and variable to variable (e.g., attitude—subjective, income—objective)

Figure 5.1   The difference between concepts and variables

Concepts, indicators and variables

If you are using a concept in your study, you need to consider its operationalisation, that is, how it will be measured. In most cases, to operationalise a concept you first need to go through the process of identifying indicators—a set of criteria reflective of the concept—which can then be converted into variables. The choice of indicators for a concept might vary with the researcher but those selected must have a logical link with the concept. Some concepts, such as 'rich', can easily be converted into indicators and then variables. For example, to decide objectively if a person is 'rich', one first needs to decide upon the indicators of richness. Assume that we decide upon income and assets as the indicators. Income is also a variable since it can be measured in dollars, therefore, you do not need to convert this into a variable. Although the assets owned by an individual are indicators of his/her 'richness', they still belong to the category of concepts. You need to look further at the indicators of assets. For example, house, boat, car and investments are indicators of assets. Converting the value of each one into dollars will give the total value of the assets owned by a person. Next, fix a level, based upon available information on income distribution and an average level of assets owned by members of a community, which acts as the basis for classification. Then analyse the information on income and the total value of the assets to make a decision about whether the person should be classified as 'rich'. The operationalisation of other concepts, such as the 'effectiveness' or 'impact' of a program, may prove more difficult. Figure 5.2 shows some examples that will help you to understand the process of converting concepts into variables.

Concepts →	Indicators →	Indicators →	Variables

Concepts	Indicators	Variables	Decision level (working definitions)
Rich	a) Income b) Assets	a) Income per year a) Total value of: Home(s); Boat; Car(s); investments	a) if > $100 000 b) if > $250 000
High academic achievement	a) Average marks obtained in examinations b) Average marks obtained in practical work c) Aggregate marks d) etc.	a) Percentage of marks b) Percentage of marks c) Percentage of marks	a) if > 75% b) if > 75% c) if > 80%
Effectiveness (of a health program) b) Changes in morbidity	a) Number of patients 1 Changes in the *extent* of morbidity 2 Changes in the *pattern* of morbidity	a) # of patients serviced in a month/year. b) 1 Changes in morbidity rate (# of illness episodes per 1000 pop) 2 Changes in morbidity typology	Whether the difference in before and after levels is statistically significant *or* Point-prevalence increase or decrease in each variable as decided by the researcher or other experts.
	c) Changes in mortality	1. Changes in the *Crude Death Rate* (CDR) 2. Changes in the *Age–Specific–Death Rate* (ASDR)	c) 1 Changes in CDR. 2 Changes in ASDR	
	d) Changes in nutritional status	1 Changes in *weight* 2 Changes in *illness episodes* 3 Changes in *morbidity*	d) 1 Changes in weight. 2 Illness episodes in a year 3 Changes in morbidity type.	

Figure 5.2   Converting concepts into variables

Types of variable

A variable can be classified in a number of ways. The classification developed here results from looking at variables in three different ways (see Figure 5.4):

- the causal relationship;
- the design of the study; and
- the unit of measurement.

From the viewpoint of causation

In studies that attempt to investigate a causal relationship or association, four sets of variables may operate (see Figure 5.3):

- **change** variables, which are responsible for bringing about change in a phenomenon;
- **outcome** variables, which are the effects of a change variable;
- variables which **affect** the link between cause and effect variables; and
- **connecting** or **linking** variables, which in certain situations are necessary to complete the relationship between cause and effect variables.

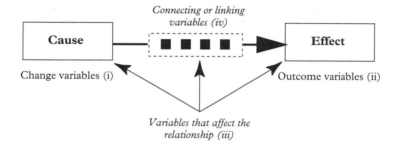

Figure 5.3   Types of variables in a causal relationship

In research terminology, change variables are called *independent variables*, outcome/effect variables are called *dependent variables*, the unmeasured variables affecting the cause and effect relationship are called *extraneous variables* and the variables that link a cause and effect relationship are called *intervening variables*. Hence:

- **Independent variable**—the cause supposed to be responsible for bringing about change(s) in a phenomenon or situation.
- **Dependent variable** —the outcome of the change(s) brought about by changes in an independent variable.
- **Extraneous variable**—several other factors operating in real-life situation may affect changes attributed to independent variables. These factors, not measured in the study, may increase or decrease the magnitude or strength of the relationship between independent and dependent variables.

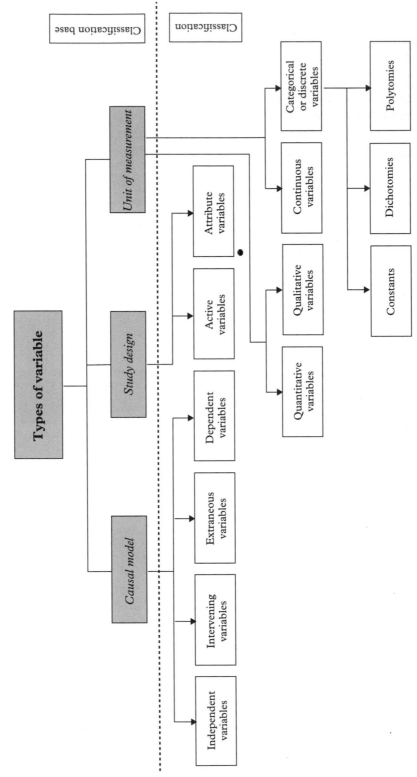

Note: Classification across a classification base is not mutually exclusive but classification within a classification base is. Within a study an independent variable can be an active variable, a quantitative or a qualitative variable and it can also be a continuous or a categorical variable but it cannot be a dependent, an extraneous or an intervening variable.

Figure 5.4   Types of variable

- **Intervening variable**—sometimes called the confounding variable (Grinnell 1988: 203), links the independent and dependent variables. In certain situations the relationship between an independent and a dependent variable cannot be established without the intervention of another variable. The cause variable will have the assumed effect only in the presence of an intervening variable.

To explain these variables let us take some examples. Suppose you want to study the relationship between smoking and cancer. You assume that smoking is a cause of cancer. Studies have shown that there are many factors affecting this relationship, such as: the number of cigarettes or the amount of tobacco smoked every day; the duration of smoking; the age of the smoker; dietary habits; and the amount of exercise undertaken by the individual. All of these factors may affect the extent to which smoking might cause cancer. These variables may either increase or decrease the magnitude of the relationship but you are not interested in measuring their impact.

In the above example the extent of smoking is the independent variable, cancer is the dependent variable and all the variables that might affect this relationship, either positively or negatively, are extraneous variables.

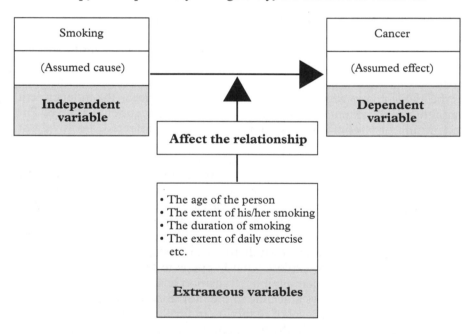

Figure 5.5 **Independent, dependent and extraneous variables in a causal relationship**

Let us take another example. Suppose you want to study the effects of a marriage counselling service on marital problems among clients of an agency providing such a service. Figure 5.6 shows the sets of variables that may operate in studying the relationship between counselling and marriage problems.

Figure 5.6   Sets of variables in counselling and marriage problems

In studying the relationship between a counselling service and marriage problems, it is assumed that the counselling service will influence, either positively or negatively, the extent of marital problems. Hence, in the study of the above relationship, the type of counselling service is the independent variable and the extent of marriage problems is the dependent variable. The magnitude or strength of this relationship can be affected, positively or negatively, by a number of other factors that are not the focus of the study. These extraneous variables might be: the birth of a child; improvement in a couple's economic situation; the couple's motivation to change the situation; the involvement of another person; self-realisation; and pressure from relatives and friends. Extraneous variables that work both ways can increase or decrease the strength of the relationship.

The example in Figure 5.7 should help you to understand intervening variables. Suppose you want to study the relationship between fertility and mortality. Your aim is to explore what happens to fertility when mortality declines. The history of demographic transition has shown that a reduction in the fertility level follows a decline in the mortality level, though the time taken to attain the same level of reduction in fertility varies markedly from country to country. As such, there is no direct relationship between fertility and mortality. With the reduction in mortality, fertility will only decline if people attempt to limit their family size. History has shown that for a multiplicity of reasons (the discussion of which is beyond the scope of this book) people have used one method or another to control their fertility, resulting in lower fertility levels. It is thus the intervention of contraceptive methods that completes the relationship: the greater the use of contraceptives, the greater the decline in the fertility level. The extent of the use of contraceptives is also affected by a number of other factors, for example, attitudes towards contraception, level of education, socio-economic status and age, religion and provision and quality of health services. These are classified as extraneous variables.

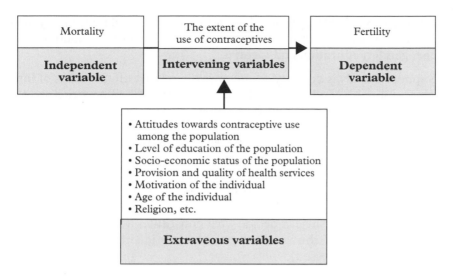

Figure 5.7   Independent, dependent, extraneous and intervening variables

In the above example, decline in mortality is assumed to be the cause of a reduction in fertility, hence, the mortality level is the independent variable and fertility is the dependent variable. But this relationship will be completed only if another variable intervenes, i.e., the use of contraceptives. A reduction in mortality (especially child mortality) increases family size, and an increase in family size creates a number of social, economic and psychological pressures on families, which in turn create attitudes favourable to a smaller family size. This change in attitudes is eventually operationalised in behaviour through the adoption of contraceptives. If people do not adopt methods of contraception, a change in mortality levels will not be reflected in fertility levels. The population explosion in developing countries is primarily due to lack of acceptance of contraceptives. The extent of the use of contraceptives determines the level of the decline in fertility. The extent of contraceptive adoption by a population is dependent upon a number of factors. In this causal model, the fertility level is the dependent variable, the extent of contraceptive use is the intervening variable, the mortality level is the independent variable, and the unmeasured variables such as attitudes, education, age, religion, the quality of services, etc. are all extraneous variables. Without the intervening variable the relationship between the independent and dependent variables will not be complete.

From the viewpoint of the study design

A study that examines association or causation may be a controlled/contrived experiment, a quasi-experiment, or an *ex post facto* study. In controlled experiments the independent (cause) variable may be introduced or manipulated either by the researcher or by someone else who is providing the service. In these situations there are two sets of variables:

- **active variables**—those variables that can be manipulated, changed or controlled.

- **attribute variables**—those that cannot be manipulated, changed or controlled, and reflect the characteristics of the study population, e.g., age, gender, education and income.

Suppose a study is designed to measure the relative effectiveness of three teaching models (Model A, Model B and Model C). The structure and contents of these models could vary and any model might be tested on any population group. The contents, structure and testability of a model on a population group may also vary from researcher to researcher. On the other hand, a researcher does not have any control over characteristics of the student population such as their age, gender or motivation to study. These characteristics of the study population are called attribute variables. However, a researcher does have the ability to control and/or change the teaching models. He/she can decide what constitutes a teaching model and on which group of the student population it should be tested (if randomisation is not used).

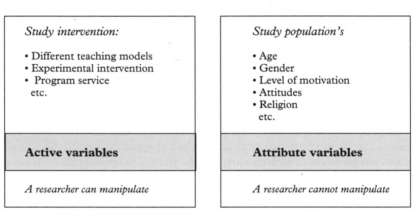

Figure 5.8   Active and attribute variables

From the viewpoint of the unit of measurement

From the viewpoint of the unit of measurement, there are two ways of categorising variables:

- whether the unit of measurement is categorical (as in nominal and ordinal scales) or continuous in nature (as in interval and ratio scales); and
- whether it is qualitative (as in nominal and ordinal scales) or quantitative in nature (as in interval and ratio scales).

The variables thus classified are called *categorical and continuous*, and *qualitative and quantitative*. On the whole there is very little difference between categorical and qualitative, and between continuous and quantitative, variables. The slight difference between them is explained below.

Categorical variables are measured on nominal or ordinal measurement scales whereas for continuous variables the measurements are made either on an interval or a ratio scale. Categorical variables can be of three types:

1 constant;
2 dichotomous; and
3 polytomous.

When a variable can have only one value or category, e.g., taxi, tree, water, it is known as a *constant*. When a variable can have only two categories as in yes/no; good/bad; rich/poor, it is known as a *dichotomous variable*. When a variable can be divided into more than two categories, e.g., religion (Christian, Muslim, Hindu); political parties (Labor, Liberal, Democrat); attitudes (strongly favourable, favourable, uncertain, unfavourable, strongly unfavourable), it is called a *polytomous variable*.

Continuous variables, on the other hand, have continuity in their measurement. For example, age, income, and attitude score. They can take on any value on the scale on which they are measured. Age can be measured in years, months and days. Similarly, income can be measured in dollars and cents.

In many ways qualitative variables are similar to categorical ones as both use either nominal or ordinal measurement scales. However, there are some differences. For example, it is possible to develop categories on the basis of measurements made on a continuous scale, such as measuring the income of a population in dollars and cents and then developing categories such as 'low', 'middle' and 'high' income. The measurement of income in dollars and cents is classified as the measurement on a continuous variable whereas its subjective measurement in categories such as 'low', 'middle' and 'high' groups is a qualitative variable.

Categorical			Continuous	Qualitative	Quantitative
Constant	**Dichotomous**	**Polytomous**			
- water	- yes/no	Attitudes:	Income ($)	Gender:	Educational
		- strongly		- female	level:
- tree	- good/bad	favourable	- Age (years)	-male	X No. of years
		- favourable		Educational	completed
- taxi	- rich/poor	- uncertain	-Weight	level:	
		- strongly	(kg)	- high	Age:*
	- day/night	unfavourable		-average	X ____
		Political		- low	years/months
	- male/	Parties:		Age: ^	
	female	- Labor		- old	Income ^
		- Liberal		- young	X ____ $ per
	- hot/cold^	- Democrat		- child	year
		Age*			
		- old		- high	Temperature:+
		- young		- middle	X ____ C or F
		- child		- low	
		Income: ^		Temperature:+	
		- high		- hot	
		- middle		- cold	
		- low			

* Can be classified in qualitative categories, e.g., old, young, child; or quantitatively on a continuous scale, e.g., in years, months and days.
^ = Can be measured quantitatively in dollars and cents as well as qualitatively in categories such as high, middle and low.
+ Similarly temperature can be measured quantitatively in degrees on different scales (Centigrade, Fahrenheit) or in qualitative categories such as hot, cold.

Figure 5.9   Categorical/continuous and quantitative/qualitative variables

Although this distinction exists, for most practical purposes there is no real difference between categorical and qualitative variables or between continuous and quantitative variables. Figure 5.9 shows similarities and differences among the various types of variable.

For a beginner it is important to understand that the way a variable is measured determines the type of analysis that can be performed, the statistical procedures that can be applied to the data, the way the data can be interpreted and the findings that can be communicated. You may not realise in the beginning that the style of your report is entirely dependent upon the way the different variables have been measured. The way you measure the variables in your study determines whether a study is 'qualitative' or 'quantitative' in nature. It is therefore important to know about the measurement scales for variables.

Types of measurement scales

The frame into which we wish to make everything fit is one of our own construction; but we do not construct it at random, we construct it by measurement so to speak; and that is why we can fit the facts into it without altering their essential qualities (Poincaré 1952: xxv).

Measurement is central to any scientific inquiry. The greater the refinement in the unit of measurement of a variable, the greater the confidence, other things being equal, one can place in the findings. One of the main differences between the physical and the social sciences is the units of measurement used and the degree of importance attached to them. In the physical sciences measurements are to be absolutely accurate and precise, whereas in the social sciences they may vary from the very subjective to the very quantifiable. Within the social sciences the emphasis on precision in measurement varies markedly from one discipline to another. An anthropologist normally uses very 'subjective' units of measurement, whereas an economist or an epidemiologist emphasises 'objective' measurement.

There are two main classification systems in the social sciences for measuring different types of variable. One was developed by S. S. Stevens (1946) and the other by Duncan (1984). According to Smith (1991: 72), 'Duncan (1984) has enumerated, in increasing order of interest to scientists, five types of measurement: nominal classification, ordinal scaling, cardinal scaling, ratio scaling, and probability scaling (1991: 72).' Duncan writes about Stevens' classification as follows:

the theory of scale types proposed in 1946 by S S Stevens focused on nominal, ordinal, interval, and ratio scales of measurement. Some of his examples of these types—notably those concerning psychological test scores—are misleading (1984: viii).

However, Bailey considers that, 'S S Stevens constructed a widely adopted classification of levels of measurement ...' (1978: 52). As this book is written for the beginner and as Stevens' classification is easier, it is used for discussion in this chapter. Stevens has classified the different types of measurement scale into four categories:

- nominal or classificatory;
- ordinal or ranking;
- interval; and
- ratio.

The nominal or classificatory scale

A nominal scale enables the classification of individuals, objects or responses based on a common/shared property or characteristic. These people, objects or responses are divided into a number of sub-groups in such a way that each member of the sub-group has a common characteristic. A variable measured on a nominal scale may have one, two or more sub-categories depending upon the extent of variation. For example, 'water' and 'tree' have only one sub-group whereas the variable 'gender' can be classified into two sub-categories: male and female. Political parties in Australia can similarly be classified into four sub-categories: Labor, Liberal, Democrats and Greens. Those who identify themselves, either by membership or belief, as belonging to the Labor Party are classified as 'Labor', those identifying with the Liberals are classified as 'Liberal', etc. The name chosen for a sub-category is notional, but for effective communication it is best to choose something that describes the characteristic of the sub-category.

Classification by means of a nominal scale ensures that individuals, objects or responses within the same sub-group have a common characteristic or property as the basis of classification. The sequence in which sub-groups are listed makes no difference as there is no relationship among sub-groups.

The ordinal or ranking scale

An ordinal scale has all the properties of a nominal scale plus one of its own. Besides categorising individuals, objects, responses or a property into sub-groups on the basis of a common characteristic, it ranks the sub-groups in a certain order. They are arranged either in ascending or descending order according to the extent a sub-category reflects the magnitude of variation in the variable. For example, income can be measured either quantitatively (in dollars and cents) or qualitatively, using sub-categories: 'above average', 'average', and 'below average'. (These categories can also be developed on the basis of quantitative measures, for example, <\$10 000 = below average, \$10 000–\$25,000 = average and above \$25 000 = above average). The sub-category 'above-average' indicates that people so grouped have more income than people in the 'average' category, and people in the 'average' category have more income than those in the 'below average' category. These sub-categories of income are related to one another in terms of the magnitude of people's income, but the magnitude itself is not quantifiable, and hence, the difference between 'above average' and 'average' or between 'average' and 'below average' sub-categories cannot be ascertained. The same is true for other variables such as socio-economic status and attitudes measured on an ordinal scale.

Therefore, an ordinal scale has all the properties/characteristics of a nominal scale, in addition to its own. Sub-categories are arranged in the order of the magnitude of the property/characteristics. Also, the 'distance' between the sub-categories is not equal as there is no quantitative unit of measurement.

The interval scale

An interval scale has all the characteristics of an ordinal scale, i.e., individuals or responses belonging to a sub-category have a common characteristic and the sub-categories are arranged in an ascending or descending order. In addition, an interval scale uses a unit of measurement that enables the individuals or responses to be placed at equally spaced intervals in relation to the spread of the variable. This scale has a starting and a terminating point that is divided into equally spaced units/intervals. The starting and terminating points and the number of units/intervals between them are arbitrary and vary from scale to scale.

Centigrade and Fahrenheit scales are examples of the interval scale. In the Centigrade system the starting point (considered as freezing point) is zero and the terminating point (considered as boiling point) is 100 C°. The gap between freezing and boiling points is divided into 100 equally spaced intervals, known as degrees. In the Fahrenheit system the freezing point is 32°F and the boiling point, 212°F, and the gap between the two points is divided into 180 equally spaced intervals. Each degree or interval is a measurement of temperature. The higher the degree, the higher the temperature. As the starting and terminating points are arbitrary, they are not absolute, i.e., you cannot say that 60°C is twice as hot as 30°C or 30°F is three times hotter than 10°F. This means that while no mathematical operation can be performed on the readings, it can be performed on the differences between readings. For example, if the difference in temperature between two objects, A and B, is 15°C and the difference in temperature between two other objects, C and D, is 45°C, you can say that the difference in temperature between C and D is three times greater than that between A and B. An attitude towards an issue measured on the Likert scale is similar. The Likert scale does not measure the absolute intensity of the attitude but simply measures it in relation to another person.

The interval scale is relative, i.e., it plots the position of individuals or responses in relation to one another with respect to the magnitude of the measurement variable. Hence, an interval scale has all the properties of an ordinal scale, plus it has a unit of measurement with an arbitrary starting and terminating point. Therefore, it is relative in nature. It helps to place individuals or responses in relation to each other with respect to the magnitude of the measuring variable. As it is a relative scale no mathematical operations can be performed on its readings.

	Nominal or classificatory	Ordinal or ranking	Interval	Ratio

Examples	A Tree, house, taxi, etc.
	B Gender: male/female
	  Attitude: favourable/ unfavourable
	C Political parties:
	  Labor
	  Liberal
	  Democrat
	  Green
	Psychiatric disorders:
	  Schizophrenic
	  Paranoid
	  Manic-depressive
	  etc.
	Religions:
	  Christian
	  Islam
	  Hindu
	  etc.
		Income:
		  above average
		  average
		  below average
		
		Socio-economic status:
		  upper
		  middle
		  low
		
		Attitudes:
		  strongly favourable
		  favourable
		  uncertain
		  unfavourable
		  strongly unfavourable
		Attitudinal scale (Likert scale):
		  10–30
		  31–40
		  41–50
		  etc.
			Temperature:
			  Centigrade → °C
			  Fahrenheit → 32°F
			
			Attitudinal Scale (Thurstone Scale):
			  10–20
			  21–30
			  31–40
			  41–50
			  etc.
				Height: cm, inches
				
				Income $
				
				Age: years/months
				
				Weight: kg
				
				Attitudinal score: Guttman Scale

Measurement Scale Characteristics of the scale	1 Each sub-group has a characteristic/property which is common to all classified within that sub-group	1 Have all the characteristics of a Nominal scale, e.g., individuals, groups, characteristic classified under a sub-group have a common characteristic PLUS 2 Sub-groups have a relationship to one another. They are arranged in ascending or descending order.	1 Has all the characteristics of an Ordinal scale (which also includes a Nominal scale). PLUS 2 It has a unit of measurement with an arbitrary starting and terminating point.	1 Has all the properties of an interval scale. PLUS 2 It has a fixed starting point e.g., a zero point.

Figure 5.10 Characteristics and examples of the four measurement scales

The ratio scale

A ratio scale has all the properties of nominal, ordinal and interval scales plus its own property: the zero point of a ratio scale is fixed, which means it has a fixed starting point. Therefore, it is an absolute scale—the difference between the intervals is always measured from a zero point. This means the ratio scale can be used for mathematical operations. The measurement of income, age, height and weight are examples of this scale. A person who is 40 years of age is twice as old as a 20-year-old. A person earning \$60 000 per year earns three times the salary of a person earning \$20 000. Figure 5.10 summarises the characteristics of the four scales.

Summary

Knowledge of the different types of variables and the way they are measured plays a crucial role in research. Variables are important in bringing clarity and specificity to the conceptualisation of a research problem, to the formulation of hypotheses, and to the development of a research instrument. They affect how the data can be analysed, what statistical tests can be applied to the data, what interpretations can be made, how the data can be presented, and what conclusions can be drawn. The way you ask a question determines its categorisation on a measurement scale, which in turn affects how the data can be analysed, what statistical tests can be applied to the data, what interpretations can be made, how the data can be presented and what conclusions can be drawn. Also, the way a variable is measured at the data collection stage to a great extent determines whether a study is considered to be predominantly 'qualitative' or 'quantitative' in nature. It is important for a beginner to understand the different ways in which a variable can be measured and the implications of this for the study. A variable can be classified from three perspectives that are not mutually exclusive: causal relationship, design of the study, and unit of measurement.

There are four measurement scales used in the social sciences: nominal, ordinal, interval, and ratio. Any concept that can be measured on these scales is called a variable. Measurement scales enable highly subjective responses, as well as responses that can be measured with extreme precision, to be categorised. The choice of measuring a variable on a measurement scale is dependent upon the purpose of your study and the way you want to communicate the findings to readers.

6

Constructing hypotheses

Almost every great step [in the history of science] has been made by the 'anticipation of nature', that is, by the invention of hypotheses which, though verifiable, often had very little foundation to start with. (T H Huxley cited in Cohen and Nagel 1966: 197).

The definition of a hypothesis

The second important consideration in the formulation of a research problem is the construction of hypotheses. Hypotheses bring clarity, specificity, and focus to a research problem, but are not essential for a study. You can conduct a valid investigation without constructing a single formal hypothesis. On the other hand, within the context of a research study, you can construct as many hypotheses as you consider to be appropriate. Some believe that one must formulate a hypothesis to undertake an investigation, however, the author does not hold this opinion. Hypotheses primarily arise from a set of 'hunches' that are tested through a study and one can conduct a perfectly valid study without having these hunches or speculations. However, in epidemiological studies, to narrow the field of investigation, it is important to formulate hypotheses.

The importance of hypotheses lies in their ability to bring direction, specificity and focus to a research study. They tell a researcher what specific information to collect, and thereby provide greater focus.

Let us imagine you are at the races and you place a bet. You bet on a hunch that a particular horse will win. You will only know if your hunch was right after the race. Take another example. Suppose you have a hunch that there are more smokers than non-smokers in your class. To test your hunch, you ask either all or just some of the class if they are smokers. You can then conclude whether your hunch was right or wrong.

Now let us take a slightly different example. Suppose you work in the area of public health. Your clinical impression is that a higher rate of a particular condition prevails among people coming from a specific population sub-group. You want to find out the probable cause of this condition. There could be many causes. To explore every conceivable possibility would require an enormous amount of time and resources. Hence, to narrow the choice, based on your knowledge of the field, identify what you assume to be the most probable cause. Design a study to collect the information needed to verify your hunch. If on verification you are able to conclude that the assumed cause is the real cause of the condition, your assumption was right.

In these examples, you started with a superficial hunch or assumption. In one case (horse racing) you waited for the event to take place and in the other two instances you designed a study to assess the validity of your assumption, and only after careful investigation did you reach a conclusion about the validity of your assumptions.

Hypotheses are based upon similar logic. As a researcher you *do not know* about a phenomenon, a situation, the prevalence of a condition in a population or about the outcome of a program but you *do have a hunch* to form the basis of certain *assumptions or guesses*. You test these by collecting information that will enable you to conclude if your hunch was right. The verification process can have one of the three outcomes. Your hunch may prove to be

1 right;
2 partially right; or
3 wrong.

Without this process of verification, you cannot conclude anything about the validity of your assumption.

Hence, a hypothesis is a hunch, assumption, suspicion, assertion or an idea about a phenomenon, relationship or situation, the reality or truth of which you do not know. A researcher calls these assumptions, assertions, statements or hunches hypotheses and they become the basis of an inquiry. In most studies the hypothesis will be based upon either previous studies or on your own or someone else's observation.

There are many definitions of a hypothesis. According to Kerlinger, 'A hypothesis is a conjectural statement of the relationship between two or more variables' (1986: 17). *Webster's New International Dictionary of English Language*, defines a hypothesis as

> a proposition, condition, or principle which is assumed, perhaps without belief, in order to draw out its logical consequences and by this method to test its accord with facts which are known or may be determined.

Black and Champion define a hypothesis as, 'a tentative statement about something, the validity of which is usually unknown' (1976: 126). In another definition, Bailey defines a hypothesis as:

> a proposition that is stated in a testable form and that predicts a particular relationship between two (or more) variables. In other words, if we think that a relationship exists, we first state it as a hypothesis and then test the hypothesis in the field (1978: 35).

According to Grinnell and Stothers,

> A hypothesis is written in such a way that it can be proven or disproven by valid and reliable data—it is in order to obtain these data that we perform our study (Grinnell 1988: 200).

From the above definitions it is apparent that a hypothesis has certain characteristics:

1 it is a tentative proposition;
2 its validity is unknown; and
3 in most cases, it specifies a relationship between two or more variables.

The functions of a hypothesis

While some researchers believe that to conduct a study requires a hypothesis, as already mentioned, having a hypothesis is not essential. However, a hypothesis is important in terms of bringing clarity to the research problem. Specifically, it serves the following functions.

Figure 6.1   The process of testing a hypothesis

- The formulation of a hypothesis provides a study with focus. It tells you what specific aspects of a research problem to investigate.
- A hypothesis tells you what data to collect and what not to collect thereby providing focus to the study.
- As it provides a focus, the construction of a hypothesis enhances objectivity in a study.
- A hypothesis may enable you to add to the formulation of theory and help you to bridge the gaps in the body of knowledge. According to Kerlinger, '... hypotheses are a particularly potent means of objectively bridging the gap between one's beliefs and empirical reality (1979: 36).'

The characteristics of a hypothesis

There is a number of considerations to keep in mind, as they are important for valid verification, when constructing hypotheses.

- *A hypothesis should be simple, specific and conceptually clear*–there is no place for ambiguity in the construction of a hypothesis, as ambiguity will make the verification of your hypothesis almost impossible. It should be 'uni-dimensional', that is, it should test only one relationship at a time. To be able to develop a good hypothesis you must be familiar with the subject area (the literature review is of immense help). The more insight you have into a problem, the easier it is to construct a hypothesis. For example:
—the average age of the male students in this class is higher than that of the female students.
The above hypothesis is clear, specific, and easy to test. It tells you what you are attempting to compare (average age of this class), which population groups are being compared (female and male students), and what you want to establish (higher average age of the male students).
—'Suicide rates vary inversely with social cohesion' (Black and Champion 1976: 126).
This hypothesis is clear and specific, but a lot more difficult to test. There are three aspects of this hypothesis: 'suicide rates'; 'vary inversely', which stipulates the direction of the relationship; and 'social cohesion'. To find out the suicide rates and to establish whether the relationship is inverse or otherwise are comparatively easy, but to ascertain social cohesion is a

lot more difficult. What determines social cohesion? How can it be measured? This problem makes it more difficult to test this hypothesis.

- *A hypothesis should be capable of verification*—methods and techniques must be available for data collection and analysis. There is no point in formulating a hypothesis if it cannot be subjected to verification because there are no techniques to verify it. However, this does not necessarily mean that you should not formulate a hypothesis for which there are no methods of verification. You might, in the process of doing your research, develop new techniques to verify it.
- *A hypothesis should be related to the body of knowledge*—it is important that your hypothesis emerges from the existing body of knowledge, and that it adds to it, as this is an important function of research. This can only be achieved if the hypothesis has its roots in the existing body of knowledge.
- *A hypothesis should be operationalisable*—that is, it can be expressed in terms that can be measured. If it cannot be measured, it cannot be tested and, hence, no conclusions can be drawn.

Types of hypothesis

As explained, any assumption that you seek to validate through an inquiry is called a hypothesis. Hence, theoretically there should be only one type of hypothesis, that is, the research hypothesis—the basis of your investigation. However, because of the conventions in scientific inquiries and because of the wording used in the construction of a hypothesis, hypotheses can be classified into several types. Broadly, there are two categories of hypothesis:

1 research hypotheses; and
2 alternate hypotheses.

The formulation of an alternate hypothesis is a convention in scientific circles. Its main function is to explicitly specify the relationship that will be considered as true in case the research hypothesis proves to be wrong. In a way, an alternate hypothesis is the opposite of the research hypothesis. Again, conventionally, a null hypothesis, or hypothesis of no difference, is formulated as an alternate hypothesis.

Let us take an example. Suppose you want to test the effect different combinations of maternal and child health services (MCH) and nutrition supplements (NS) have on the infant mortality rate. To test this a two-by-two factorial experimental design is adopted (see Figure 6.2).

There are several ways of formulating a hypothesis. For example:

1 There will be no difference in the level of infant mortality among the different treatment modalities.
2 The MCH and NS treatment group will register a greater decline in infant mortality than either the MCH, the NS treatment or the control group.
3 Infant mortality in the MCH treatment group will reach a level of 30/1000 over five years.

Maternal and Child Health Services (MCH)

	Yes	No
Yes	MCH + NS	NS
No	MCH	Control

Nutrition supplements (NS)

Figure 6.2   **2 x 2 factorial experiment to study the relationship between MCH, NS and infant mortality**

4 Decline in the infant mortality rate will be three times greater in the MCH treatment group than in the NS one over five years.

Let us take another example. Suppose you want to study the smoking pattern in a community in relation to gender differentials. The following hypotheses could be constructed.

1 There is no significant difference in the proportion of male and female smokers in the study population.
2 A greater proportion of females than males are smokers in the study population.
3 Sixty per cent of females and thirty per cent of males in the study population are smokers.
4 There are twice as many female smokers as male smokers in the study population.

In both sets of examples, the way the first hypothesis has been formulated indicates that there is no difference either in the extent of the impact of different treatment modalities on the infant mortality rate or in the proportion of male and female smokers. When you construct a hypothesis stipulating that there is no difference between two situations, groups, outcomes, or the prevalence of a condition or phenomenon, this is called a *null hypothesis* and is usually written as Ho.

The second hypothesis in each example implies that there is a difference either in the extent of the impact of different treatment modalities on infant mortality or in the proportion of male and female smokers among the population, though the extent of the difference is not specified. A hypothesis in which a researcher stipulates that there will be a difference but does not specify its magnitude is called a *hypothesis of difference*.

A researcher may have enough knowledge about the smoking behaviour of the community or the treatment program and its likely outcomes to speculate almost the exact prevalence of the situation or the outcome of a treatment program in quantitative units. Examine the third hypothesis in both sets of examples: the level of infant mortality is 30/1000 and the proportion of male and female smokers is sixty and thirty per cent respectively. This type of hypothesis is known as a *hypothesis of point-prevalence*.

The fourth hypothesis in both sets of examples speculates a relationship between the impact of different combinations of MCH and NS programs on the dependent variable (infant mortality) or the relationship between the prevalence of a phenomenon (smoking) among different populations (male and female). This type of hypothesis stipulates the extent of the relationship in terms of the effect of different treatment groups on the dependent variable ('three times greater in the MCH treatment group than in the NS one over five years') or the prevalence of a phenomenon in different population groups ('twice as many female as male smokers'). This type of hypothesis is called a *hypothesis of association*.

There may be some confusion about null and research hypotheses as in Figure 6.3 the null hypothesis is also classified under 'research hypothesis'. Any type of hypothesis, including a null hypothesis, can become the basis of an inquiry. When a null hypothesis becomes the basis of an investigation, it becomes a research hypothesis.

Figure 6.3   Types of hypothesis

Errors in testing a hypothesis

As already mentioned, a hypothesis is an assumption thay may prove to be either correct or incorrect. It is possible to arrive at an incorrect conclusion about a hypothesis for a variety of reasons. Incorrect conclusions about the validity of a hypothesis may be drawn if:

- the study design selected is faulty;
- the sampling procedure adopted is faulty;
- the method of data collection is inaccurate;
- the analysis is wrong;
- the statistical procedures applied are inappropriate; or
- the conclusions drawn are incorrect.

Any, some or all of these aspects of the research process could be responsible for the inadvertent introduction of error in your study, making conclusions meaningless. Hence, in the testing of a hypothesis there is always the possibility of errors attributable to the reasons identified above. Figure 6.4 shows the types of error that can result in the testing of a hypothesis.

When a null hypothesis is actually:

	True	False
Accept	Correct decision	Type I error
Reject	Type II error	Correct decision

When your decision is to:

Figure 6.4   **Type I and Type II errors in testing a hypothesis**

Hence in drawing conclusions about a hypothesis, two types of error can occur:

- *rejection* of a null hypothesis when it is true. This is known as a Type I error.
- *acceptance* of a *null* hypothesis when it is false. This is known as a Type II error.

Summary

Hypotheses, though important, are not essential for a study. A perfectly valid study can be conducted without constructing a single hypothesis. Hypotheses are important for bringing clarity, specificity and focus to a research study.

A hypothesis is a speculative statement that is subjected to verification through a research study. In formulating a hypothesis it is important to ensure that it is simple, specific, conceptually clear, able to be verified, rooted in a body of knowledge and able to be operationalised.

There are two broad types of hypothesis: a research hypothesis, and an alternate hypothesis. A research hypothesis can be further classified, based upon the way it is formulated, as a null hypothesis, a hypothesis of difference, a hypothesis of point-prevalence, and a hypothesis of association.

The testing of a hypothesis becomes meaningless if any one of the aspects of your study—design, sampling procedure, method of data collection, analysis of data, statistical procedures applied or conclusions drawn—is faulty or inappropriate. This can result in erroneous verification of a hypothesis: Type I where you reject a null hypothesis when it is true and should not have been rejected; or Type II where you accept a null hypothesis when it is false and should not have been accepted.

Step II

Conceptualising a research design

7

The research design

Having decided *what* you want to study *about*, the next question is, *how* are you going to conduct your study? What procedures will you adopt to obtain answers to research questions? How will you carry out the tasks needed to complete the different components of the research process? What should you do and what should you not do in the process of undertaking the study? These are some of the questions that need to be answered before you can proceed with the study. Basically, answers to these questions constitute the core of a research design.

The definition of a research design

A research design is a plan, structure and strategy of investigation so conceived as to obtain answers to research questions or problems. The plan is the complete scheme or program of the research. It includes an outline of what the investigator will do from writing the hypotheses and their operational implications to the final analysis of data (Kerlinger 1986: 279).

A traditional research design is a blueprint or detailed plan for how a research study is to be completed—operationalizing variables so they can be measured, selecting a sample of interest to study, collecting data to be used as a basis for testing hypotheses, and analysing the results (Thyer 1993: 94).

A research design is a procedural plan that is adopted by the researcher to answer questions validly, objectively, accurately, and economically. According to Jahoda et al., 'A research design is the arrangement of conditions for collection and analysis of data in a manner that aims to combine relevance to the research purpose with economy in procedure' (1962: 50).

The functions of a research design

The above definitions suggest that a research design has two main functions. The first relates to the identification and/or development of procedures and logistical arrangements required to undertake a study, and the second emphasises the importance of quality in these procedures to ensure their validity, objectivity and accuracy. Hence, through a research design you:

- conceptualise an operational plan to undertake the various procedures and tasks required to complete your study; and
- ensure that these procedures are adequate to obtain valid, objective and accurate answers to the research questions. Kerlinger calls this function the 'control of variance' (1986: 280).

Let us explain the second function first by taking a few examples. Suppose you want to find out the effectiveness of a marriage counselling service provided by an agency, that is, the extent to which the service has been able to resolve the marital problems of its clients. In studying this relationship there are several variables that can affect the dependent variable (the extent of marital problems):

- the independent variable (the type of counselling service);
- extraneous variables (the items listed in the box in Figure 7.1);
- and chance or random variables (variables that can be associated with the respondents and/or the research instrument).

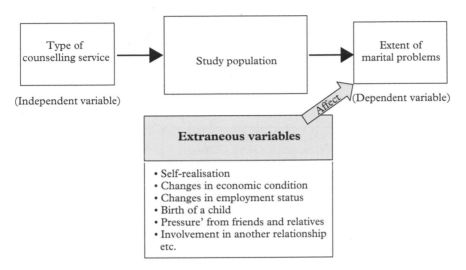

Figure 7.1 Factors affecting the relationship between a counselling service and the extent of marital problems

Extraneous as well as chance variables can affect the dependent variable in both positive and negative ways. In some cases they may help in resolving marital problems (positive effect), thereby adding to the assumed effect of the independent variable on the dependent variable whereas they may stand in the way of resolving the marital problem, thus, decreasing the assumed effect of the independent variable on the dependent variable (negative effect). For example, a change in economic conditions can work both ways. An improvement may resolve some of the problems while deterioration may increase them. If you closely study this relationship, the change in the dependent variable (the extent of marital problems) can be attributed to three sets of variable.

Total change in extent of marital problems =

> change attributable to counselling service ±
> change attributable to extraneous variables ±
> change attributable to chance variables

Let us take another example. Suppose you want to study the impact of different teaching models on the level of comprehension of students for which you adopt a comparative study design. In this study, the change in the level of comprehension can be attributed to a number of factors, some of which are shown in Figure 7.2.

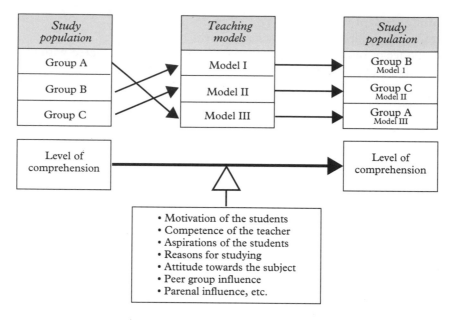

Figure 7.2   The relationship between teaching models and comprehension

Change in level of comprehension =

> change attributable to the teaching model ±
> change attributable to extraneous variables ±
> change attributable to chance variables.

In fact, in any study that attempts to establish a causal relationship, you will discover that there are three sets of variables operating to bring about a change in the dependent variable. This can be expressed as an equation:

> change in the outcome variable =
>
> change because of the cause variable ±
> change because of extraneous variables ±
> change because of chance or random variables

or in technical terms:

> change in the dependent variable =
>
> change attributable to the independent variable ±
> change attributable to extraneous variables ±
> change attributable to chance variables

or

> total variance =
>
> variance attributable to the independent variable ±
> variance attributable to extraneous variables ±
> random or chance variance

or graphically (see figure 7.4).

Figure 7.3   The proportion attributable to the three components may vary markedly

As the total change measures the combined effect of all three components it is difficult to isolate the impact of each of them (see Figure 7.3). Since your aim as a researcher is to determine the change that can be attributed to the independent variable, design your study to ensure that the independent variable has the maximum opportunity to have its full effect on the dependent variable, whilst the effects that are attributed to extraneous and chance variables are minimised. This is what Kerlinger (1986: 286) calls the 'maxmincon' principle of variance.

One of the most important questions is: how do we minimise the effect attributable to extraneous and chance variables? The answer is that we cannot minimise it, but it can be quantified. The sole purpose of having a control group is to measure the change that is a result of extraneous variables. The effect of chance variables is often assumed to be none or negligible. As discussed, chance variation comes primarily from two sources: respondents and the research instrument. It is assumed that if some respondents affect the dependent variable positively, others will affect it negatively. For example, if some respondents are extremely positive in their attitude towards an issue, being very liberal or positively biased, there are bound to be others who are extremely negative (being very conservative or negatively biased). Hence, they tend to cancel each other out so the net effect is assumed to be zero. Therefore, in most studies chance variance is considered to be nil. However, if in a study population most individuals are either negatively or positively biased, a systematic error in the findings will be introduced. Similarly, if a research instrument is not reliable, that is, it is not measuring correctly what it is supposed to measure, a systematic bias may be introduced into the study.

In the physical sciences a researcher can control extraneous variables as experiments are usually done in a laboratory. By contrast, in the social sciences, the laboratory is society, over which the researcher lacks control. Since no researcher has control over extraneous variables their effect, as mentioned, is extremely difficult to minimise. The best option is to quantify their impact through the use of a control group, though the introduction of a control group creates the problem of ensuring that the extraneous variables have a similar effect on both control and experimental groups. In some situations their impact can be eliminated (this is possible only where one or two variables have a marked impact on the dependent variable). There are two methods used to ensure that extraneous variables have a similar effect on control and experimental groups and two methods for eliminating extraneous variables.

1 *Ensure that extraneous variables have a similar impact on control and experimental groups.* It is assumed that if two groups are comparable, the extent to which the extraneous variables will affect the dependent variable will be similar in both groups. The following two methods ensure that the control and experimental groups are comparable to one another:

   • **Randomisation**—ensures that the two groups are comparable with respect to the variable(s). It is assumed that if the groups are comparable, the extent to which extraneous variables are going to affect the dependent variable is the same in each group.

   • **Matching**—another way of ensuring that the two groups are comparable so that the effect of extraneous variables will be the same in both groups (discussed in Chapter 8).

2 *Eliminate extraneous variable(s).* Sometimes it is possible to eliminate the extraneous variable, or to build it into the study design. This is usually done when there is strong evidence that the extraneous variable has a high correlation with the dependent variable, or when you want to isolate the impact of the extraneous variable separately. There are two methods used to achieve this:

   • **Build the affecting variable into the design of the study**—to explain this concept let us take an example. Suppose you want to study the impact of maternal health services on the infant mortality of a population. It can be assumed that the nutritional status of children also has a marked effect on infant mortality. To study the impact of maternal health services *per se*, you adopt a two-by-two factorial design as explained in Figure 7.4.

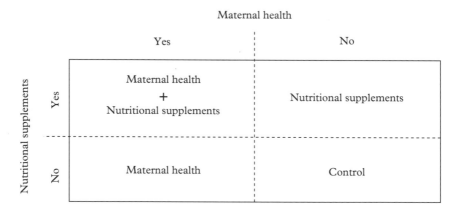

Figure 7.4   Building into the design

   • **Eliminate the variable**—to understand this, let us take another example. Suppose you want to study the impact of a health education program on the attitudes towards and beliefs about the causation and treatment of a certain illness among Europeans and Aboriginal people living in a particular community. As attitudes and beliefs vary markedly from culture to culture, studying Europeans and Aboriginal people as one group will not provide an accurate picture. In such studies it is appropriate to eliminate the cultural variation in the study population by selecting and studying the populations separately or by constructing culture-specific cohorts at the time of analysis.

Let us now come back to the first function of a research design, which relates to the overall plan of the study. It details for you, your supervisor and other readers all the procedures you plan to use and the tasks you are going to perform to obtain answers to your research questions. One of the most important requirements of a research design is to specify everything clearly so a reader will understand what procedures to follow and how to follow them. A research design, therefore, should:

- name the study design *per se*, that is, 'cross-sectional', 'before-and-after', 'comparative', 'control experiment' or 'random control'; and
- provide detailed information about the following aspects of the study:
  –who will constitute the study population?
  –how will the study population be identified?
  –will a sample or the whole population be selected?
  –if a sample is selected, how will it be contacted?
  –how will consent be sought?
  –what method of data collection will be used and why?
  –in the case of a questionnaire, where will the responses be returned?
  –how should respondents contact you if they have queries?
  –in the case of an interview, where will they be conducted?

Chapter 8 describes some of the commonly used study designs. The rest of the topics that constitute a research design are covered in the following chapters.

Summary

In this chapter you have learnt about the functions of a research design: to detail the procedures for undertaking a study (e.g., study design, sampling, measurement); and to ensure that, if a study seeks to establish a causal relationship, the independent variable has the maximum opportunity to have its effect on the dependent variable whilst the effect of extraneous and chance variables is minimised.

A study without a control measures the total change (change attributable to independent variable ± extraneous variables ± chance variables) in a phenomenon or situation. The purpose of introducing a control group is to quantify the impact of extraneous and chance variables.

The study design is a part of the research design. It is the design of the study *per se*, whereas the research design also includes other details related to the carrying out of the study.

Selecting a study design

The number of contacts:
- The cross-sectional study design
- The before-and-after study design
- The longitudinal study design

The reference period:
- The retrospective study design
- The prospective study design
- The retrospective–prospective study design

The nature of the investigation:
- The experimental study designs
- Some other commonly used designs

Summary

In this chapter we will discuss some of the most commonly used study designs. The various designs have been classified by examining them from three different perspectives:

- the number of contacts with the study population;
- the reference period of the study; and
- the nature of the investigation.

Every study design can be classified from each one of these perspectives. These perspectives are arbitrary bases of classification, hence, the terminology used to describe them is not universal, but the names of the designs within each classification-base are universally used. Note that the designs within each category are mutually exclusive, i.e., if a particular study is cross-sectional in nature it cannot be at the same time a before-and-after or a longitudinal study but it can be a non-experimental or experimental, as well as a retrospective or a prospective study.

The number of contacts

Based on the number of contacts with the study population, designs can be classified into three groups:

- cross-sectional studies;
- before-and-after studies; and
- longitudinal studies.

The cross-sectional study design

Cross-sectional studies, also known as one-shot or status studies, are the most commonly used design in the social sciences. This design is best suited to studies aimed at finding out the prevalence of a phenomenon, situation, problem, attitude or issue, by taking a cross-section of the population. They are useful in obtaining an overall 'picture' as it stands at the time of the study. They are 'designed to study some phenomenon by taking a cross-section of it at one time.' (Babbie 1989: 89). Such studies are cross-sectional with regard to both the study population and the time of investigation.

A cross-sectional study is extremely simple in design. You decide what you want to find out, identify the study population, select a sample (if you need to), and contact your respondents to find out the required information. For example, a cross-sectional design would be the most appropriate for a study of the following topics:

- The attitude of the study population towards uranium mining in Australia.
- The socio-economic–demographic characteristics of immigrants in Western Australia.
- The incidence of HIV positive cases in Australia.
- The reasons for homelessness among young people.
- The quality assurance of a service provided by an organisation.

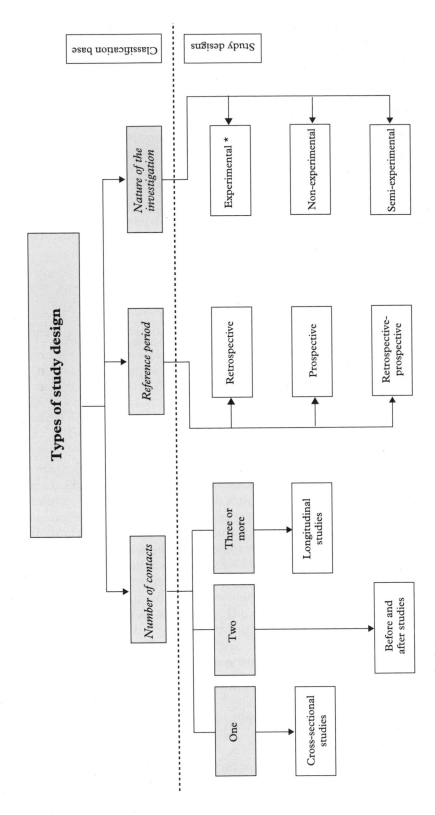

Figure 8.1   Types of study design

- The impact of unemployment on street crime (this could also be a before-and-after study).
- The relationship between the home environment and the academic performance of a child at school.
- The attitude of the community towards equity issues.
- The extent of unemployment in a city.
- Consumer satisfaction with a product.
- The effectiveness of random breath testing in preventing road accidents (this could also be a before-and-after study).
- The health needs of a community.
- The attitudes of students towards the facilities available in their library.

As these studies involve only one contact with the study population, they are comparatively cheap to undertake and easy to analyse. However, their biggest disadvantage is that they cannot measure change. To measure change it is necessary to have at least two observations, that is, at least two cross-sectional studies, at two points in time, on the same population.

The before-and-after study design

The main advantage of the before-and-after design (also known as the pre-test/post-test design) is that it can measure change in a situation, phenomenon, issue, problem or attitude. It is the most appropriate design for measuring the impact or effectiveness of a program. A before-and-after design can be described as two sets of cross-sectional observations on the same population to find out the change in the phenomenon or variable(s) between two points in time. The change is measured by comparing the difference in the phenomenon or variable(s) at the before and after observations.

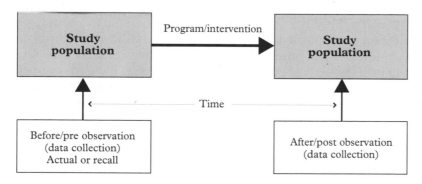

Figure 8.2   Before-and-after (pre-test/post-test) study design

A before-and-after study is carried out by adopting the same process as a cross-sectional study except that it is comprised of two cross-sectional observations, the second being undertaken after a certain period. Depending upon how it is set up, a before-and-after study may be either an experiment or a non-experiment. It is one of the most commonly used designs in evaluation studies. The difference between the two sets of observations with respect to the dependent variable is considered to be the impact of the program. The following are examples of topics that can be studied using this design:

- The impact of administrative restructuring on the quality of the services provided by an organisation.
- The effectiveness of a marriage counselling service.
- The impact of sex education on sexual behaviour among school children.
- The effect of a drug awareness program on the knowledge about and use of drugs among young people.
- The impact of incentives on the productivity of employees in an organisation.
- The impact of increased funding on the quality of teaching in universities.
- The impact of maternal and child health services on the infant mortality rate.
- The effect of random breath testing on road accidents.
- The effect of an advertisement on the sale of a product.

Though a before-and-after design has advantages—the main one being its ability to measure change in a phenomenon or to assess the impact of an intervention—it can also have certain disadvantages. However, these do not occur, individually or collectively, in every study. The prevalence of a particular disadvantage or combination of disadvantages is dependent upon the nature of the investigation, the study population and the method of data collection. The disadvantages are:

- Instead of collecting one set of data, two must be collected, which means two contacts with the study population. It is therefore more expensive and more difficult to implement. It requires a longer time to complete, particularly if you are using an experimental design, and hence, need to wait until your intervention is completed.
- In some cases the time lapse between the two contacts may result in attrition in the study population. It is possible that of those who participated in the pre-test, some may move out of the area or withdraw from the experiment for other reasons.
- One of the main limitations of this design is that, as it measures *total change*, you cannot ascertain whether independent or extraneous variables are responsible for producing change in the dependent variable. Also, is it not possible to quantify the contribution of independent and extraneous variables separately.
- If the study population is very young and if there is a significant time lapse between the before-and-after observations, changes in the study population may be because it is maturing. This is particularly true when you are studying young children. The effect of this maturation, if it is significantly correlated with the dependent variable, is reflected at the 'after' observation and is known as the *maturation effect*.
- Sometimes the instrument itself educates the respondents. This is known as the *reactive effect* of the instrument. For example, suppose you want to ascertain the impact of a program designed to create awareness of drugs

in a population. To do this, you design a questionnaire listing various drugs and asking respondents to indicate whether they have heard of them. At the pre-test stage, a respondent, while answering questions, which include the names of the various drugs, is being made aware of them, and this will be reflected in his/her responses at the post-test stage. Thus, the research instrument itself has educated the study population and, hence, has affected the dependent variable. Another example of this effect is a study designed to measure the impact of a family planning education program on respondents' awareness of contraceptive methods. Most studies designed to measure the impact of a program on participants' awareness face the difficulty that a change in the level of awareness, to some extent, may be because of this reactive effect.

Another disadvantage that may occur when you use a research instrument twice to gauge the attitude of a population towards an issue is a possible shift in attitude between the two observations. Sometimes people who place themselves on the extreme positions of a measurement scale at the pre-test stage, may, for a number of reasons, shift towards the mean at the post-test stage. They might feel that they have been too negative or too positive at the pre-test stage. Therefore, the mere expression of an attitude in response to a questionnaire or interview has caused them to alter their attitude at the time of the post-test. This type of effect is known as the *regression effect*.

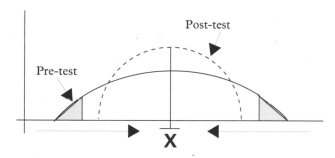

Figure 8.3   The regression effect

The longitudinal study design

The before-and-after study design is appropriate for measuring the extent of change in a phenomenon, situation, problem, attitude, etc., but is less helpful for studying the pattern of change. To determine the pattern of change in relation to time, a longitudinal design is used, for example, when you wish to study the proportion of people adopting a program in relation to time. Longitudinal studies are also useful when you need to collect factual information on a continuing basis. You may want to ascertain the trends in the demand for labour, immigration trends, changes in the incidence of a disease or in the mortality, morbidity and fertility patterns of a population.

In longitudinal studies the study population is visited a number of times, at regular intervals, usually over a long period, to collect the required information. These intervals are not fixed so their length may vary from study to study. Intervals might be as short as a week or longer than a year. Irrespective of the size of the interval, the information gathered each time is identical. Although the data collected is from the same study population, it may or may not be from the same respondents. A longitudinal study can be seen as a series of repetitive cross-sectional studies.

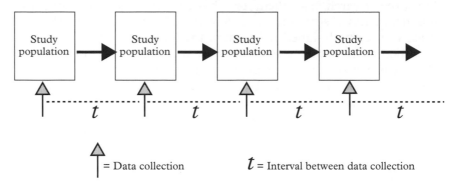

Figure 8.4   The longitudinal study design

Longitudinal studies have the same disadvantages as before-and-after studies, in some instances to an even greater degree. In addition, longitudinal studies can suffer from the conditioning effect. This describes a situation where, if the same respondents are contacted frequently, they begin to know what is expected of them and may respond to questions without thought, or they may lose interest in the inquiry, with the same result.

The main advantage of a longitudinal study is that it allows the researcher to measure the pattern of change and obtain factual information requiring collection on a regular or continuing basis.

The reference period

The *reference period* refers to the time-frame in which a study is exploring a phenomenon, situation, event or problem. Studies within this perspective are thus categorised as:

- retrospective;
- prospective; and
- retrospective–prospective.

The retrospective study design

Retrospective studies investigate a phenomenon, situation, problem or issue that has happened in the past. They are usually conducted either on the basis of the data available for that period or on the basis of respondents' recall of the situation. For example, studies conducted on the following topics are classified as retrospective studies:

- The living conditions of Aboriginal people in Australia in the early twentieth century.
- The utilisation of land before World War II in Western Australia.
- A historical analysis of migratory movements in Eastern Europe between 1915 and 1945.
- The relationship between levels of unemployment and street crime.

The prospective study design

Prospective studies refer to the likely prevalence of a phenomenon, situation, problem, attitude or outcome in the future. Such studies attempt to establish the outcome of an event or what is likely to happen. Experiments are usually classified as prospective studies as the researcher must wait for an intervention to register its effect on the study population. The following topics are classified as prospective studies:

- To determine, under field conditions, the impact of maternal and child health services on the level of infant mortality.
- To establish the effects of a counselling service on the extent of marital problems.
- To determine the impact of random breath testing on the prevention of road accidents.
- To find out the effect of parental involvement on the level of academic achievement of their children.
- To measure the effects of a change in migration policy on the extent of immigration in Australia.

The retrospective–prospective study design

Retrospective–prospective studies focus on past trends in a phenomenon and study it into the future. A study is classified under this category when you measure the impact of an intervention without having a control group. In fact, most before-and-after studies, if carried out without having a control— where the base-line is constructed from the same population before introducing the intervention—will be classified as retrospective–prospective studies. In a retrospective–prospective study a part of the data is collected retrospectively from the existing records before the intervention is introduced and then the study population is followed to ascertain the impact of the intervention. Trend studies, which become the basis of projections, fall into this category. Some examples are:

- The effect of random breath testing on road accidents.
- The impact of incentives on the productivity of the employees of an organisation.
- The impact of maternal and child health services on the infant mortality rate.
- The effect of an advertisement on the sale of a product.

The nature of the investigation

On the basis of the nature of the investigation, studies can be classified as:

*   experimental;
*   non-experimental; and
*   quasi or semi-experimental.

To understand the differences, let us consider some examples. Suppose you want to test: the impact of a particular teaching method on the level of comprehension of students; the effectiveness of a program such as random breath testing on the level of road accidents; or, the usefulness of a drug such as AZT in treating people who are HIV positive. Imagine any similar situation in your own academic or professional field. In such situations there is assumed to be a *cause and effect* relationship. There are two ways of studying this relationship. The first involves the researcher (or someone else) introducing the intervention that is assumed to be the 'cause' of change, and waiting until it has produced—or has been given sufficient time to produce—the change. The second consists of the researcher observing a phenomenon and attempting to establish what caused it. In this instance the researcher starts from the effect(s) or outcome(s) and attempts to determine causation. If a relationship is studied in the first way, starting from the cause to establish the effects, the study is classified as an experimental one. If the second path is followed, that is, starting from the effects to trace the cause, it is classified as a non-experimental study (see Figure 8.5). In the former case the independent variable can be either 'observed', introduced, controlled or manipulated by the researcher or someone else, whereas in the latter, this cannot happen as the assumed cause has already occurred. Instead, the researcher retrospectively links the cause(s) to the outcome(s). A semi-experimental design has the properties of both experimental and non-experimental studies; part of the study may be non-experimental and the other part experimental.

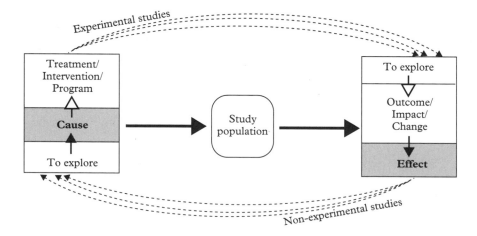

Figure 8.5   **Experimental and non-experimental studies**

An experimental study can be carried out in either a 'controlled' or a 'natural' environment. For an experiment in a controlled environment, the researcher (or someone else) introduces the intervention or stimulus to study its effects. The study population is in a 'controlled' situation such as a room. For an experiment in a 'natural' environment, the study population is exposed to an intervention in its own environment.

Experimental studies can be further classified on the basis of whether or not the study population is randomly assigned to different treatment groups. One of the biggest problems in comparable designs (those in which you compare two or more groups) is a lack of certainty that the different groups are in fact comparable in every respect except the treatment. The process of randomisation is designed to ensure that the groups are comparable. In a random design, the study population, the experimental treatments, or both, are not predetermined but randomly assigned (see Figure 8.6). Random assignment in experiments means that any element of a study population group has an equal and independent chance of becoming a part of an experimental or control group, or, in the case of multiple treatment modalities, any treatment has an equal and independent chance of being assigned to any of the population groups. It is important to note that the concept of randomisation can be applied to any of the experimental designs we discuss.

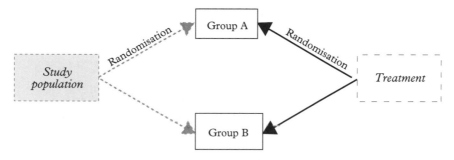

Figure 8.6   Randomisation in experiments

The experimental study design

There are so many types of experimental design that not all of them can be considered within the scope of this book. This section, therefore, is confined to describing the most commonly used ones in the social sciences, the humanities, public health, marketing, education, epidemiology, social work, etc. These designs have been categorised as:

- the after-only design;
- the before-and-after design;
- the control design;
- the double control design;
- the comparative design;
- the'matched control experimental design; and
- the placebo design.

The 'after-only' design

In an 'after-only' design the researcher knows that a population is being, or has been, exposed to an intervention and wishes to study its impact on the population. In this design, information on base-line (pre-test or before observation) is usually 'constructed' on the basis of respondents' recall of the situation before the intervention, or from information available in existing records (see Figure 8.7). The change in the dependent variable is measured by the difference between the 'before' (base-line) and 'after' observations. Technically, this is a very faulty design for measuring the impact of an intervention as there is no proper base-line data to compare the 'after' observation with. Therefore, one of the major problems of this design is that the two sets of data are not strictly comparable. Accordingly, some of the changes in the dependent variable may be attributable to the difference in the way the two sets of data were compiled. Another problem with this design is that it measures total change, including change attributable to extraneous variables, hence, it cannot identify the net effect of an intervention. However, this design is widely used in impact assessment studies for in real-life many programs operate without the benefit of a planned evaluation at the program planning stage (though this is fast changing) in which case it is just not possible to follow strictly the sequence—collection of base-line information, implementation of the program, and then program evaluation. An evaluator therefore has no choice but to adopt this design.

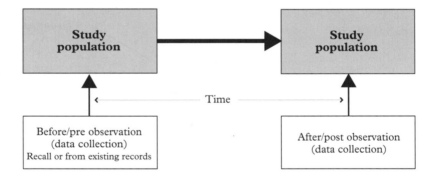

Figure 8.7 'After-only' design

In practice, the adequacy of this design depends on having reasonably accurate data available about the prevalence of a phenomenon before the intervention is introduced. This might be the case for situations such as: the impact of random breath testing on road accidents; the impact of a health program on the mortality of a population; the impact of an advertisement on the sale of a product; the impact of a decline in mortality on the fertility of a population; or the impact of a change in immigration policy on the extent of immigration. In these situations it is expected that accurate records are kept about the phenomenon under study and any change in trends is primarily because of the introduction of the intervention or change in the policy.

The 'before-and-after' design

The 'before-and-after' design overcomes the problem of retrospectively constructing the 'before' observation by establishing it before the intervention is introduced to the study population (see Figure 8.2). Then, when the program has been completely implemented or is assumed to have had its effect on the population, the 'after' observation is carried out to ascertain the impact attributable to the intervention (see Figure 8.8).

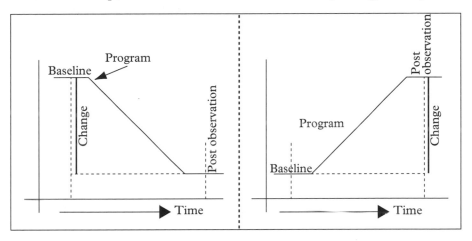

Figure 8.8   Measurement of change

The before-and-after design takes care of only one problem of the after-only design, i.e., the comparability of the before and after observations. It still does not enable one to conclude that any change—in whole or in part—can be attributed to the program intervention. To overcome this, a 'control' group is used. Before-and-after designs may also suffer from the problems identified earlier in this chapter in the discussion of before-and-after study designs. The impact of the intervention in before-and-after design is calculated as follows:

> Change in dependent variable =
>
> [status of the dependent variable at the 'after' observation] –
> [status of the dependent variable at the 'before' observation].

The control group design

In a study utilising the control group design the researcher selects two population groups instead of one, a 'control' group, and an 'experimental' group (Figure 8.9). These groups are expected to be comparable as far as possible in every respect except the intervention. The experimental group either receives or is exposed to the intervention, whereas the control group is not. First, 'before' observations are made on both groups, at the same time. The experimental group is then exposed to the intervention. When it is assumed that the intervention has had an impact, an 'after' observation is made on both groups. Any difference in the 'before' and 'after' observations between the groups regarding the dependent variable(s) is attributed to the intervention.

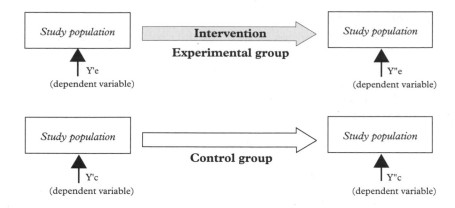

Figure 8.9   The control experimental design

In the experimental group, total change in the dependent variable,

(Ye) = (Y"e – Y'e), where
Y"e = 'after' observation on the experimental group
Y'e = 'before' observation on the experimental group.

In other words:

(Y"e – Y'e) = (Impact of program intervention) ± (Impact of extraneous variables) ± (Impact of chance variables).

In the control group, total change in the dependent variable,

(Yc) = (Y'c-Y'c), where
Y'c = post-test observation on the control group
Y'c = pre-test observation on the control group.

In other words:

(Y'c -Y'c) = (Impact of extraneous variables) ± (Impact of chance variables).

The difference between control and experimental groups =

(Y"e – Y'e) – (Y"c – Y'c), which is
{(Impact of program intervention) ± (Impact of extraneous variables★) ± (Impact of chance variables#)} – {(Impact of extraneous variables★) ± (Impact of chance variables#)}.

Using a simple arithmetic operation this = Impact of the intervention.

Therefore, the impact of any intervention is equal to the difference in the 'before' and 'after' observations in the dependent variable between the 'experimental' and 'control' groups.

It is important to remember that the chief objective of the control group is to quantify the impact of extraneous variables. This helps you to ascertain the impact of the intervention only.

The double control design

Although the control group design helps the researcher to quantify the impact that can be attributed to extraneous variables, it does not separate out other effects that may be due to the research instrument (such as the reactive effect), or, respondents (such as the maturation or regression effects). When the researcher needs to identify and separate out these effects, a double-control design is required.

In a double-control study, the researcher has two control groups instead of one. To quantify, say, the reactive effect of an instrument, the researcher excludes one of the control groups from the before observation (Figure 8.10).

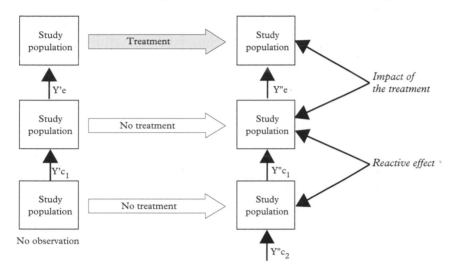

Figure 8.10   Double control designs

The different effects are calculated as follows:

$(Y'e - Y'e)$ = (Impact of program intervention)$\pm$(Impact of extraneous variables)$\pm$(Reactive effect)$\pm$(Random effect).

$(Y''c_1 - Y'c_1)$ = (Impact of extraneous variables)$\pm$(Reactive effect)$\pm$(Random effect).

$(Y''c2 - Y'c1\star)$ = (Impact of extraneous variables)$\pm$(Random effect).

(Note: $(Y''c2 - Y'c1)$ and not $(Y''c2 - Y'c2)$ as there is no before-observation for the second control group).

$(Y''e - Y'e) - (Y''c1 - Y'c1)$ = Impact of program intervention.

$(Y''c1-Y'c1) - (Y'c2 - Y'c1)$ = Reactive effect.

The net effect of the program intervention can be calculated in the same manner as for the control group designs as explained earlier.

The comparative design

Sometimes a researcher seeks to compare the effectiveness of different treatment modalities. In such situations a comparative design is appropriate.

With a comparative design, as with most others, a study can be carried out either as an experiment or as a non-experiment. In the comparative experimental design, the study population is divided into the same number of groups as the number of treatments to be tested. For each group the base-line with respect to the dependent variable is established. The different treatment models are then introduced to the different groups. After a certain period, when it is assumed that the treatment models have had their effect, the 'after' observation is carried out to ascertain any change in the dependent variable. The degree of change in the dependent variable in the different population groups is then compared to establish the relative effectiveness of the various interventions.

In the non-experimental form of comparative design, groups already receiving different interventions are identified, and only the 'post-observation' with respect to the dependent variable is conducted. The 'pre-test observation' is constructed either by asking the study population in each group to recall the required information relating to the period before the introduction of the treatment or by extracting such information from existing records. Sometimes a 'pre-test observation' is not constructed at all, on the assumption that if the groups are comparable the base-line must be identical. As each group is assumed to have the same base-line, the difference in the post-test observation is assumed to be because of the intervention.

To illustrate this, imagine you want to compare the effectiveness of three teaching models (A, B and C) on the level of comprehension of students in a class (see Figure 8.11). To undertake the study, you divide the class into three groups (X, Y and Z), through randomisation, to ensure their comparability. Before exposing these groups to the teaching models, you first establish the base-line for each group's level of comprehension of the chosen subject. You then expose each group to a different teaching model to teach the chosen subject. Afterwards, you again measure the groups' levels of comprehension of the material. Suppose Xa is the average level of comprehension of group X before the material is taught, using model A, and Xa' is this group's average level of comprehension after the completion of the program. The change in the level of comprehension, Xa'– Xa, is therefore attributed to model A. Similarly, changes in group Y and Z, Yb'–Yb and Zc'–Zc respectively, are attributed to teaching models B and C respectively. The changes in the average level of comprehension for the three groups are then compared to establish which teaching model is the most effective. (Note that extraneous variables will affect the level of comprehension in all groups equally, as they have been formed randomly).

It is also possible to set up this study as a non-experimental one, simply by exposing each group to the three teaching models, following up with an 'after' observation. The difference in the levels of comprehension is attributed to the difference in the teaching models as it is assumed that the three groups are comparable with respect to their original level of comprehension of the topic.

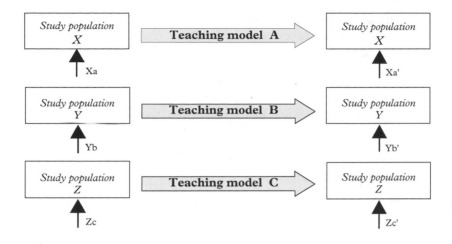

Figure 8.11 Comparative experimental design

The 'matched control' experimental design

Comparative groups are usually formed on the basis of their overall comparability with respect to a relevant characteristic in the study population, such as socio-economic status, the prevalence of a certain condition, or the extent of a problem in the study population. In matched studies, comparability is determined on an individual-by-individual basis. Two individuals from the study population who are almost identical with respect to a selected characteristic and/or condition, such as age, gender, or type of illness, are matched and then each is allocated to a different group (the matching is usually done on an easily identifiable characteristic). In the case of a 'matched control' experiment, once the two groups are formed, the researcher decides through randomisation or otherwise which group is to be considered control, and which, experimental.

The matched design can pose a number of problems:

- Matching increases in difficulty when done on more than one variable.
- Matching on variables that are hard to measure, such as attitude or opinion, is extremely difficult.
- Sometimes it is hard to know which variable to choose as a basis for matching. You may be able to base your decision upon previous findings or you may have to undertake a preliminary study to determine your choice of variable.

Matched groups are most commonly used in the testing of new drugs. Patients are matched on certain characteristics (type of illness, age or gender) to form pairs. The individuals forming each pair are then allocated to two different groups. On a random basis, one is provided with the treatment and the other is considered a control.

The 'placebo' design

A patient's belief that s/he is receiving treatment can play an important role in his/her recovery from an illness even if treatment is ineffective. This psychological effect is known as the placebo effect. A placebo design attempts to determine the extent of this effect. A placebo design involves two or three groups, depending on whether or not the researcher wants to have a control group (see Figure 8.12). If the researcher decides to have a control group, the first group receives the treatment, the second receives the placebo treatment and the third—the control group—receives nothing. The decision as to which group will be the treatment, the placebo or the control group, can also be made through randomisation.

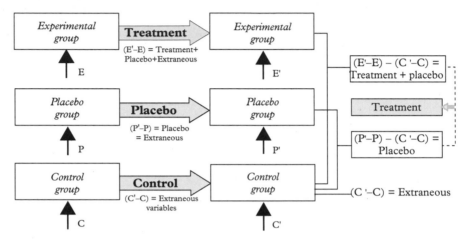

Figure 8.12 The placebo design

Some other commonly used designs

This section describes some additional designs, experimental and non-experimental, commonly used in the social sciences and the humanities.

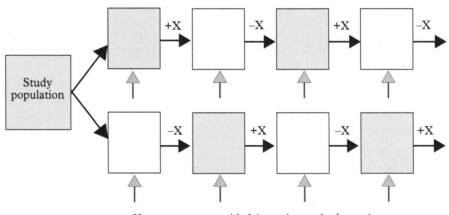

+X = treatment provided (experimetnal sebment)
–X = no treatment (control segment)

Figure 8.13 The cross-over experimental design

The cross-over comparative experimental design

The denial of treatment to the control group is considered unethical by some professionals. In addition, the denial of treatment may be unacceptable to some individuals in the control group, which could result in them dropping out of the experiment and/or going elsewhere to receive treatment. The former increases 'experimental mortality' and the latter may contaminate the study. The cross-over experimental design makes it possible to measure the impact of a treatment without denying treatment to any group, though this design has its own problems.

In the cross-over design, also called the ABAB design (Grinnell 1993: 104) two groups are formed, the intervention is introduced to one of them, and, after a certain period, the impact of this intervention is measured. Then the interventions are 'crossed over', i.e., the experimental group becomes the control, and vice versa (see Figure 8.13). However, in this design, population groups do not constitute experimental or control groups but only segments upon which experimental and control observations are conducted.

One of the main disadvantages of this design is discontinuity in treatment. The main question is, what impact would intervention have produced had it not been provided in segments?

The replicated cross-sectional design

In practice one usually examines programs already in existence and ones in which clients are at different stages of an intervention. Evaluating the effectiveness of such programs within a conventional experimental design is impossible because it is not possible to establish a base-line, the intervention having been introduced already. In this situation, the usual method of selecting a group of people who were recently recruited to the program and following them through till the intervention has been completed, may take a long time. The clients who are at different stages of a program are randomly selected. However, it is possible to choose clients who are at different phases of the program to form the basis of your study (see Figure 8.13).

This design is based upon the assumption that participants at different stages of a program are similar in terms of their socio-economic– demographic characteristics and the problem for which they are seeking intervention.

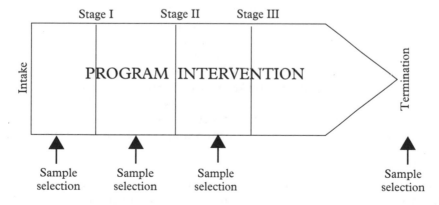

Figure 8.14 The replicated cross-sectional design

Trend studies

If you want to map change over a period, a trend study is the most appropriate method of investigation. Trend analysis enables you to find out what has happened in the past, what is happening now and what is likely to happen in the future in a population group. Trend studies are also useful in forecasting trends by extrapolating from present and past trends.

This design involves selecting a number of data observation points in the past, together with a picture of the present or immediate past with respect to the phenomenon under study and then making certain assumptions as to future trends. On the basis of the classification system developed in this chapter, this design can be classified under 'retrospective–prospective' studies.

Trends regarding the phenomenon under study can be correlated with other characteristics of the study population. For example, you may want to examine the changes in political preference of a study population in relation to age, gender, income, or ethnicity.

Cohort studies

Cohort studies are based upon the existence of a common characteristic such as year of birth, graduation or marriage, within a sub-group of a population. Suppose you want to study the employment pattern of a batch of accountants who graduated from a university in 1975, or to study the fertility behaviour of women who were married in 1930. To study the accountants' career paths you contact all who graduated from the university in 1975 to find out their employment histories. Similarly, you investigate the fertility history of those women who married in 1930. Both of these studies can be carried out either as cross-sectional or longitudinal designs. In the case of a longitudinal design, it is not important for the required information to be collected from the same respondents, however, it is important that the respondents belong to the cohort. (In the above examples they must have graduated in 1975 or married in 1930.)

Panel studies

Trend, cohort and panel studies are similar except that panel studies are longitudinal and prospective in nature and collect information from the same respondents. In trend and cohort studies the information can be collected in a cross-sectional manner and the observation points can be retrospectively constructed, whereas in a panel study the observations are made over a period of time and are prospective in nature. Suppose you want to study the changes in the pattern of expenditure on household items in a community. To do this, you select a few families to find out the amount they spend every fortnight on household items. You keep collecting the same information from the same families over a period of time to ascertain the changes in the expenditure pattern. Such a study is called a panel study. Similarly, a panel study design can be used to study the morbidity pattern in a community.

Blind studies

The concept of a blind study can be used with comparable and placebo experimental designs and is applied to studies measuring the effectiveness of a drug. In a blind study, the study population does not know whether it is getting real or fake treatment. The main objective of designing a blind study is to isolate the placebo effect: the psychological effect on the recovery process of a patient's knowledge that s/he is receiving the treatment.

Double-blind studies

The concept of a double-blind study is very similar to that of a blind-study except that it also tries to eliminate the researcher's bias: the researcher does not know the identity of experimental and placebo groups. In a double-blind study neither the researcher nor the subjects know who is receiving real and who is receiving fake treatment.

Case studies

The case study method is an approach to studying a social phenomenon through a thorough analysis of an individual case. The case may be a person, group, episode, process, community, society or any other unit of social life. All data relevant to the case are gathered and organised in terms of the case. It provides an opportunity for the intensive analysis of many specific details often overlooked by other methods. This approach rests on the assumption that the case being studied is typical of cases of a certain type so that, through intensive analysis, generalisations may be made that will be applicable to other cases of the same type.

Summary

In this chapter the various study designs have been examined from three perspectives. The terminology used to describe these perspectives is that of the author but the names of the study designs are universally used. The different designs across each category are mutually exclusive but not so within a category. Some commonly used designs have been discussed.

The three perspectives are: the number of contacts, the reference period, and the nature of the investigation. The first comprises cross-sectional studies, before-and-after studies, and longitudinal studies. The second categorises the studies as retrospective, prospective and retrospective–prospective. The third perspective classifies studies into experimental, non-experimental, and semi-experimental studies.

Step III

Constructing an instrument for data collection

9

Selecting a method of data collection

Collecting data using primary sources
- Observation
- The interview
- The questionnaire

Collecting data using secondary sources
- Problems with using data from secondary sources

Summary

There are two major approaches to gathering information about a situation, person, problem or phenomenon. Sometimes, information required is already available and need only be extracted. However, there are times when the information must be collected. Based upon these broad approaches to information gathering, data are categorised as:

• secondary data; and
• primary data.

Information gathered using the first approach is said to be collected from *secondary sources* whereas the sources used in the second approach are called *primary sources*. Examples of secondary sources include the use of census data to obtain information on the age–sex structure of a population; the use of hospital records to find out the morbidity and mortality patterns of a community; the use of an organisation's records to ascertain its activities; and the collection of data from sources such as articles, journals, magazines, books and periodicals to obtain historical and other types of information. On the other hand, finding out first-hand the attitudes of a community towards health services, ascertaining the health needs of a community, evaluating a social program, determining the job satisfaction of the employees of an organisation, and ascertaining the quality of services provided by a worker, are examples of information collected from primary sources. In summary, primary sources provide first-hand information and secondary sources provide second-hand data. Figure 9.1 shows the various methods of data collection.

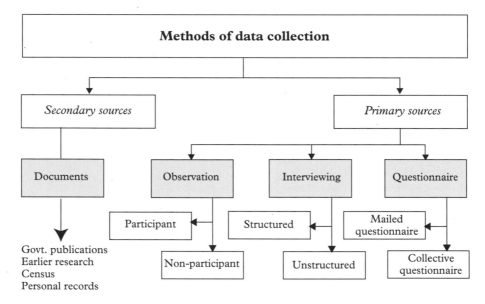

Figure 9.1   Methods of data collection

None of the methods of data collection provides 100 per cent accurate and reliable information. The quality of the data gathered is dependent upon a number of other factors, which we will identify as we discuss each method. Your skill as a researcher lies in your ability to take care of the factors that could affect the quality of your data. One of the main differences between experienced and amateur researchers lies in their understanding of, and ability to control, these factors. It is therefore important for a beginner to be aware of them.

Collecting data using primary sources

Several methods can be used to collect primary data. The choice of a method depends upon the purpose of the study, the resources available and the skills of the researcher. There are times when the method most appropriate to achieve the objectives of a study cannot be used because of constraints such as a lack of resources and/or required skills. In such situations you should be aware of the problems these limitations impose on the quality of the data.

In selecting a method of data collection, the socio-economic–demographic characteristics of the study population play an important role: you should know as much as possible about characteristics such as educational level, age-structure, socio-economic status and ethnic background. If possible, it is helpful to know the study population's interest in, and attitude towards, participation in the study. Some populations, for a number of reasons, may not feel either at ease with a particular method of data collection, (such as being interviewed) or comfortable to express opinions in a questionnaire. Furthermore, people with little education may respond differently to certain methods of data collection compared to people with more education.

Another important determinant of the quality of your data is the way the purpose of the study is explained to potential respondents. Whatever method of data collection is used, make sure that respondents clearly understand the purpose and relevance of the study. This is particularly important when you use a questionnaire to collect data because in an interview situation you can answer a respondent's questions but in a questionnaire you will not have this opportunity.

In the following sections each method of data collection is discussed from the point of view of its applicability and suitability to a situation, and the problems and limitations associated with it.

Observation

Observation is one way to collect primary data. Observation is a purposeful, systematic and selective way of watching and listening to an interaction or phenomenon as it takes place. There are many situations in which observation is the most appropriate method of data collection, for example, when you want to learn about the interaction in a group, study the dietary patterns of a population, ascertain the functions performed by a worker, or study the behaviour or personality traits of an individual. It is also appropriate in situations where full and/or accurate information cannot be elicited by questioning, because respondents either are not co-operative or are unaware of the answers because it is difficult for them to detach themselves from the interaction. In summary, when you are more interested in the behaviour than in the perceptions of individuals, or when subjects are so involved in the interaction that they are unable to provide objective information about it, observation is the best approach to collect the required information.

Types of observation

There are two types of observation:

- participant observation; and
- non-participant observation.

Participant observation is when a researcher participates in the activities of the group being observed in the same manner as its members, with or without their knowing that they are being observed. For example, you might want to examine the reactions of the general population towards people in wheelchairs. You can study their reactions by sitting in a wheelchair yourself. Alternatively, you might want to study the life of prisoners and pretend to be a prisoner in order to do this.

Non-participant observation, on the other hand, is when the researcher does not get involved in the activities of the group but remains a passive observer, watching and listening to its activities and drawing conclusions from this. For example, you might want to study the functions carried out by nurses in a hospital. As an observer, watch, follow, and record the activities as they are performed. After making a number of observations, conclusions can be drawn about the functions nurses carry out in the hospital. Any occupational group in any setting can be observed in the same manner.

Problems with using observation as a method of data collection

The use of observation as a method of data collection may suffer from a number of problems, which is not to suggest that all or any of these necessarily prevails in every situation. But as a beginner you should be aware of these problems.

- When individuals or groups become aware that they are being observed, they may change their behaviour. Depending upon the situation, this change could be positive or negative—it may increase or decrease, for example, their productivity—and may occur for a number of reasons. When a change in the behaviour of persons or groups is attributed to their being observed it is known as the *Hawthorne Effect*. The use of observation in such a situation introduces distortion: what is observed does not represent their normal behaviour.
- There is always the possibility of observer bias. If an observer is biased, he/she can easily introduce bias and there is no easy way to verify the observations and the inferences drawn from them.
- The interpretations drawn from observations may vary from observer to observer.
- There is the possibility of incomplete observation and/or recording, which varies with the method of recording. An observer may watch keenly but at the expense of detailed recording. The opposite problem may occur when the observer takes detailed notes but in doing so, misses some of the interaction.

Situations in which observations can be made

Observations can be made under two conditions:

- natural; and
- controlled.

Observing a group in its natural operation rather than intervening in its activities is classified as observation under natural conditions. Introducing a stimulus to the group for it to react to and observing the reaction is called controlled observation.

The recording of observation

There are many ways of recording observation. The selection of a method of recording depends upon the purpose of the observation. Keep in mind that each method has its advantages and disadvantages.

- **Narrative**—in this form of recording the researcher records a description of the interaction in his or her own words. Usually, s/he makes brief notes while observing the interaction and soon after the observation makes detailed notes in narrative form. In addition, some researchers may interpret the interaction and draw conclusions from it. The biggest advantage of narrative recording is that it provides a deeper insight into the interaction. However, a disadvantage is that an observer may be biased in his/her observation and, therefore, the interpretations and conclusions drawn from the observation will also be biased. Also, if a researcher's attention is on observing, s/he might forget to record an important piece of interaction, and, obviously, in the process of recording, part of the interaction may be missed. Hence, there is always the possibility of incomplete recording and/or observation. In addition, with different observers the comparability of narrative recording can be a problem.
- **Scales**—at times some observers may prefer to develop a scale in order to rate various aspects of the interaction or phenomenon. The recording is done on a scale developed by the observer/researcher. A scale may be one-, two- or three-directional, depending upon the purpose of the observation. For example, in the scale in Figure 9.2—designed to record the nature of the interaction within a group—there are three directions: positive, negative, and neutral.

  One of the problems with using a scale to record observations is that it does not provide in-depth information about the interaction. In addition, it may suffer from any of the following problems:

  —Unless the observer is extremely confident of his/her ability to assess an interaction, s/he may tend to avoid the extreme positions on the scale, using mostly the central part. The error this tendency creates is called the *error of central tendency*.

  —Some observers may prefer certain sections of the scale in the same way that some teachers are strict markers and others are not. When observers have a tendency to use a particular part of the scale in recording an interaction, this phenomenon is known as the *elevation effect*.

A study of the nature of interaction in a group

Aspects of interaction		Positive				Neutral				Negative		
Participation	5	4	3	2	1	0	1	2	3	4	5
Rapport	5	4	3	2	1	0	1	2	3	4	5
Confidence	5	4	3	2	1	0	1	2	3	4	5
Aggressiveness	5	4	3	2	1	0	1	2	3	4	5
Withdrawnness	5	4	3	2	1	0	1	2	3	4	5
Friendliness	5	4	3	2	1	0	1	2	3	4	5
Aloofness	5	4	3	2	1	0	1	2	3	4	5

Figure 9.2   A three-directional rating scale

—Another type of error that may be introduced is when the way an observer rates an individual on one aspect of the interaction influences the way s/he rates that individual on another aspect of the interaction. Again something similar to this can happen in teaching when a teacher's assessment of the performance of a student in one subject may influence his/her rating of that student's performance in another. This type of effect is known as the *halo effect.*

- **Categorical recording**—sometimes an observer may decide to record her/his observation using categories. The type and number of categories depend upon the type of interaction and the observer's choice about how to classify the observation. For example: passive/active (two categories); introvert/extrovert (two categories); always/sometimes/never (three categories); strongly agree/agree/uncertain/disagree/strongly disagree (five categories). The use of categories to record an observation may suffer from the same problems as those associated with scales.
- **Recording on mechanical devices**—observation can also be recorded on a video tape and then analysed. The advantage of taping the interaction is that the observer can see it a number of times before drawing any conclusions, and can invite other professionals to view the tape in order to arrive at more objective conclusions. However, one of the disadvantages is that some people may feel uncomfortable or may behave differently before a camera. Therefore the interaction may not be a true reflection of the situation.

The choice of a particular method for recording your observation is dependent upon the purpose of the observation, the complexity of the interaction and the type of population being observed. It is important to consider these factors before deciding upon the method for recording your observation.

The interview

Interviewing is a commonly used method of collecting information from people. In many walks of life we collect information through different forms of interaction with others. Any person-to-person interaction between two or more individuals with a specific purpose in mind is called an interview. On the one hand interviewing can be very flexible, when the interviewer has the freedom to formulate questions as they come to mind around the issue being investigated, and on the other hand it can be inflexible, when the investigator is to keep strictly to the questions decided beforehand. Interviews are classified according to the degree of flexibility as:

- unstructured; and
- structured.

Unstructured interviews

In an *unstructured interview*, also known as an in-depth interview, the interviewer develops a framework, called an *interview guide*, within which to conduct the interview. Within this structure the interviewer formulates questions spontaneously during an interview. Unstructured interviews can be carried out in a one-to-one situation or collectively with a group of respondents (called group interviews or focused group interviews).

This approach to data collection is extremely useful in situations where either in-depth information is needed or little is known about the area. The flexibility allowed to the interviewer in what s/he asks of a respondent is an asset as it can elicit extremely rich information. As it provides in-depth information, many researchers use this technique for constructing a structured research instrument. On the other hand, since an interview guide does not list specific questions to be asked of respondents, the comparability of questions asked and responses obtained may become a problem. As the researcher gains experience during the interviews, the questions asked of respondents change, hence, the type of information obtained from those who are interviewed at the beginning may be markedly different from that obtained from those interviewed towards the end. Also, this freedom can introduce investigator bias into the study. Using an interview guide as a means of data collection requires much more skill on the part of the investigator than does using a structured interview.

Structured interviews

In a *structured interview* the investigator asks a pre-determined set of questions, using the same wording and order of questions as specified in the interview schedule. An *interview schedule* is a written list of questions, open or closed-ended, prepared for use by an interviewer, in a person-to-person interaction (this may be face-to-face, by telephone or by other electronic media). Note that an interview schedule is a research tool/instrument for collecting data, whereas interviewing is a method of data collection.

One of the main advantages of the structured interview is that it provides uniform information, which assures the comparability of data. Structured interviewing requires fewer interviewing skills than does unstructured interviewing.

The questionnaire

A questionnaire is a written list of questions, the answers to which are recorded by respondents. In a questionnaire respondents read the questions, interpret what is expected and then write down the answers. The only difference between an interview schedule and a questionnaire is that, in the former it is the interviewer who asks the questions (and if necessary, explains them), and records the respondent's replies on an interview schedule. This distinction is important in accounting for the respective strengths and weaknesses of the two methods.

In the case of a questionnaire, as there is no one to explain the meaning of questions to respondents, it is important that questions are clear and easy to understand. Also, the layout of a questionnaire should be such that it is easy to read and pleasant to the eye, and the sequence of questions should be easy to follow. A questionnaire should be developed in an interactive style. This means respondents should feel as if someone is talking to them. In a questionnaire, a sensitive question or a question respondents may feel hesitant about answering should be prefaced by an interactive statement explaining the relevance of the question. It is a good idea to use a different font for these statements to distinguish them from the actual questions. Examples in Figures 9.3 and 9.4 taken from two surveys recently carried out by the author with the help of two students explain some of the above points.

Choosing between an interview schedule and a questionnaire

The choice between a questionnaire and an interview schedule is important and should be considered thoroughly as the strengths and weaknesses of the two methods can affect the validity of the findings. The nature of the investigation and the socio-economic–demographic characteristics of the study population are central in this choice. The selection between an interview schedule and a questionnaire should be based upon the following criteria.

- **The nature of the investigation**—if the study is about issues that respondents may feel reluctant to discuss with an investigator, a questionnaire may be the better choice as it ensures anonymity. This may be the case with studies on drug use, sexuality, indulgence in criminal activities and personal finances. However, there are situations where better information about sensitive issues can be obtained by interviewing respondents. It depends on the type of study population and the skills of the interviewer.
- **The geographical distribution of the study population**—if potential respondents are scattered over a wide geographical area, you have no choice but to use a questionnaire, as interviewing in these circumstances would be extremely expensive.
- **The type of study population**—if the study population is illiterate, very young or very old, or handicapped, there may be no option but to interview respondents.

Where to Go?

A study of occupational mobility among immigrants

The questionnaire opened with the following interactive statement.

Personal circumstances, and educational and occupational background, to a great extent determine the occupational mobility of an individual. This is especially true for immigrants. We would therefore like to ask you some questions about you and your family background. Knowledge of these factors is also important for assessing the representativeness of the sample who participated in the study in reflecting the immigrants and to understand the extent, nature and reasons of occupational mobility in relation to your background. We would appreciate your answering these questions as the information you provide will be very useful to us. We would like to emphasise that your responses are extremely valuable to us and we would immensely appreciate your answering all questions. However, if you feel that you do not want to answer a particular question, we will gladly accept your decision. We can assure you that your responses will be completely anonymous and will not be used for any other purpose.

Before asking questions about family background, the following interactive statement was inserted in the questionnaire.

Now, we would like to ask some questions about your family. Your family circumstances can affect your choice of an occupation after immigration. Again, we assure you of the complete anonymity of your responses.

Before ascertaining respondents' experiences with respect to recognition of their qualifications in Australia, the following interactive statement prepared them to be at ease with the area of inquiry.

Recognition of educational and professional qualifications, in addition to other factors, plays a major role in determining an individual's occupational mobility in a new country. In this section we would like to ask your opinion about the process of getting your qualifications recognised. We would also like to know how satisfied or dissatisfied you are with the outcome. If you are dissatisfied, we would like to know your reasons as this information may help decision makers to improve the process. Again, we assure you that your answers will be completely confidential. However, if you still feel that you do not want to answer a particular question, please feel free to omit it.

Figure 9.3 Example 1 — Where to Go? A study of occupational mobility among immigrants.

Occupational Redeployment

A study of occupational redeployment among State Government
employees

The following interactive statement was inserted in the questionnaire
before questions asking about the socio-economic–demographic
background of respondents.

*In order to gain an understanding of the situation of employees who have
experienced occupational redeployment in State Government departments
during the last three years, we would like to ask some questions about your
background. Your answers will help us to determine the types of occupation
where redeployment has occurred and the backgrounds of the employees who
have been affected by it. Please do not feel obliged to answer a question if you
do not wish to, though we assure you that any information you provide will
be treated with strict confidentiality.*

Questions about occupational history were prefaced by the following
statement.

*We would like to ask some questions about your work history. The answers
to these questions will enable us to compare the type of work you have been
doing since entering the workforce with the job you have been assigned after
redeployment. This will help us to establish the nature and extent of change
in your job before and after redeployment. Again, there is no obligation to
answer a question if you do not want to. However, answers to these questions
are extremely important to us. We assure you of the anonymity of the
information you provide.*

Before asking questions about the impact of redeployment, the following interactive statement was incorporated into the questionnaire.

*The following questions ask you to express your opinion about different
aspects of your job* after *and* before *redeployment. Your answers will help
us to gauge the impact of redeployment on different aspects of your work
and family situation. We would appreciate your honest opinions. Be assured
that your responses will be completely anonymous.*

Figure 9.4   Example 2 — Occupational Redeployment—A study of occupational redeployment
among State Government employees.

The different ways of administering a questionnaire

A questionnaire can be administered in different ways.

- **The mailed questionnaire**—the most common approach to collecting information is to send the questionnaire to prospective respondents by mail. Obviously this approach presupposes that you have access to their addresses. Usually it is a good idea to send a pre-paid, self-addressed envelope with the questionnaire as this might increase the response rate. A mailed questionnaire *must* be accompanied by a covering letter (see below for details). One of the major problems with this method is the low response rate. In the case of an extremely low response rate, the findings have extremely limited applicability to the population studied.

- **Collective administration**—one of the best ways of administering a questionnaire is to obtain a captive audience such as students in a class-room, people attending a function, participants of a program or people assembled in one place. This ensures a very high response rate as you will find very few people refuse to participate in your study. Also, as you have personal contact with the study population, you can explain the purpose, relevance and importance of the study and can clarify any questions that respondents may have. The author's advice is that if you have a captive audience for your study, don't miss the opportunity—it is the quickest way of collecting data and you save money on postage.

- **Administration in a public place**—sometimes you can administer a questionnaire in a public place such as a shopping centre, health centre, hospital, school, or pub. Of course this depends upon the type of study population you are looking for and where it is likely to be found. Usually the purpose of the study is explained to potential respondents as they approach and their participation in the study is requested. Apart from being slightly more time-consuming, this method has all the advantages of administering a questionnaire collectively.

The contents of the covering letter

It is essential that you write a covering letter with your mailed questionnaire. It should very briefly:

- introduce you and the institution you are representing;
- describe in two or three sentences the main objectives of the study;
- explain the relevance of the study;
- convey any general instructions;
- indicate that participation in the study is voluntary—if recipients do not want to respond to the questionnaire, they have the right not to;
- assure respondents of the anonymity of the information provided by them;
- provide a contact number in case they have any questions;
- give a return address for the questionnaire and a deadline for its return; and
- thank them for their participation in the study.

The advantages of a questionnaire

A questionnaire has several advantages.

- **It is less expensive**—as you do not interview respondents, you save time and human and financial resources. The use of a questionnaire, therefore, is comparatively convenient and inexpensive. Particularly, when it is administered collectively to a study population, it is an extremely inexpensive method of data collection.
- **It offers greater anonymity**—as there is no face-to-face interaction between respondents and interviewer, this method provides greater anonymity. In some situations when sensitive questions are asked it helps to increase the likelihood of obtaining accurate information.

The disadvantages of a questionnaire

Although a questionnaire has several disadvantages, it is important to note that not all data collection using this method has these disadvantages. The prevalence of a disadvantage depends on a number of factors, but you need to be aware of them to understand their possible bearing on the quality of the data. These are:

- **Limited application**—one main disadvantage is that its application is limited to a study population that can read and write. It cannot be used on a population that is illiterate, very young, very old, or handicapped.
- **A low response rate**—questionnaires are notorious for their low response rates, i.e., people fail to return them. If you plan to use a questionnaire, keep in mind that because not everyone will return their questionnaire, your sample size will in effect be reduced. The response rate depends upon a number of factors: the interest of the sample in the topic of the study; the layout and length of the questionnaire; the quality of the letter explaining the purpose and relevance of the study; and the methodology used to deliver the questionnaire. You should consider yourself lucky to obtain a 50 per cent response rate and sometimes it may be as low as 20 per cent. However, as mentioned, the response rate is not a problem when a questionnaire is administered in a collective situation.
- **Self-selecting bias**—not everyone who receives a questionnaire returns it, so there is a self-selecting bias. Those who return their questionnaire may have attitudes, attributes or motivations that are different from those who do not. Hence, if the response rate is very low, the findings may not be representative of the total study population.
- **Lack of opportunity to clarify issues**—if, for any reason, respondents do not understand some questions, there is no opportunity for them to have the meaning clarified. If different respondents interpret questions differently, this will affect the quality of the information provided.
- **Spontaneous responses are not allowed for**—mailed questionnaires are inappropriate when spontaneous responses are required, as a questionnaire gives them time to reflect before answering.
- **The response to a question may be influenced by the response to other questions**—as respondents can read all the questions before answering (which usually happens), the way they answer a particular question may be affected by their knowledge of other questions.

- **It is possible to consult others**—with mailed questionnaires respondents may consult other people before responding. In situations where an investigator wants to find out only the study population's opinions, this method may be inappropriate, though requesting respondents to express their own opinion may help.
- **A response cannot be supplemented with other information**—an interview can sometimes be supplemented with information from other methods of data collection such as observation. However, a questionnaire lacks this advantage.

The advantages of the interview

- **The interview is more appropriate for complex situations**—it is the most appropriate approach for studying complex and sensitive areas as the interviewer has the opportunity to prepare a respondent before asking sensitive questions and to explain complex ones to respondents in person.
- **It is useful for collecting in-depth information**—in an interview situation, it is possible for an investigator to obtain in-depth information by probing. Hence, in situations where in-depth information is required, interviewing is the preferred method of data collection.
- **Information can be supplemented**—an interviewer is able to supplement information obtained from responses with those gained from observation of non-verbal reactions.
- **Questions can be explained**—it is less likely that a question will be misunderstood as the interviewer can either repeat a question or put it in a form that is understood by the respondent.
- **Interviewing has a wider application**—an interview can be used with almost any type of population: children, handicapped, illiterate or the very old.

The disadvantages of the interview

- **Interviewing is time-consuming and expensive**—this is especially so when potential respondents are scattered over a wide geographical area. However, if you have a situation such as an office, a hospital or an agency where potential respondents come to obtain a service, interviewing them in that setting may be less expensive and less time-consuming.
- **The quality of data depends upon the quality of the interaction**— in an interview the quality of interaction between an interviewer and interviewee is likely to affect the quality of the information obtained. Also, because the interaction in each interview is unique, the quality of the responses obtained from different interviews may vary significantly.
- **The quality of data depends upon the quality of the interviewer**— in an interview situation the quality of the data generated is affected by the experience, skills and commitment of the interviewer.
- **The quality of data may vary when many interviewers are used**— use of multiple interviewers may magnify the problems identified in the two previous points.
- **The researcher may introduce his/her bias**—researcher bias in the framing of questions and the interpretation of responses is always possible.

• **The interviewer may be biased**—if the interviews are conducted by a person or persons, paid or voluntary, other than the researcher, it is also possible that they may exhibit bias in the way they interpret responses, select response categories or choose words to summarise respondents' expressed opinions.

Forms of question

The form and wording of questions is extremely important in a research instrument as they have an effect on the type and quality of information obtained. The questions should therefore be appropriate, relevant and free from any of the problems discussed under 'considerations in formulating questions'. This section discusses open-ended and closed-ended questions, which are both commonly used in the social sciences.

In an interview schedule or a questionnaire, questions may be formulated as:

• open-ended; or
• closed-ended.

In an open-ended question the possible responses are not given. In the case of a questionnaire, the respondent writes down the answers in his/her words whereas in the case of an interview schedule the investigator records the answers either verbatim or a in summary describing a respondent's answer. In a closed-ended question the possible answers are set out in the questionnaire or schedule and the respondent or the investigator ticks the category that best describes the respondent's answer. It is usually wise to provide a category, 'other/please explain' to accommodate any response not listed. The questions in Figure 9.5 are classified as closed-ended questions. The same questions could be asked as open-ended questions, as shown in Figure 9.6.

When deciding whether to use open-ended or closed-ended questions to obtain information about a variable, visualise how you plan to use the information generated. This is important because the way you frame your questions determines the unit of measurement by which the responses will be classified. In turn the unit of measurement dictates what statistical procedures can be applied to the data and the way the information can be analysed and displayed.

Let us take, as an example, the question about the variable, 'income'. In closed-ended questions income can be qualitatively recorded in categories such as 'above average/average/below average', or quantitatively, in categories such as 'under $10 000/$10 000–$19 999/...' Your choice will affect the unit of measurement for income, which in turn will affect the application of statistical procedures. For example, you cannot calculate the average income of a person from the responses to question (C a) in Figure 9.5; nor can you calculate the median or mode category of income. But from the responses to question (C), you can accurately calculate mode category of income. However, the average and the median income cannot be accurately calculated (such calculations are usually made under certain assumptions). From the responses to question (C) in Figure 9.6 the different descriptors of income can be calculated very accurately. In addition, information on income can be displayed in any form. The same is true for any other information obtained in response to open and closed-ended questions.

A. Please indicate your age by placing a tick in the appropriate category.

Under 15 ☐
15–19 years ☐
20–24 years ☐

B. How would you describe your current marital status?

Married ☐
Single ☐
De facto ☐
Divorced ☐
Separated ☐

C. What is your average annual income?

Under 10 000 ☐
10 000–19 999 ☐
20 000–29 999 ☐
30 000–39 999 ☐
40 000+ ☐

OR

C(a) How would you categorise your average annual income?

Above average ☐
Average ☐
Below average ☐

D. What, in your opinion, are the qualities of a good administrator?

Able to make decisions ☐
Fast decision maker ☐
Able to listen ☐
Impartial ☐
Skilled in interpersonal communication ☐
Other, please specify

_____

_____

Figure 9.5   Examples of closed-ended questions

A. What is your current age? _____ years

B. How would you describe your current marital status? _____

C. What is your average annual income? _____ $

D. What, in your opinion, are the qualities of a good administrator?

1 _____

2 _____

3 _____

4 _____

5 _____

Figure 9.6   Examples of open-ended questions

Both open-ended and closed-ended questions have their advantages and disadvantages in different situations. To some extent, their advantages and disadvantages depend upon whether they are being used in an interview or in a questionnaire and on whether they are being used to seek information about facts or opinions. As a rule, closed-ended questions are extremely useful for eliciting factual information and open-ended questions for seeking opinions, attitudes and perceptions. The choice of open or closed-ended questions should be made according to the purpose for which a piece of information is to be used, the type of study population from which information is going to be obtained, the method proposed for communicating the findings and the readership.

The advantages and disadvantages of open-ended questions

Open-ended questions have a number of advantages and disadvantages.

* Open-ended questions provide in-depth information if used in an interview by an experienced interviewer. In a questionnaire, open-ended questions can provide a wealth of information provided respondents feel comfortable about expressing their opinions and are fluent in the language used. On the other hand, analysis of open-ended questions is more difficult. The researcher usually needs to go through another process—content analysis—in order to classify the data.
* In a questionnaire, open-ended questions provide respondents with the opportunity to express themselves freely, resulting in a greater variety of information. Thus respondents are not 'conditioned' by having to select answers from a list. The disadvantage of free choice is that, in a questionnaire, some respondents may not be able to express themselves, so information can be lost.
* As open-ended questions allow respondents to express themselves freely, they virtually eliminate the possibility of investigator bias (investigator bias is introduced through the response pattern presented to respondents). On the other hand, there is a greater chance of interviewer bias in open ended questions.

The advantages and disadvantages of closed-ended questions

Closed-ended questions, like open-ended questions, have many advantages and disadvantages.

- One of the main disadvantages of closed-ended questions is that the information obtained through them lacks depth and variety.
- There is a greater possibility of investigator bias because the researcher may list only the response patterns that he/she is interested in or those that come to mind. Even if the category of 'other' is offered, most people will usually select from the given responses, so the findings may still reflect the researcher's bias.
- In a questionnaire, the given response pattern for a question could condition the thinking of respondents, so the answers provided may not truly reflect respondents' opinions. Rather, they may reflect the extent of agreement or disagreement with the researcher's opinion or analysis of a situation.
- The ease of answering a ready-made list of responses may create a tendency among some respondents and interviewers to tick a category or categories without thinking through the issue.
- Closed-ended questions, as they provide 'ready made' categories within which respondents reply to the questions asked by the researcher, help to ensure that the information needed by the researcher is obtained.
- Because the possible responses are already categorised, they are easy to analyse.

Considerations in formulating questions

The wording and tone of your questions is important because the information and its quality largely depend upon these factors. It is therefore important to be careful about the way you formulate questions. Some considerations to keep in mind when formulating questions are as follows.

- **Always use simple and everyday language**—your respondents may not be highly educated, and even if they are, they still may not know some of the 'simple' technical jargon that you are used to. Particularly in a questionnaire, take extra care to use words that your respondents will understand as you will have no opportunity to explain questions to them. A pre-test should show you what is and what is not understood by your respondents. For example:

  'Is anyone in your family a *dipsomaniac*?' (Bailey 1978: 100).

  In this question many respondents, even some who are well educated, will not understand 'dipsomaniac' and, hence, may answer the question wrongly or not at all.
- **Do not use ambiguous questions**—an ambiguous question is one that contains more than one meaning and that can be interpreted differently by different respondents. This will result in different answers, making it difficult, if not impossible, to draw any valid conclusions from the information. The following questions fall in this category:

'Is your work made difficult because you are expecting a baby?' (Moser and Kalton 1989: 323)   Yes ☐ No ☐

In the survey all women were asked if they were pregnant. Those women who were not pregnant ticked 'no', meaning no they were not pregnant and those who were pregnant and who ticked 'no', meant pregnancy had not made their work difficult. The question has other ambiguities as well: it does not specify the type of work and the stage of pregnancy.

'Are you satisfied with your canteen?' (Moser and Kalton 1989: 319).

This question is also ambiguous as it does not ask respondents to indicate the aspects of the canteen with which they may be satisfied or dissatisfied. Is it with the service, the prices, the physical facilities, the attitude of the staff or the quality of the meals? Respondents may have any one of these aspects in mind when they answer the question.

- **Do not ask double-barrelled questions**—a double-barrelled question is a question within a question. The main problem with this type of question is that one does not know which particular question a respondent has answered. Some respondents may answer both 'questions' and others, only one of them.

'How often and how much time do you spend on each visit?'

This question was asked in a survey in Western Australia to ascertain the need for child minding services in one of the hospitals. The question has two parts: how often do you visit and how much time is spent on each visit? In this type of question some respondents may answer the first part whereas others may answer the second and some may answer both parts. Incidentally, this question is also ambiguous in that it does not specify 'how often' in terms of a period of time. Is it in a week, a fortnight, a month or a year?

'Does your department have a special recruitment policy for racial minorities and women?' (Bailey 1978: 97).

This question is double-barrelled in that it asks respondents to indicate whether their office has a special recruitment policy for two population groups: racial minorities and women. A 'yes' response does not necessarily mean that the office has a special recruitment policy for both groups.

- **Do not ask leading questions**—a leading question is one which, by its contents, structure or wording, leads a respondent to answer in a certain direction. Such questions are judgemental and lead respondents to answer either positively or negatively.

'Unemployment is increasing, isn't it?'

'Smoking is bad, isn't it?'

The first problem is that these are not questions but statements. Because the statements suggest that 'unemployment is increasing' and 'smoking is bad', respondents may feel that to disagree with them is to be in the wrong, especially if they feel that the researcher is an authority and that if she or he is saying that 'unemployment is increasing' or 'smoking is bad', it must be so. The feeling that there is a 'right' answer can 'force' people to respond in a way that is contrary to their true position.

- **Do not ask questions that are based on presumptions**—in such questions the researcher assumes that respondents fit into a particular category and seeks information based upon that assumption.

> 'How many cigarettes do you smoke in a day? (Moser and Kalton 1989: 325).
>
> 'What contraceptives do you use?'

Both these questions were asked without ascertaining whether or not respondents were smokers or sexually active. In situations like this it is important to first ascertain whether or not a respondent fits into the category about which you are inquiring.

The construction of a research instrument

The construction of a research instrument or tool is the most important aspect of a research project because anything you say by way of findings or conclusions is based upon the type of information you collect, and the data you collect is entirely dependent upon your research instrument. The famous saying about computers—'garbage in garbage out'—is also applicable to data collection. The research tool provides the input into a study and therefore the quality and validity of the output, the findings, are solely dependent upon it.

In spite of its immense importance, to the author's knowledge, no specific guidelines for beginners on how to construct a research tool exist. Students are left to learn for themselves under the guidance of their research supervisor. The guidelines suggested below outline a broad approach especially for beginners. The underlying principle is to ensure the validity of your instrument by ensuring that the objectives of your study are achieved. Therefore, clearly defined objectives play an extremely important role as each question in the instrument must stem from the objectives, research questions and/or hypotheses of the study. It is suggested that a beginner should follow the following procedure.

> Step 1: If you have not already done so, clearly define and individually list all the specific objectives, research questions, or hypotheses to be tested.
>
> Step 2: For each objective, research question or hypothesis, list all the associated questions that you want to answer through your study.
>
> Step 3: Take each question identified in step 2 and list the information required to answer it.
>
> Step 4: Formulate question(s) to obtain this information.

Objectives/research questions/hypotheses Step I	Main and associated research questions Step II	Information required Step III	Questions Step IV	
1 To find out the understanding of the concept 'community responsiveness' among health administrators, managers, service providers and connsumer of health services	What is community responsiveness? What does it mean when people use the term 'community responsiveness?'	1 Perception of community responsiveness	Q1.1	When you use the term 'community responsiveness', what do you mean by it?
			Q1.2	What comes to your mind when you use the term 'community responsiveness' in the delivery of health services?
			Q1.3	What, in your opinion, are the characteristics of 'community responsiveness'?
	What are the differences in the perception of community responsiveness among health administrators, planners managers, service providers and consumers of health services		Q1.4	What, in your opinion, is the difference between 'community development and community responsiveness'?
2 To identify the strategies needed to foster community responsiveness in the delivery of health services		2 Occupational status, i.e. health administrator, planner, service provider or consumer	Q2.1	What would you categorise your job as? Health administrator/planner Service provider Health consumer
		3 age gender education	Q3.1	How old are you? _____
3 To develop a set of indicators to evaluate the effectiveness of strategies to foster community responsiveness.			Q3.2	Are you _____ female _____ male?
			Q3.3	What is the highest level of educational achievement you have attained?

Figure 9.7   Guidelines for constructing a research instrument, illustrated using Figure 4.3 in Chapter 4: a study to evaluate community responsiveness in a health program.

In the above process you may find that the same piece of information is required for a number of questions. In such a situation the question should be asked once only. To illustrate this process see Figure 9.7 for which we have already developed a set of objectives in Chapter 4, Figure 4.3.

Asking personal and sensitive questions

In the social sciences, sometimes one needs to ask questions that are of a personal nature. Some respondents may find this offensive. It is important to be aware of this as it may affect the quality of information or even result in an interview being terminated or failure to return questionnaires. Researchers have used a number of approaches to deal with this problem. Which approach is best is a difficult question to answer. According to Bradburn and Sudman,

> '... no data collection method is superior to other methods for all types of threatening questions. If one accepts the results at face value, each of the data gathering methods is best under certain conditions' (1976: 12–13).

In terms of the best technique for asking sensitive or threatening questions, there appears to be two opposite opinions, and these are that a question of a personal nature should be asked in:

- a direct manner; and
- an indirect manner.

The advantage with the first approach is that one can be sure that an affirmative answer is accurate. Those who advocate the second approach believe that direct questioning is likely to offend respondents and hence they are unlikely to answer even the non-sensitive questions. Some ways of asking personal questions in an indirect manner are as follows:

- by showing drawings or cartoons;
- by asking a respondent to complete a sentence;
- by asking a respondent to sort cards containing statements; and
- by using random devices. To describe these methods is beyond the scope of this book.

The order of questions

The order of questions in a questionnaire or in an interview schedule is important as it affects the quality of information, the interest and even willingness of a respondent to participate in a study. Again there are two categories of opinions as to the best way to order questions. The first is that questions should be asked in a random order and the second is that they should follow a logical progression based upon the objectives of the study. The author believes that the latter procedure is better as it gradually leads respondents into the themes of the study, starting with simple themes and progressing to complex ones. This approach sustains the interest of respondents and gradually stimulates them to answer the questions. However, the random approach is useful in situations where a researcher wants respondents to express their agreement or disagreement with different aspects of an issue. In this case a logical listing of statements or questions may 'condition' a respondent to the opinions expressed by the researcher through the statements.

Prerequisites for data collection

Before you start obtaining information from potential respondents it is imperative that you make sure of their:

- **motivation to share the required information**—it is essential for respondents to be willing to share information with you. You should make every effort to motivate them by explaining clearly and in simple terms the objectives and relevance of the study, either at the time of the interview or through the questionnaire.
- **clear understanding of the questions**—respondents must understand what is expected of them in the questions. If respondents do not understand a question clearly, the response given may either be wrong or irrelevant, or make no sense.
- **possession of the required information**—the third prerequisite is that respondents must have the information sought. This is of particular importance when you are seeking factual or technical information. If respondents do not have the required information, they cannot provide it. In the case of opinions this does not necessarily apply as all of us have opinions.

Collecting data using secondary sources

So far we have discussed the primary sources of data collection where the required data was collected either by you or by someone else for the specific purpose you have in mind. There are occasions when your data has already been collected by someone else and you need only to extract the required information for the purpose of your study. This section lists some of the many secondary sources that can be grouped into the following categories:

- **Government or semi-government publications**—there are many government and semi-government organisations that collect data on a regular basis in a variety of areas and publish it for use by members of the public and interest groups. Some common examples are: the census, vital statistics registration, labour force surveys, health reports, economic forecasts, demographic information.
- **Earlier research**—for some topics, an enormous number of research studies that have already been done by others can provide you with the required information.
- **Personal records**—some people write historical and personal records that may provide the information you need.
- **Mass media**—reports published in newspapers, magazines etc. may be another good source of data.

Problems with using data from secondary sources

When using data from secondary sources you need to be careful as there may be certain problems with the availability, format and quality of data. The extent of these problems varies from source to source. While using such data some issues you should keep in mind are:

- **Validity and reliability**—the validity of information may vary markedly from source to source. For example, information obtained from a census is likely to be more valid and reliable than that obtained from most personal diaries.
- **Personal bias**—the use of information from personal diaries, newspapers and magazines may have the problem of personal bias as these writers are likely to exhibit less rigorousness and objectivity than one would expect in research reports.
- **Availability of data**—it is common for beginning researchers to assume that the required data will be available, but you cannot and should not make this assumption. Therefore, it is important to make sure that the required data is available before you proceed further with your study.
- **Format**—before deciding to use data from secondary sources it is equally important to ascertain that the data are available in the required format. For example, you might need to analyse age in the categories 23–33, 34–48 etc., but in your source, age may be categorised differently, e.g., 21–24, 25–29, etc.

Summary

In this chapter you have learnt about the various methods of data collection. The methods used to collect information about a situation, phenomenon, issue or group of people can be classified as:

- primary sources; and
- secondary sources.

Interviewing, observation and the use of questionnaires are the three main methods classified under primary sources. All other sources, where the information required is already available, such as government publications, reports and previous research, are called secondary sources.

The choice of a particular method of collecting data depends upon the purpose of collecting information, the type of information being collected, the resources available to the researcher, the skills of the researcher and the socio-economic–demographic characteristics of the study population. Each method has its own advantages and disadvantages and each is appropriate for certain situations. The choice of a particular method for collecting data is important in itself for ensuring the quality of the information. No method of data collection will guarantee 100 per cent accurate information. The quality of your information is dependent upon several methodological, situational, and respondent-related factors and your ability as a researcher lies in either controlling or minimising the effect of these factors in the process of data collection.

The use of open-ended and closed-ended questions is appropriate for different situations. Both of them have strengths and weaknesses. You should be aware of these so that you can use them appropriately.

The construction of a research instrument is the most important aspect of any research endeavour as it determines the nature and quality of the information. This is the input of your study and the output is entirely dependent upon it. A research instrument must be developed in the light of the objectives of your study. The method suggested in this chapter ensures that questions in an instrument have a direct link to your objectives. The wording of questions can have several problems.

Collecting data using attitudinal scales

Functions of attitudinal scales

Difficulties in developing an attitudinal scale

Types of attitudinal scale:
- The summated rating or Likert scale
- The equal-appearing-interval or Thurstone scale
- The cumulative or Guttman scale
- The relationship between attitudinal and measurement scales

Summary

Functions of attitudinal scales

A researcher using a questionnaire or an interview schedule to investigate respondents' attitudes towards an issue may use a series of either questions, or statements. To do so, s/he constructs or selects questions or statements that reflect the issue in question. Respondents are asked to indicate their degree of agreement/disagreement or satisfaction/dissatisfaction by selecting the appropriate response category or a number on a numerical scale.

An issue may have many aspects. For example, the attitude of a community towards the provision of a particular service is comprised of their attitude towards the need for the service; its manner of delivery; its location; the physical facilities provided to users; the behaviour of the staff; the competence of the staff; the effectiveness and efficiency of the service; and so on. Similarly, other examples—such as the attitude of employees towards the management of their organisation; the attitude of employees towards occupational redeployment and redundancy; the attitude of nurses towards death and dying; the attitude of consumers towards a particular product; the attitude of students towards a lecturer; or the attitude of staff towards the strategic plan for their organisation—can be broken down in the same manner.

Respondents may have different attitudes towards different aspects. Researchers, when ascertaining attitudes in the usual manner, construct questions designed to tap respondents' attitudes towards all these aspects separately, either on a categorical or on a numerical scale. The main limitation of this method is that it is difficult to draw any conclusion about the overall attitude of a respondent from the responses. For example, suppose you want to find out the attitude of students towards a lecturer. There are different aspects of teaching: the contents of lectures; the organisation of material; the lecturer's ability to communicate material; the presentation and style; knowledge of the subject; responsiveness; punctuality; and so on. Students may rate the lecturer differently on different aspects. That is, the lecturer might be considered extremely competent and knowledgeable in his/her subject but may not be considered a good communicator by a majority of students. Further, students may differ markedly in their opinion regarding any one aspect of a lecturer's teaching. Some might consider the lecturer to be a good communicator and others might not. The main problem is: how do we find out the 'overall' attitude of the students towards the lecturer? How do we combine the responses to different aspects of any issue to come up with one indicator that is reflective of an overall attitude towards an issue? Attitudinal scales play an important role in overcoming this problem.

Attitudinal scales measure the intensity of respondents' attitudes towards the various aspects of a situation or issue and provide techniques to combine the attitudes towards different aspects into one overall indicator. This reduces the risk of an expression of opinion by respondents being influenced by their opinion on only one or two aspects of that situation or issue.

Difficulties in developing an attitudinal scale

In developing an attitudinal scale there are three main problems:

1 Which aspects of a situation or issue should be included when seeking to measure an attitude? For instance, in the example cited above, what aspects of teaching should be included in a scale to find out the attitude of students towards their lecturer?
2 What procedure should be adopted for combining the different aspects to obtain an overall picture?
3 How can one ensure that a scale really is measuring what it is supposed to measure?

The first problem is extremely important as it largely determines the third problem: the extent to which the statements on different aspects are reflective of the main issue largely determines the validity of the scale. You can solve the third problem by ensuring that your statements on the various aspects have a logical link with the main issue under study. The greater the link, the higher the validity. The different types of attitudinal scale (Likert, Thurstone and Guttman) provide an answer to the second problem. They guide you as to the procedure for combining the attitudes towards various aspects of an issue, though the degree of difficulty in following the procedure for these scales varies from scale to scale. For example, the Guttman scale is much more difficult to construct than the Likert scale.

Types of attitudinal scale

There are three major types of attitudinal scale:

1 the summated rating scale, also known as the Likert scale;
2 the equal-appearing-interval scale or differential scale, also known as the Thurstone scale; and
3 the cumulative scale, also known as the Guttman scale.

The summated rating or Likert scale

The summated rating scale, more commonly known as the Likert scale, is the easiest to construct. This scale is based upon the assumption that each statement/item on the scale has equal 'attitudinal value', 'importance' or 'weight' in terms of reflecting an attitude towards the issue in question. This assumption is also the main limitation of this scale as statements on a scale seldom have equal attitudinal value. For instance, in the examples in Figures 10.1 and 10.2, 'knowledge of subject' is not as important in terms of the degree to which it reflects the attitude of the students towards the lecturer as 'has published a great deal' or 'some students like, some do not', but, on the Likert scale, each is treated as having the same 'weight'. A student may not bother much about whether a lecturer has published a great deal, but may be more concerned about 'knowledge of the subject', 'communicates well' and 'knows how to teach'.

The lecturer:	Strongly agree	Agree	Uncertain	Disagree	Strongly disagree
1 Knows the subject well	☐	☐	☐	☐	☐
2 Is unenthusiastic about teaching	☐	☐	☐	☐	☐
3 Shows concern for students	☐	☐	☐	☐	☐
4 Makes unreasonable demands	☐	☐	☐	☐	☐
5 Has *poor* communication skills	☐	☐	☐	☐	☐
6 Knows how to teach	☐	☐	☐	☐	☐
7 Can explain difficult concepts in simple terms	☐	☐	☐	☐	☐
8 Is hard to approach	☐	☐	☐	☐	☐
9 Is liked by some students and not by others	☐	☐	☐	☐	☐
10 Is difficult to get along with	☐	☐	☐	☐	☐

Figure 10.1 An example of a categorical scale

The lecturer:							
1 Knows the subject well	7	6	5	4	3	2	1
2 Is enthusiastic about teaching	7	6	5	4	3	2	1
3 Shows no concern for students	7	6	5	4	3	2	1
4 Demands too much	7	6	5	4	3	2	1
5 Communicates well	7	6	5	4	3	2	1
6 Knows how to teach	7	6	5	4	3	2	1
7 Can explain difficult concepts in simple terms	7	6	5	4	3	2	1
8 Is seldom available to the students	7	6	5	4	3	2	1
9 Is liked by some students and not by others	7	6	5	4	3	2	1
10 Has published a great deal	7	6	5	4	3	2	1

Figure 10.2 An example of a seven-point numerical scale

It is important to remember that the Likert scale does not measure attitude *per se*. It does help to place different respondents in relation to each other in terms of the intensity of their attitude towards an issue: it shows the strength of one respondent's view in relation to another.

Considerations in constructing a Likert scale

In developing a Likert scale, there is a number of things to consider. First, decide whether the attitude to be measured is to be classified into one-, two- or three-directional categories (that is, whether you want to determine positive, negative and neutral positions in the study population) with respect to their attitude towards the issue under study. Next, consider whether you want to use categories or a numerical scale. This should depend upon whether you think that the study population can express itself better on a numerical scale or in categories. The decision about the number of points and the number of categories on a categorical scale depends upon how finely you want to measure the intensity of the attitude in question and on the capacity of the population to make fine distinctions. Figure 10.1 shows a five-point categorical scale that is three-directional and Figure 10.2 illustrates a seven-point numerical scale that is one-directional. Sometimes researchers develop statements reflecting opinion about an issue in varying degrees (Figure 10.3). In this instance a respondent is asked to select the statement which best describes the opinion.

1: The lecturer

a   knows the subject *extremely well*
b   knows the subject *well*
c   has an *average* knowledge of the subject
d   *does not know* the subject
e   has an *extremely poor knowledge* of the subject

Figure 10.3   An example of a scale with statements reflecting varying degrees of attitudes

The procedure for constructing a Likert scale

Figure 10.5 shows the procedure used in constructing a Likert scale.

Calculating attitudinal scores

Suppose you have developed a questionnaire/interview schedule to measure the attitudes of a class of students towards their lecturer. Also, assume you have decided to use a categorical scale using five categories (a smaller or larger number could also have been used).

The lecturer:	SA	A	U	D	SD
1 Knows the subject well (+)	5	4	3	2	1
2 Is unenthusiastic about teaching (–)	1	2	3	4	5
3 Shows concern for students (+)	5	4	3	2	1
4 Makes unreasonable demands (–)	1	2	3	4	5
5 Communicates poorly (–)					
6 Knows how to teach (+)					
7 Can explain difficult concepts in simple terms (+)					
8 Is hard to approach (–)					
9 Is liked by some students and not by others (+/–)					
10 Is difficult to get along with (–)					

SA = strongly agree, A = agree, U = uncertain, D = disagree, SD = strongly disagree

Figure 10.4   Scoring positive and negative statements

In the above example, statement no. 1 is a positive statement, hence, if a respondent ticks 'strongly agree', s/he is assumed to have a more positive attitude on this item than a person who ticks 'agree'. The person who ticks 'agree' has a more positive attitude than a person who ticks 'uncertain', and so on. Therefore, a person who ticks 'strongly agree' has the most positive attitude compared with all of the others with different responses. Hence, the person is given the highest score, 5, as there are only five response categories. If there were four categories you could assign a score of 4. As a matter of fact, any score can be assigned as long as the intensity of the response pattern is reflected in the score and the highest score is assigned to the response with the highest intensity.

Procedure

Step 1	Assemble or construct statements that are reflective of the attitudes towards the main issue in question. Statements should be worded to reflect both positive and negative attitudes towards the issue, that is, they should be for, as well as against, the issue. (If your scale is one-directional, you need only positive statements). Make sure that all the statements have a logical link with the main issue. you also need to decide whether you want respondents to answer in categories or on a numerical scale.
Step 2	Administer the statements to a small group of people.
Step 3	Analyse the responses by assigning a weighting—a numerical value—to the responses. Numerical values are assigned differently to positive and negative statements. For a positive statement the response indicating the most favourable attitude is to be given the highest score. For example, on a five-category or five-point scale, 5 is assigned to the response that indicates the most favourable attitude and 1 to the response which indicates the least favourable attitude. By contrast, a person who agrees strongly with a negative statement indicates that s/he does not have a favourable attitude, hence, the scoring is reversed, i.e., 1 is assigned to the response where a respondent strongly agrees with a negative statement and 5 to the response where s/he strongly disagrees with it.
Step 4	Calculate each respondent's attitudinal score by adding numerical values assigned in step 3 to the responses s/he gave to each statement.
Step 5	compare all respondents' scores for each item to identify non-discriminative items. Non-discriminative statements do not help you to distinguish respondents with respect to attitude as almost everyone responds to them in the same way. (Refer to a book specifically written for measuring attitudes.)
Step 6	Eliminate non-discriminative items.
Step 7	Construct a questionnaire/interview schedule comprised of the selected statements/items.

Figure 10.5 The procedure for constructing a Likert scale

Statement number 2 is a negative statement. In this case a person who ticks 'strongly disagree' has the most positive attitude on this item, hence, is assigned the highest score, 5. On the other hand a respondent who ticks 'strongly agree' has the least positive attitude on the item and therefore is assigned the lowest score, 1. The same scoring system is followed for the other statements.

Note statement 9. There will always be some people who like a lecturer and some who do not, hence this type of statement is neutral. There is no point in including it as most respondents are likely to answer in the same way.

To illustrate how to calculate an individual's attitudinal score, let us take the example of two respondents who have ticked the different statements marked in our example by # and @ (see Figure 10.6).

The lecturer:	SA	A	U	D	SD
1 Knows the subject well (+)	@				#
2 Is unenthusiastic about teaching (−)		#			@
3 Shows concern for students (+)			@		#
4 Makes unreasonable demands (−)		#			@
5 Communicates poorly (−)		#			@
6 Knows how to teach (+)		@		#	
7 Can explain difficult concepts in simple terms (+)	@	#			
8 Is hard to approach (−)			@#		
9 Is liked by some students and not by others (+/−)				@#	
10 Is difficult to get along with (−)			#		@

SA = strongly agree, A = agree, U = uncertain, D = disagree, SD = strongly disagree

Figure 10.6 Calculating an attitudinal score

Let us work out their attitudinal score.

Statement no.   1   2   3   4   5   6   7   8   9   10

Respondent @ =   5 + 5 + 4 + 5 + 4 + 5 + 5 + 2 + 2 + 5 = 42
Respondent # =   1 + 2 + 2 + 1 + 1 + 3 + 4 + 2 + 2 + 1 = 19

The analysis shows that, overall, respondent @ has a 'more' positive attitude towards the lecturer than respondent #. You cannot say that the attitude of respondent @ is twice (42/19 = 2.21) as positive as that of respondent #. The attitudinal score only places respondents in a position relative to one another. Remember that the Likert scale does not measure the attitude *per se* but helps you to rate a group of individuals in descending or ascending order with respect to their attitudes towards the issues in question.

The equal-appearing interval or Thurstone scale

To overcome this problem with the Likert scale, the Thurstone scale calculates a 'weight' or 'attitudinal value' for each statement. The weight (equivalent to the median value) for each statement is calculated on the basis of rating assigned by a group of judges. Each statement with which respondents express agreement (or to which they respond in the affirmative) is given an attitudinal score equivalent to the 'attitudinal value' of the statement. The procedure for constructing the Thurstone scale is as follows:

Step 1   Assemble or construct statements reflective of attitudes towards the issue in question.

Step 2   Select a panel of judges who are experts in the field of attitudes being explored.

Step 3   Send the statements to these judges with a request to rate each statements importance in reflecting an attitude towards the issue being studied. Ask them to rate each statement on an 11-point scale.

Step 4   On the basis of the judges' ratings, calculate the median value of their ratings for each item.

Step 5   If the judges' ratings of any item are scattered over the scale, this indicates that even among the experts, there is no agreement as to the degree to which that statement reflects an attitude towards the issue in question. Discard such statements.

Step 6   From the remaining statements select items that best reflect attitudes towards various aspects of the issue.

Step 7   Construct a questionnaire/interview schedule comprised of the selected items.

Figure 10.7   The procedure for constructing the Thurstone scale

The main advantage of this scale is that, as the importance of each statement is determined by judges, it reflects the 'absolute' rather than relative attitudes of respondents. The scale is thus able to indicate the intensity of people's attitudes and any change in this intensity should the study be replicated. On the other hand, the scale is difficult to construct, and a major criticism is that judges and respondents may assess the importance of a particular statement differently and, therefore, the respondents' attitudes might not be reflected.

The cumulative or Guttman scale

The Guttman scale is one of the most difficult scales to construct and therefore is rarely used. This scale does not have much relevance for beginners in research and therefore is not discussed in this book. For information about this scale, consult books specifically dealing with attitudinal scales.

The relationship between attitudinal and measurement scales

Different attitudinal scales use different measurement scales. It is important to know which attitudinal scale belongs to which measurement scale as this will help you in the interpretation of respondents' scores. Table 10.1 shows attitudinal scales in relation to measurement scales.

Table 10.1 The relationship between attitudinal and measurement scales

Attitudinal scales	*Measurement scales*
Likert scale	Ordinal scale
Thurstone scale	Interval scale
Guttman scale	Ratio scale

Summary

Attitudinal scales measure attitudes towards an issue. Their strength lies in their ability to combine attitudes towards different aspects of an issue and to provide an indicator that is reflective of an overall attitude. There are problems in developing an attitudinal scale. Which aspects should be included when measuring attitudes towards an issue? How should the responses given by a respondent to ascertain the overall attitude be combined? How does one ensure the scale developed really measures attitude towards the issue in question?

There are three types of scale that measure attitude: the Likert, Thurstone and Guttman scales. The Likert scale is the most common because it is easy to construct. The main assumption of the scale is that each statement is 'equally important'. The 'importance' of each item for the Thurstone scale is determined by a panel of judges. Arranging statements in a perfect cumulative order is the main problem in developing the Guttman scale.

11

Establishing the validity and reliability of a research instrument

The concept of validity
- Types of validity

The concept of reliability
- Factors affecting the reliability of a research instrument
- Methods of determining the reliability of an instrument

Summary

In the last two chapters we discussed various methods of data collection. The questions asked of your respondents are the basis of your findings and conclusions. These questions constitute the 'input' for your conclusions (the 'output'). This input passes through a series of steps—the selection of a sample, the collection of information, the processing of data, the application of statistical procedures and the writing of a report—and the manner in which all of these are done can affect the accuracy and quality of your conclusions. Accordingly, it is natural for a researcher to attempt to establish (and for a reader to question) the quality of the results, that is, to seek to establish their validity. As inaccuracies can be introduced into a study at any stage, the concept of validity can be applied to the research process as a whole or to any of its steps. We can talk about the validity of the study design used, the sampling strategy adopted, the conclusions drawn, the statistical procedures applied or the measurement procedures used. Broadly, there are two perspectives on validity:

1 Is the research investigation providing answers to the research questions for which it was undertaken?
2 If so, is it providing these answers using appropriate methods and procedures?

In this chapter we are concerned with the concept of validity as applied to measurement procedures.

The concept of validity

To examine the concept of validity, let us take a very simple example. Suppose you have designed a study to ascertain the health needs of a community. In doing so, you have developed an interview schedule. Most of the questions in the interview schedule relate to the attitude of the study population towards the health services being provided to them. Note that your aim was to find out about health needs but the interview schedule is finding out what attitudes respondents have to the health services, thus, the instrument is not measuring what it was designed to measure. The author has come across many similar examples among students and less skilled researchers.

In terms of measurement procedures, therefore, validity is the ability of an instrument to measure what it is designed to measure. 'Validity is defined as the degree to which the researcher has measured what he has set out to measure' (Smith 1991: 106). According to Kerlinger, 'The commonest definition of validity is epitomised by the question: Are we measuring what we think we are measuring?' (1973: 457). Babbie writes, '... validity refers to the extent to which an empirical measure adequately reflects the real meaning of the concept under consideration' (1990: 133). These definitions raise some questions:

• Who decides that an instrument is measuring what it is supposed to measure?
• How can it be established that an instrument is measuring what it is supposed to measure?

Obviously the answer to the first question is the person who has designed the study and experts in the field. The second question is extremely important. On what basis does a researcher or an expert make this judgement? In the social sciences there appear to be two approaches to establishing the validity of a research instrument: logic and statistical evidence. Establishing validity through logic implies justification of each question in relation to the objectives of the study, whereas the statistical procedures provide hard evidence by way of calculating the coefficient of correlations between the questions and the outcome variables.

Establishing a logical link between the questions and the objectives is both simple and difficult. It is simple in the sense that you may find it easy to see a link for yourself, and difficult because your justification may lack the backing of experts and the statistical evidence to convince others. Establishing a logical link between questions and objectives is easier when the questions relate to tangible matters. For example, if you want to find out about age, income, height, or weight, it is relatively easy to establish the validity of the questions, but to establish whether a set of questions is measuring, say, the effectiveness of a program, the attitudes of a group of people towards an issue, or the extent of satisfaction of a group of consumers with the service provided by an organisation, is more difficult. When a less tangible concept is involved, such as effectiveness, attitude, or satisfaction, you need to ask several questions in order to cover different aspects of the concept and demonstrate that the questions asked are actually measuring it. Validity in such situations becomes more difficult to establish.

It is important to remember that the concept of validity is only pertinent to a particular instrument and it is an ideal state that researchers aim to achieve.

Types of validity

There are three types of validity:

1 Face and content validity;
2 Concurrent and predictive validity; and
3 Construct validity.

Face and content validity

The judgement that an instrument is measuring what it is supposed to is primarily based upon the logical link between the questions and the objectives of the study. Hence, one of the main advantages of this type of validity is that it is easy to apply. Each question or item on the scale must have a logical link with an objective. Establishment of this link is called *face validity*. It is equally important that the items and questions cover the full range of the issue or attitude being measured. Assessment of the items of an instrument in this respect is called *content validity*. In addition, the coverage of the issue or attitude should be balanced, that is, each aspect should have similar and adequate representation in the questions or items. Content validity is also judged on the basis of the extent to which statements or questions represent the issue they are supposed to measure, as judged by the researcher and experts in the field. Although it is easy to present logical arguments to establish validity, there are certain problems:

1 The judgement is based upon subjective logic, hence, no definite conclusions can be drawn. Different people may have different opinions about the face and content validity of an instrument.
2 The extent to which questions reflect the objectives of a study may differ. If the researcher substitutes one question for another, the magnitude of the link may be altered. Hence, the validity or its extent may vary with the questions selected for an instrument.

Concurrent and predictive validity

'In situations where a scale is developed as an indicator of some observable criterion, the scale's validity can be investigated by seeing how good an indicator it is.' (Moser and Kalton 1971: 356). Suppose you develop an instrument to determine the suitability of applicants for a profession. The instrument's validity might be determined by comparing it with another assessment, for example, by a psychologist, or with a future observation of how well these applicants have done in the job. If both assessments are similar, the instrument used to make the assessment is assumed to have higher validity. These types of comparisons establish two types of validity: *predictive* and *concurrent*. Predictive validity is judged by the degree to which an instrument can forecast an outcome. Concurrent validity is judged by how well an instrument compares with a second assessment concurrently done. 'It is usually possible to express predictive validity in terms of the correlation coefficient between the predicted status and the criterion. Such a coefficient is called a validity coefficient.' (Burns 1994: 220).

Construct validity

Construct validity is a more sophisticated technique for establishing the validity of an instrument. It is based upon statistical procedures. It is determined by ascertaining the contribution of each construct to the total variance observed in a phenomenon.

Suppose you are interested in carrying out a study to find out the degree of job satisfaction among employees of an organisation. You consider status, the nature of the job and remuneration as the three most important factors indicative of job satisfaction, and construct questions to ascertain the degree to which people consider each important for job satisfaction. After the pre-test or data analysis you use statistical procedures to establish the contribution of each construct (status, the nature of the job, and remuneration) to the total variance (job satisfaction). The contribution of these factors to the total variance is an indication of the degree of validity of the instrument. The greater the variance attributable to the constructs, the higher the validity of the instrument.

One of the main disadvantages of construct validity is that a researcher needs to know the required statistical procedures.

The concept of reliability

We use the word 'reliability' so often in our lives. When we say that a person is reliable, what do we mean? We infer that she or he is dependable, consistent, predictable, stable, and honest.

The concept of reliability in relation to a research instrument has a similar meaning: if a research tool is consistent and stable, and hence, predictable and accurate, it is said to be reliable. The greater the degree of consistency and stability in an instrument, the greater is its reliability. Therefore, 'a scale or test is reliable to the extent that repeat measurements made by it under constant conditions will give the same result.' (Moser and Kalton 1989: 353).

The concept of reliability can be looked at from two sides:

1 How reliable is an instrument?
2 How unreliable is it?

The first question focuses on the ability of an instrument to produce consistent measurements. When you collect the same set of information more than once, using the same instrument and get the same or similar results, under the same or similar conditions, an instrument is considered to be reliable. The second question focuses on the degree of inconsistency in the measurements made by an instrument, that is, the extent of difference in the measurements when a you collect the same set of information more than once, by using the same instrument under the same or similar conditions. Hence, the degree of inconsistency in the different measurements is an indication of the extent of its inaccuracy. This 'error' is a reflection of an instrument's unreliability. Therefore, reliability is the degree of accuracy or precision in the measurements made by a research instrument. The lower the degree of 'error' in an instrument, the higher is the reliability.

Let us take an example. Suppose you develop a questionnaire to ascertain the prevalence of domestic violence in a community. You administer this questionnaire and find that domestic violence is prevalent in, say, five per cent of households. If you follow this with another survey using the same questionnaire on the same population under the same conditions, and discover that the prevalence of domestic violence is, say, fifteen per cent, the questionnaire has not given a comparable result, which may mean it is unreliable. The less the difference between the two sets of results, the higher the reliability of the instrument.

Factors affecting the reliability of a research instrument

In the social sciences it is impossible to have a research tool which is 100 per cent accurate not only because a research instrument cannot be so, but also because it is impossible to control the factors affecting reliability. Some of these factors are:

- **The wording of questions**—a slight ambiguity in the wording of questions or statements can affect the reliability of a research instrument as respondents may interpret the questions differently at different times, resulting in different responses.

- **The physical setting**—in the case of an instrument being used in an interview, any change in the physical setting at the time of the repeat interview may affect the responses given by a respondent, which may affect reliability.
- **The respondent's mood**—a change in a respondent's mood when responding to questions or writing answers in a questionnaire can change and may affect the reliability of that instrument.
- **The nature of interaction**—in an interview situation, the interaction between the interviewer and the interviewee can affect responses significantly. During the repeat interview the responses given may be different due to a change in interaction, which could affect reliability.
- **The regression effect of an instrument**—when a research instrument is used to measure attitudes towards an issue, some respondents, after having expressed their opinion, may feel that they have been either too negative or too positive towards the issue. The second time they may express their opinion differently, affecting reliability.

Methods of determining the reliability of an instrument

There is a number of ways of determining the reliability of an instrument. The various procedures can be classified into two groups:

1 external consistency procedures; and
2 internal consistency procedures.

External consistency procedures

External consistency procedures compare cumulative test results with each other as a means of verifying the reliability of the measure. The two methods are as follows.

- **Test/re-test**—this is a commonly used method for establishing the reliability of a research tool. In the test/re-test (repeatability test) an instrument is administered once, and then again, under the same or similar conditions. The ratio between the test and re-test scores (or any other finding, e.g., prevalence of domestic violence, a disease or incidence of an illness) is an indication of the reliability of the instrument. The greater the value of the ratio, the higher the reliability of the instrument. As an equation:

$$(\text{Test score})/(\text{Re-test}) = 1$$
or
$$(\text{Test score})-(\text{Re-test}) = 0$$

A ratio of 1 shows 100 per cent reliability (no difference between test and re-test) and any deviation from it indicates less reliability. The less the value of this ratio, the less the reliability of the instrument. Expressed in another way, zero difference between the test and re-test scores is an indication of 100 per cent reliability. The greater the difference between the test scores/findings, the greater the unreliability of the instrument. The main advantage of the test/re-test procedure is that it permits the instrument to be compared with itself, thus avoiding the sort of problems that could arise with the use of another instrument.

The main disadvantage is that a respondent may recall the responses that he or she gave in the first round, which in turn may affect the reliability of the instrument. Where an instrument is reactive in nature (when an instrument educates the respondent with respect to what the researcher is trying to find out) this method will not provide an accurate assessment of its reliability. One of the ways of overcoming this problem is to increase the time-span between the two tests, but this may affect reliability for other reasons, such as the maturation of respondents and the impossibility of achieving conditions similar to those under which the questionnaire was first administered.

- **Parallel forms of the same test**—in this procedure, the researcher constructs two instruments that are intended to measure the same phenomenon. The two instruments are then administered to two similar populations. The results obtained from one test are compared with those obtained from the other. If they are similar, it is assumed that the instruments are reliable.

The main advantage of this procedure is that it does not suffer from the problem of recall found in the test/re-test procedure. Also, a time lapse between the two tests is not required. A disadvantage is that a researcher needs to construct two instruments, instead of one. Moreover, it is extremely difficult to construct two instruments that are comparable in their measurement of a phenomenon. It is equally difficult to achieve comparability in the two population groups and in the two conditions under which the tests are administered.

Internal consistency procedures

The idea behind internal consistency procedures is that items measuring the same phenomenon should produce similar results. The following method is commonly used for measuring the reliability of an instrument.

- **The split-half technique**—this technique is designed to correlate half of the items with the other half and is appropriate for instruments that are designed to measure attitudes towards an issue or phenomenon. The questions or statements are divided in half in such a way that any two questions or statements intended to measure the same aspect fall into different halves. The scores obtained by administering the two halves are correlated. Reliability is calculated by using the product moment correlation between scores obtained from the two halves. Because the product moment correlation is calculated on the basis of only half the instrument, to assess reliability for the whole it needs to be corrected. This is known as *stepped-up* reliability. The stepped-up reliability for the whole instrument is calculated by a formula called the Spearman-Brown formula.

Summary

The concept of validity refers to quality and can be applied to any aspect of the research process. With respect to measurement procedures it relates to whether a research instrument is measuring what it set out to measure. There are two approaches used to establish the validity of an instrument: the establishment of a logical link between the objectives of a study and the questions used in an instrument, and the use of statistical analysis to demonstrate this link. There are three types of validity: face and content, concurrent and predictive, and construct validity.

The reliability of an instrument refers to its ability to produce consistent measurements each time. When we administer an instrument under the same or similar conditions to the same population and obtain similar results, we say that the instrument is 'reliable'. The more similar the results, the greater the reliability. We can look at reliability from two sides: reliability (the extent of accuracy) and unreliability (the extent of inaccuracy). Ambiguity in the wording of questions, a change in the physical setting for data collection, a respondent's mood when providing information, the nature of the interaction between interviewer and interviewee, and the regressive effect of an instrument, are factors that can affect the reliability of a research instrument.

There are external and internal consistency procedures for determining reliability. Test/re-test and parallel forms of the same test are the two procedures that determine the external reliability of a research instrument, whereas the split-half technique is classified under internal consistency procedures.

Step IV

Selecting a sample

Sampling **Chapter 12**

12
Sampling

The concept of sampling

Let us take a very simple example to explain the concept of sampling. Suppose you want to estimate the average age of the students in your class. There are two ways of doing this. The first method is to contact all students in the class, find out their ages, add them up, then divide this by the number of students (the definition of an average). The second method is to select a few students from the class, ask them their ages, add them up, then divide by the number of students you have asked, which enables you to make an *estimate* of the average age of the class. Take another example: suppose you want to find out the average income of families living in a city. You could follow the procedures described above, but imagine the amount of effort and resources required to go to each family in the city to find out their income! You could follow the second method by selecting a few families to become the basis of your inquiry and then make an *estimate* of the average income of families in the city. A further example would be the outcome of an election: the result is decided after voting on election day, but predictions about the outcome are usually made on the basis of opinion polls. These polls are based upon a very small group of people who are questioned about their voting preferences. On the basis of these results, a *prediction* is made about the outcome.

Sampling, therefore, is the process of selecting a few (a sample) from a bigger group (the sampling population) to become the basis for estimating or predicting a fact, situation or outcome regarding the bigger group. A sample is a sub-group of the population you are interested in.

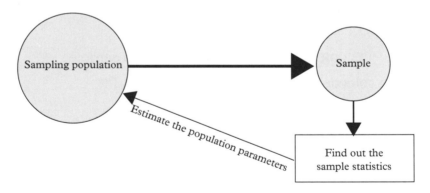

Figure 12.1 The concept of sampling

This process of selecting a sample from the total population has advantages and disadvantages. The advantages are that it saves time as well as financial and human resources. However, the disadvantage is that you *do not find out the facts* about the population's characteristics of interest to you but *only estimate* or *predict* them. Hence, the possibility of an error in your estimation exists.

Sampling is thus a trade-off between certain gains and losses. While on the one hand you save time and resources, on the other, you may compromise the level of accuracy in your findings. Through sampling you only make an estimate about the actual situation prevalent in the total population from which the sample is drawn. If you ascertain a piece of information from the total sampling population, and if your method of inquiry is correct, your findings should be reasonably accurate. However, if you select a sample and use this as the basis from which to estimate the situation in the total population, an error is possible. Tolerance of this possibility of error is an important consideration in selecting a sample.

Sampling terminology

Let us, again, consider the examples used above. Our main aims are to find out the average age of the class, the average income of the families living in the city, and the likely election outcome for a particular state or country. Let us assume that we adopt the second method, that is, we select a few students, families or electorates, to achieve these aims.

- **Population** or **study population**—the class/city/electorates from which you select a few students/ families/electors, to sample.
- **Sample**—the small group of students, families or electors from whom you obtain the information to make an estimate of the average age, average income or election outcome.
- **Sample size**—the number of students, families or electors from whom you obtain the required information.
- **Sampling design** or **strategy**—the way we selected the students, families or electors.
- **Sampling unit** or **element**—each student, family or elector that becomes the basis of selection of the sample.
- **Sampling frame**—a list identifying each student, family or elector.
- **Sample statistics**—your findings on the basis of the information obtained from the respondents (sample), e.g., the average age of the students (calculated from information obtained from those who were questioned); the average income of families in the city (calculated from the information obtained from those families who participated in your study); and the expected election outcome (from the responses obtained from those questioned). The sample statistics become the basis of estimating the prevalence of a characteristic in the study population.
- **Population parameters** or **mean**—the population characteristics you want to investigate, which are the average age of the class, the average income of the families living in the city, and the expected outcome of the election.

Principles of sampling

The theory of sampling is guided by three principles. To effectively explain these, we will take an extremely simple example. Suppose there are four individuals: A, B, C and D. A is 18 years of age, B is 20, C is 23 and D is 25. As you know their ages, you can *find out* (calculate) their average age by simply adding 18+20+23+25=86 and dividing by 4. This gives the average age of A, B, C and D as 21.5 years.

Now let us suppose that we want to select a sample of two individuals to make an *estimate* of the average age of the four individuals. If we adopt the theory of probability, we can have six possible combinations of two: A and B; A and C; A and D; B and C; B and D; and C and D. Let us take each of these pairs to calculate the average age of the sample:

- A+B = 18+20 = 38/2 = 19.0 years;
- A+C = 18+23 = 41/2 = 20.5 years;
- A+D = 18+25 = 43/2 = 21.5 years;
- B+C = 20+23 = 43/2 = 21.5 years;
- B+D = 20+25 = 45/2 = 22.5 years; and
- C+D = 23+25 = 48/2 = 24.0 years.

Notice that in most cases the average age (sample statistics) calculated on the basis of these samples of two is different. Now compare these sample statistics with the average of all four individuals, the population mean (population parameter) of 21.5 years. Out of a total of six possible sample combinations, only in the case of two is there no difference between the sample statistics and the population mean. Where there is a difference, this is attributed to the sample and is known as *sampling error*. Again, the size of the sampling error varies markedly. Let us consider the difference in the sample statistics and the population mean for each of the six samples.

Table 12.1 The difference between sample statistics and the population mean

Sample	Sample average (Sample statistics) (1)	Population mean (Population parameter) (2)	Difference between (1) and (2)
1	19.0	21.5	−2.5
2	20.5	21.5	−1.5
3	21.5	21.5	0.0
4	21.5	21.5	0.0
5	22.5	21.5	+1.0
6	24.0	21.5	+2.5

This analysis suggests a very important principle of sampling:

> **Principle one**—In a majority of cases where sampling is done there will be a difference between the sample statistics and the true population mean, which is attributable to the selection of the units in the sample.

To understand the second principle, let us continue with the above example but instead of a sample of two individuals, take a sample of three. There are four possible combinations of three that can be drawn.

- A+B+C = 18+20+23 = 61/3 = 20.67 years;
- A+B+D = 18+20+25 = 63/3 = 21.00 years;
- A+C+D = 18+23+25 = 66/3 = 22.00 years; and
- B+C+D = 20+23+25 = 68/3 = 22.67 years.

Now, let us compare the difference between the sample statistics and the population mean.

Table 12.2 The difference between a sample and a population average

Sample	Sample average (1)	Population average (2)	Difference between (1) and (2)
1	20.67	21.5	−0.83
2	21.00	21.5	−0.5
3	22.00	21.5	+0.5
4	22.67	21.5	+1.17

Compare the difference between the differences calculated in this table and the previous one. In the first table the difference between the sample statistics and the population mean lies between −2.5 to +2.5 years, whereas in the second, it is between −0.83 to +1.17 years. The gap between the sample statistics and the population mean is reduced in the second table. This reduction is attributed to the increase in the sample size. This, therefore, leads to the second principle:

Principle two—The greater the sample size, the more accurate will be the estimate of the true population mean.

The third principle of sampling is particularly important as a number of sampling strategies, such as stratified and cluster sampling, are based on it. To understand this principle, let us continue with the same example but use slightly different data. Suppose the ages of four individuals are markedly different: A=18, B=26, C=32 and D=40. In other words, we are visualising a population where the individuals, with respect to age—the variable we are interested in—are markedly different.

Let us follow the same procedure, selecting samples of two individuals at a time and then three. If we work through the same procedures, described above, we will find that the difference in the average age in the case of samples of two, ranges between −7 and + 7 years and in the case of the sample of three, ranges between −3.67 and +3.67. In both cases the range of the difference is greater than previously calculated. This is attributable to the greater difference in the ages of the four individuals—the sampling population. In other words, the sampling population is more heterogeneous in regard to age.

Principle three—The greater the difference in the variable under study in a population, for a given sample size, the greater will be the difference between the sample statistics and the true population mean.

These principles are crucial to keep in mind when you are determining the sample size needed for a particular level of accuracy, and, in selecting the sampling strategy best suited to your study.

Factors affecting the inferences drawn from a sample

The above principles suggest that two factors may influence the degree of certainty about the inferences drawn from a sample:

1 **The size of the sample**—findings based upon larger samples have more certainty than those based on smaller ones. As a rule, the larger the sample size, the more accurate will be the findings.

2 **The extent of variation in the sampling population**—the greater the variation in the study population with respect to the characteristics under study, for a given sample size, the greater will be the uncertainty. (In technical terms, the greater the standard deviation, the higher will be the standard error, for a given sample size, in your estimates). If a population is homogeneous with respect to the characteristics under study, a small sample can provide a reasonably good estimate, but if it is heterogeneous, to obtain the same level of accuracy, you need to select a larger sample. Of course, if all the elements in a population are identical, then the selection of even one will provide an absolutely accurate estimate. As a rule, the higher the variation with respect to the characteristics under study in the study population, the greater will be the uncertainty for a given sample size.

Aims in selecting a sample

In selecting a sample, always try to

- achieve maximum precision in your estimates within a given sample size, and
- avoid bias in the selection of your sample.

Bias in the selection of a sample can occur if:

- sampling is done by a non-random method, i.e., if the selection is consciously or unconsciously influenced by human choice;
- the sampling frame—list, index or other population records—which serves as the basis of selection, does not cover the sampling population accurately and completely; and
- a section of a sampling population is impossible to find or refuses to co-operate.

Types of sampling

The various sampling strategies could be categorised in three different categories (Figure 12.2):

- Random/probability sampling designs;
- Non-random/probability sampling designs; and
- 'Mixed' sampling designs.

To understand these designs, we will discuss each individually.

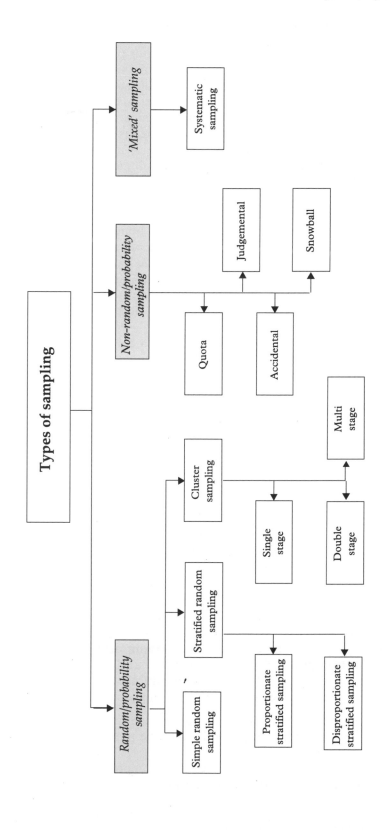

Figure 12.2 Types of sampling

Random/probability sampling designs

For a sampling design to be called a random or probability sample, each element in the population must have an *equal* and *independent* chance of selection in the sample. Equal implies that the probability of selection of each element in the population is the same, that is, the choice of an element in the sample is not influenced by other considerations such as personal preference. The concept of independence means that the choice of one element is not dependent upon the choice of another element in the sampling: the selection or rejection of one element does not affect the inclusion or exclusion of another. To explain these concepts let us return to our example of the class.

Suppose there are 80 students in the class. Assume 20 of these refuse to participate in your study. You want the entire population of 80 students in your study but as 20 refuse to participate, you can only use a sample of 60. The 20 students who refuse to participate could have strong feelings about the issues you wish to explore, but your findings will not reflect their opinions. Their exclusion from your study means that each of the 80 students does not have an equal chance of selection. Therefore your sample does not represent the total class.

The same could apply to a community. In a community, in addition to the refusal to participate, let us assume that you are unable to identify all the residents living in the community. If a significant proportion of people cannot be included in the sampling population because they either cannot be identified or refuse to participate, then any sample drawn will not provide to each element in the sampling population an equal chance of being selected in the sample. Hence, the sample will not be representative of the total community.

To understand the concept of an *independent chance of selection*, let us assume that there are five students in the class who are extremely close friends. If one of them is selected but refuses to participate because the other four are not chosen, and you are therefore forced to select either the five or none, then your sample will not be considered an independent sample since the selection of one is dependent upon the selection of others. The same could happen in the community where a small group says that either all of them or none of them will participate in the study. In these situations where you are forced either to include or to exclude a part of the sampling population, the sample is not considered to be independent, and hence is not representative of the sampling population.

A sample can only be considered a random/probability sample and therefore representative of the population under study if both these conditions are met. If not, bias can be introduced into the study.

There are two main advantages of random/probability samples:

• as they represent the total sampling population, the inferences drawn from such samples can be generalised to the total sampling population; and

• some statistical tests based upon the theory of probability can be applied only to data collected from random samples.

Methods of drawing a random sample

Of the methods that you can adopt to select a random sample the three most common are:

- **the fishbowl draw**—if your total population is small, an easy procedure is to number each element using separate slips of paper for each element, put all the slips into a box, and then pick them out one by one without looking, until the number of slips selected equals the sample size you decided upon. This method is used in some lotteries.
- **computer programs**.
- **a table of random numbers**—most books on research methodology and statistics include a table of randomly generated numbers in their appendices (see, for example, Table 12.3). You can select your sample using these tables according to the procedure described in Figure 12.3.

The procedure for selecting a sample using a table of random numbers is as follows:

Step 1 Identify the total number of elements in the study population, e.g., 50, 100, 430, 795, 1265. The total number of elements in a study population may run up to four or more digits (if your total sampling population is 9 or less, it is one digit; if it is 99 or less, it is two digits; ...).

Step 2 Number each element starting from 1.

Step 3 If the table for random numbers is on more than one page, choose the starting page by a random procedure. Again, select a column or row that will be your starting point with a random procedure and proceed from there in a predetermined direction.

Step 4 Corresponding to the number of digits to which the total population runs, select the same number, randomly, of columns or rows of digits from the table.

Step 5 Decide on your sample size.

Step 6 Select the required number of elements for your sample from the table. If you happen to select the same number twice, discard it and go to the next. This can happen as the table for random numbers is generated by sampling with replacement.

Figure 12.3 Using a table of random numbers

Let us take an example to illustrate the use of the table for random numbers. Let us assume that your sampling population consists of 256 individuals. Number each individual, from 1 to 256. Randomly select the starting page, set of column (1 to 10) or row from the table and then identify three columns or rows of numbers.

Suppose you identify the ninth column of numbers and the last three digits of this column (underlined). Assume that you are selecting 10 per cent of the total population as your sample (25 elements). Let us go through the numbers underlined in the ninth set of columns. The first number is

Table 12.3 Selecting a sample using a table for random numbers

	1	2	3	4	5	6	7	8	9	10
1	48461	14952	72619	73689	52059	37086	60050	86192	67049	64739
2	76534	38149	49692	31366	52093	15422	20498	33901	10319	43397
3	70437	25861	38504	14752	23757	29660	67844	78815	23758	86814
4	59584	03370	42806	11393	71722	93804	09095	07856	55589	50063
5	04285	58554	16085	51555	27501	73883	33427	33343	45507	50063
6	77340	10412	69189	85171	29802	44785	86368	02583	96483	76553
7	59183	62687	91778	80354	23512	97219	65921	02035	59487	91403
8	91800	04281	39979	03927	82564	28777	59049	97532	54540	79472
9	12066	24817	81099	48940	69554	55925	48379	12866	41232	21580
10	69907	91751	53512	23748	65906	91385	84983	27915	48491	91068
11	80467	04873	54053	25955	48518	13815	37707	68687	15570	08890
12	78057	67835	28302	45048	56761	97725	58438	91529	24645	18544
13	05648	39387	78191	88415	60269	94880	58812	42931	71898	61534
14	22304	39246	01350	99451	61862	78688	30339	60222	74052	25740
15	61346	50269	67005	40442	33100	16742	61640	21046	31909	72641
16	56793	37696	27965	30459	91011	51426	31006	77468	61029	57108
17	56411	48609	36698	42453	85061	43769	39948	87031	30767	13953
18	62098	12825	81744	28882	27369	88185	65846	92545	09065	22653
19	68775	06261	54265	16203	23340	84750	16317	88686	86842	00879
20	52679	19599	13687	74872	89181	01939	18447	10787	76246	80072
21	84096	87152	20719	25215	04349	54434	72344	93008	83282	31670
22	83964	55937	21417	49944	38356	98404	14850	17994	17161	98981
23	31191	75131	72386	11689	95727	05414	88727	45583	22568	77700
24	30545	68523	29850	67833	05622	89975	79042	27142	99257	32349
25	52573	91001	52315	26430	54175	30122	31796	98842	37600	26025
26	16586	81842	01076	99414	31574	94719	34656	80018	86988	79234
27	81841	88481	61191	25013	30272	23388	22463	65774	10029	58376
28	43563	66829	72838	08074	57080	15446	11034	98143	74989	26885
29	19945	84193	57581	77252	85604	45412	43556	27518	90572	00563
30	79374	23796	16919	99691	80276	32818	62953	78831	54395	30705
31	48503	26615	43980	09810	38289	66679	73799	48418	12647	40044
32	32049	65541	37937	41105	70106	89706	40829	40789	59547	00783
33	18547	71562	95493	34112	76895	46766	96395	31718	48302	45893
34	03180	96742	61486	43305	84183	99605	67803	13491	09243	29557
35	94822	24738	67749	83748	59799	25210	31093	62925	72061	69991
36	4330	60599	85828	19152	68499	27977	35611	96240	62747	89529
37	43770	81537	59527	95674	76692	86420	69930	10020	72881	12532
38	56908	77192	50623	41215	14311	42834	80651	93750	59957	31211
39	32787	07189	80539	75927	75475	73965	11796	72140	48944	74156
40	52441	78392	11733	57703	29133	71164	55355	31006	25526	55790
41	22377	54723	18227	28449	04570	18882	00023	67101	06895	08915
42	18376	73460	88841	39602	34049	20589	05701	08249	74213	25220
43	53201	28610	87957	21497	64729	64983	71551	99016	87903	63875
44	34919	78801	59710	27396	02593	05665	11964	44134	00273	76358
45	33617	92159	21971	16901	57383	34262	41744	60891	57624	06962
46	70010	40964	98780	72418	52571	18415	64362	90637	38034	04909
47	19282	68447	35665	31530	59838	49181	21914	65742	89815	39231
48	91429	73328	13266	54898	68795	40948	80808	63887	89939	47938
49	97637	78393	33021	05867	86520	45363	43066	00988	64040	09803
50	95150	07625	05255	83254	93943	52325	93230	62668	79529	66964

049 which is below 256, (total population), hence the 49th element becomes a part of your sample. The second number, 319, is more than the total elements in your population (256), hence, you cannot accept the 319th element in the sample. The same applies to the next element, 758, and indeed the next five elements, 589, 507, 483, 487 and 540. After 540 is 232, and as this number is within the sampling frame, it can be accepted as a part of the sample. Similarly, if you follow down the same three digits in the same column, you select 052, 029, 065, 246, 161, before you come to the element 029 again. As the 29th element has already been selected, go to the next number, and so on until 25 elements have been chosen. Once you have reached the end of a column, you can either move to the next set of columns or randomly select another one in order to continue the process of selection. For example the following 25 elements are selected from the ninth, tenth and second columns of Table 12.3:

Table 12.4 Selected elements using the table of random numbers

			Elements selected		
#	49	232	52	29	65
	246	161	243	61	213
	34	40			
*	63	68	108	72	25
	234	44	211	156	220
	231	(10th column)			
@	149	246			

sample selected from the 9th column
* sample selected from the 10th column
@ sample selected from the 2nd column

Several computer programs that can be used to select the required sample are available.

Different systems of drawing a random sample

There are two ways of selecting a random sample:

- sampling without replacement; and
- sampling with replacement.

Suppose you want to select a sample of 20 students out of a total of 80. The first student is selected out of the total class, so the probability of selection for the first student is 1/80. When you select the second student there are only 79 left in the class and the probability of selection for the second student is not 1/80 but 1/79. The probability of selecting the next student is 1/78. By the time you select the 20th student, the probability of his or her selection is 1/61. This type of sampling is called *sampling without replacement*. But this is contrary to our basic definition of randomisation, i.e., each element has an equal and independent chance of selection. In the second system, called *sampling with replacement*, the selected element is replaced in the sampling population and if it is selected again, it is discarded and the next one is selected. If the sampling population is fairly large, the probability of selecting the same element twice is fairly remote.

Specific random/probability sampling designs

There are three commonly used types of random sampling design.

- **Simple random sampling (SRS)**—the most commonly used method of selecting a probability sample. In line with the definition of randomisation, whereby each element in the population is given an equal and independent chance of selection, a simple random sample is selected by the following procedure.

Step 1 Identify by a number all elements or sampling units in the population.
Step 2 Decide on the sample size (n).
Step 3 Select (n) using either the fishbowl draw, the table of random numbers or a computer program.

Figure 12.4 The procedure for selecting a simple random sample

To illustrate, let us again take our example of the class. There are 80 students in the class, so the first step is to identify each student by a number from 1 to 80. Suppose you decide to select a sample of 20 using the simple random sampling technique. Use either the fishbowl draw, the table for random numbers or a computer program to select the 20 students. These 20 students become the basis of your inquiry.

- **Stratified random sampling**—as discussed, the accuracy of your estimate largely depends on the extent of variability or heterogeneity of the study population with respect to the characteristics that have a strong correlation with what you are trying to ascertain (Principle three). It follows, therefore, that if, by some means the heterogeneity in the population can be reduced, for a given sample size, you can achieve greater accuracy in your estimate. Stratified random sampling is based upon this logic.

In stratified random sampling the researcher attempts to stratify the population in such a way that the population within a stratum is homogeneous with respect to the characteristic on the basis of which it is being stratified. It is important that the characteristics chosen as the basis of stratification are clearly identifiable in the study population. For example, it is much easier to stratify a population on the basis of gender than on the basis of age, income or attitude. It is also important for the characteristic that becomes the basis of stratification to be related to the main variable the researcher is exploring. Once the sampling population has been separated into non-overlapping groups the researcher selects the required number of elements from each stratum, using the simple random sampling technique. There are two types of stratified sampling: proportionate and disproportionate stratified sampling. With proportionate stratified sampling, the number of elements from each stratum in relation to its proportion in the total population is selected, whereas in disproportionate stratified sampling, consideration is not given to the size of the stratum. The procedure for selecting a stratified sample is schematically presented in Figure 12.5.

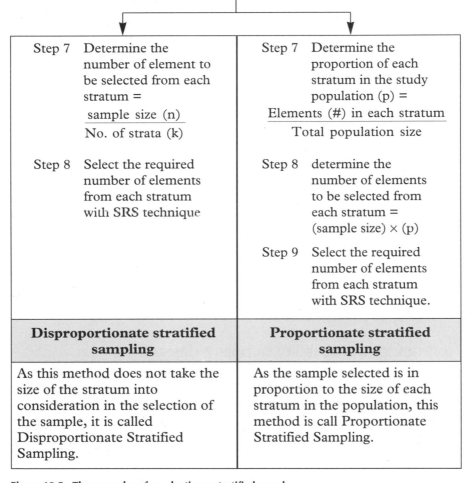

Step 1   Identify all elements or sampling units in the sampling population.

Step 2   Decide upon the different strata (k) into which you want to stratify the population.

Step 3   Place each element into the appropriate stratum.

Step 4   Number every element in each stratum separately.

Step 5   Decide the total sample size (n).

Step 6   Decide whether you want to select proportionate or disproportionate stratified sampling and follow the following steps.

Step 7 Determine the number of element to be selected from each stratum = $\dfrac{\text{sample size (n)}}{\text{No. of strata (k)}}$ Step 8 Select the required number of elements from each stratum with SRS technique	Step 7 Determine the proportion of each stratum in the study population (p) = $\dfrac{\text{Elements (\#) in each stratum}}{\text{Total population size}}$ Step 8 determine the number of elements to be selected from each stratum = (sample size) × (p) Step 9 Select the required number of elements from each stratum with SRS technique.
Disproportionate stratified sampling	**Proportionate stratified sampling**
As this method does not take the size of the stratum into consideration in the selection of the sample, it is called Disproportionate Stratified Sampling.	As the sample selected is in proportion to the size of each stratum in the population, this method is call Proportionate Stratified Sampling.

Figure 12.5   The procedure for selecting a stratified sample

- **Cluster sampling**—simple random and stratified sampling techniques are based on a researcher's ability to identify each element in a population. It is easy to do this if the total sampling population is small, but if the population is large as in the case of a city, state or country, it becomes difficult and expensive to identify each sampling unit. In such cases the use of cluster sampling is more appropriate.

Cluster sampling is based on the ability of the researcher to divide the sampling population into groups, called clusters, and then to select elements within each cluster, using the SRS technique. Clusters can be formed on the basis of geographical proximity or a common characteristic that has a correlation with the main variable of the study (as in stratified sampling). Depending on the level of clustering, sometimes, sampling may be done at different levels. These levels constitute the different stages (single, double or multi) of clustering, which will be explained later.

Imagine you want to investigate the attitude of post-secondary students in Australia towards problems in higher education in the country. Higher education institutions are in every state and territory of Australia. In addition, there are different types of institutions, e.g., universities, universities of technology, colleges of advanced education and TAFE colleges. Within each institution various courses are offered both at undergraduate and postgraduate levels. Each academic course could take three to four years. You can imagine the magnitude of the task. In such situations cluster sampling is extremely useful in selecting a random sample.

The first level of cluster sampling could be at the state or territory level. Clusters could be grouped according to similar characteristics that ensure their comparability in terms of student population. If this is not easy you may decide to select all the states and territories and select a sample at the institutional level. For example, with a simple random technique, one institution from each category within each state could be selected, e.g., one university, one university of technology, one college of advanced education and one TAFE college. This is based upon the assumption that institutions within a category are fairly similar with regards to student profile. Then, within an institution on a random basis, one or more academic programs could be selected, depending on resources. Within each study program selected, students studying in a particular year can be selected. Further selection of a proportion of students can then occur. The process of selecting a sample in this manner is called *multi-stage cluster sampling*.

Non-random/probability sampling designs

Non-probability sampling designs do not follow the theory of probability in the choice of elements from the sampling population. Non-probability sampling designs are used when the number of elements in a population is either unknown or cannot be individually identified. In such situations the selection of elements is dependent upon other considerations. There are four non-random designs, each based on a different consideration, which are commonly used in qualitative and quantitative research:

- quota sampling;
- accidental sampling;
- judgemental or purpose sampling; and
- snowball sampling.

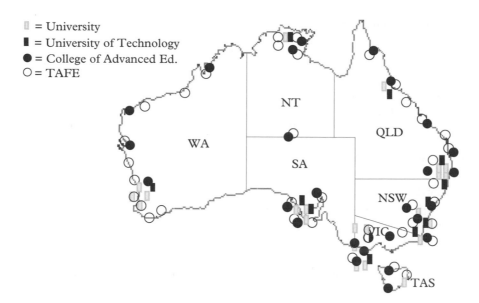

= University
= University of Technology
= College of Advanced Ed.
= TAFE

Figure 12.6 The concept of cluster sampling

Quota sampling

The main consideration directing quota sampling is the researcher's ease of access to the sample population. In addition to convenience, she or he is guided by some visible characteristic, such as gender or race, of the study population that is of interest to her/him. The sample is selected from a location convenient to the researcher and whenever a person with this visible relevant characteristic is seen, that person is asked to participate in the study. The process continues until the researcher has been able to contact the required number of respondents (quota).

Let us suppose that you want to select a sample of 20 male students in order to find out the average age of the male students in your class. You decide to stand at the entrance to the classroom, as this is convenient, and whenever a male student enters the classroom, ask his age. This process continues until you have asked 20 students their age. Alternatively, you might want to find out about the attitudes of Aboriginal students towards the facilities provided to them in your university. Stand at a convenient location and whenever you see an Aboriginal student, collect the required information through whatever method you have adopted for the study.

There are advantages and disadvantages with this design. The advantages are: it is the least expensive way of selecting a sample; you do not need any information, such as a sampling frame, the total number of elements, their location, or other information about the sampling population; and it guarantees the inclusion of the type of people you need. The disadvantages are: as the resulting sample is not a probability one, the findings cannot be generalised to the total sampling population; and the most accessible individuals might have characteristics that are unique to them and hence might not be truly representative of the total sampling population.

Accidental sampling

Accidental sampling is also based upon convenience in accessing the sampling population. Whereas quota sampling attempts to include people possessing an obvious/visible characteristic, accidental sampling makes no such attempt.

This method of sampling is common among market research and newspaper reporters. It has more or less the same advantages and disadvantages as quota sampling. As you are not guided by any obvious characteristics, some people contacted may not have the required information.

Judgemental or purposive sampling

The primary consideration in purposive sampling is the judgement of the researcher as to who can provide the best information to achieve the objectives of the study. The researcher only goes to those people who in her/his opinion are likely to have the required information and be willing to share it.

This type of sampling is extremely useful when you want to construct a historical reality, describe a phenomenon or develop something about which only a little is known.

Snowball sampling

Snowball sampling is the process of selecting a sample using networks. To start with, a few individuals in a group or organisation are selected and the required information is collected from them. They are then asked to identify other people in the group or organisation, and the people selected by them become a part of the sample. Information is collected from them, and then these people are asked to identify other members of the group, and in turn, those identified become the basis of further data collection. This process is continued until the required number or a saturation point has been reached, in terms of the information being sought.

This sampling technique is useful if you know little about the group or organisation you wish to study, as you only need to make contact with a few individuals, who can then direct you to the other members of the group. This method of selecting a sample is useful for studying communication patterns, decision making or diffusion of knowledge within a group. There are disadvantages to this technique, however. The choice of the entire sample rests upon the choice of individuals at the first stage. If they belong to a particular faction or have strong biases, the study may be biased. Also, it is difficult to use this technique when the sample becomes fairly large.

The 'mixed' sampling design

Systematic sampling design

Systematic sampling has been classified under the 'mixed sampling' category because it has the characteristics of both random and non-random sampling designs.

In systematic sampling the sampling frame is first divided into a number of segments, called intervals. Then, from the first interval, using the SRS technique, one element is selected. The selection of subsequent elements from other intervals is dependent upon the order of the elements selected in the first interval. If in the first interval it is the fifth element, the fifth element of each subsequent interval will be chosen. Notice that from the first interval the choice of an element is on a random basis, but the choice of the elements from subsequent intervals is dependent upon the choice from the first, and hence cannot be classified as a random sample. For this reason it has been classified here as 'mixed sampling'. The procedure used in systematic sampling is as follows:

Step 1   Prepare a list of all the elements in the study population (N).
Step 2   Decide on the sample size (n).
Step 3   Determine the width of the interval $= \dfrac{\text{Total population}}{\text{Sample size}} = (k)$
Step 4   Using the SRS, select an element from the first interval (nth order).
Step 5   Select the same order element from each subsequent interval.

Figure 12.7   The procedure for selecting a systematic sample

Although the general procedure for selecting a sample by the systematic sampling technique is described above, one can deviate from it by selecting a different element from each interval with the SRS technique. By adopting this, systematic sampling can be classified under probability sampling designs.

Figure 12.8   Systematic sampling

To select a random sample one must have a sampling frame. Sometimes this is impossible or obtaining one becomes too expensive. However, in real life there are situations when a kind of sampling frame exists, for example, records of clients in an agency, enrolment lists of students in a school or university, electoral lists of people living in an area, or records of the staff employed in an organisation. All these can be used as a sampling frame to select a sample with the systematic sampling technique. This convenience of having a 'ready made' sampling frame may be at a price: in some cases it may not truly be a random listing. Mostly these lists are either in alphabetical order, based upon a number assigned to a case, or are arranged in a way that is convenient to the users of the records. If the 'width of an interval' is large, say, 1 in 30 cases, and if the cases are arranged in alphabetical order, you could preclude some whose surnames start with the same letter or some adjoining letter may not be included at all.

Suppose there are 50 students in a class and you want to select 10 students using the systematic sampling technique. The first step is to determine the width of the interval (50/10 = 5). This means that from every five you need to select one element. Using the SRS technique, from the first interval (1–5 elements), select one of the elements. Suppose you selected the third element. From the rest of the intervals select every third element.

The calculation of sample size

'How big a sample should I select?' 'What should be my sample size?' 'How many cases do I need?' These are the most common questions asked. Basically, it depends on what you want to do with the findings and what type of relationships you want to establish. Your purpose in undertaking research is the main determinant of the level of accuracy required in the results, and this level of accuracy is an important determinant of sample size. In determining the size of your sample, you need to consider the following:

• At what level of confidence do you want to test your results, findings or hypotheses?
• With what degree of accuracy do you wish to estimate the population parameters?
• What is the estimated level of variation (standard deviation), with respect to the main variable you are studying, in the study population?

Answering these questions is necessary regardless of whether you intend to determine the sample size yourself or have an expert do it for you. The size of the sample is important for testing a hypothesis or establishing an association, but for other studies the general rule is *the larger the sample size, the more accurate will be your estimates*. In practice, your budget determines the size of your sample. Your skills in selecting a sample, within the constraints of your budget, lie in the way you select your elements so that they effectively and adequately represent your sampling population.

To illustrate this procedure let us take the example of a class. Suppose you want to find out the average age of the students within an accuracy of 0.5 of a year, that is, you can tolerate an error of half a year on either side of the true average age. Let us also assume that you want to find the average age within half a year of accuracy at 95% confidence level, that is, you want to be 95 per cent confident about your findings.

The formula for determining the confidence limits is:

$$\hat{x} = \bar{x} \pm (t_{.05})\frac{\sigma}{\sqrt{\eta}}$$

where

$\hat{x}$ = estimated value of the population mean

$\bar{x}$ = average age calculated from the sample

$t_{.05}$ = value of t at 95% confidence level

$\frac{\sigma}{\sqrt{\eta}}$ = standard error

$\quad\quad \sigma \quad\quad$ = standard deviation

$\quad\quad \eta \quad\quad$ = sample size

$\quad\quad \sqrt{} \quad$ = square root

If we decide to tolerate an error of 1/2 years, that means

$$\bar{x} \pm \frac{(t_{.05})\frac{\sigma}{\sqrt{\eta}}}{=} = \bar{x} \pm 0.5$$

or in other words we will like $\left[(t_{.05}) \frac{\sigma}{\sqrt{\eta}} \right] = 0.5$

$$\text{OR} \quad = (1.96) \frac{\sigma}{\sqrt{\eta}} = 0.5 \quad \text{(value of } t_{0.05} - 1.96\text{)}$$

Level	0.02	0.10	0.05	0.02	0.01	0.001
t-value	1.282	1.645	1.960	2.326	2.576	3.291

$$\therefore \sqrt{\eta} = \frac{1.96 \times \sigma}{0.5}$$

There is only one unknown quantity in the above equation: σ

Now the main problem is how to find out the value of σ without having to collect data. This is the biggest problem in estimating the sample size. Because of this it is important to know as much as possible about the study population.

The value of σ can be found by one of the following:

1 guessing;
2 consulting an expert;
3 obtaining the value of σ from previous comparable studies; or
4 carrying out a pilot study to calculate the value.

Let us assume that σ is one year.

$$\therefore \sqrt{\eta} = \frac{1.96 \times 1}{0.5} = 3.92$$

$$\therefore \eta = 15.37 \text{ say } 16$$

Hence, to determine the average age of the class at a level of 95% accuracy (assuming $\sigma = 1$ year) with $1/2$ year of error, a sample of at least 16 students is necessary.

Now assume that instead of 95%, you want to be 99% confident about the estimated age, tolerating an error of $1/2$ year.

$$\sqrt{n} = \frac{2.576 \times 1}{0.5}$$
$$= 5.15$$
$$\therefore \eta = 26.54 \text{ say } 27$$

Hence, if you want to be 99% confident and are willing to tolerate an error of $^1/_2$ year, you need to select a sample of 27 students. Similarly, you can calculate the sample size with varying values of σ.

Summary

In this chapter you have learnt about sampling, the process of selecting a few elements from a sampling population. Sampling, in a way, is a trade-off between accuracy and resources. Through sampling you *make an estimate* about the information of interest. You do not find the true population mean.

Sampling is guided by three principles. One of the most important principles of sampling is that the greater the sample size, the more accurate will be the estimate of the true population mean, given that everything else remains the same. The inferences drawn from a sample can be affected by both the size of the sample and the extent of variation in the sampling population.

Sampling designs can be classified as random/probability sampling designs, non-random/probability sampling designs, and 'mixed' sampling designs. For a sample to be called a random sample, each element in the study population must have an equal and independent chance of selection. Three random designs were discussed: simple random sampling, stratified random sampling, and cluster sampling. The procedures for selecting a sample using these designs were detailed step-by-step. The use of the fishbowl technique, the table of random numbers, and specifically designed computer programs, are three commonly used methods of selecting a probability sample.

There are four non-probability sampling designs: quota, accidental, judgemental and snowball. Each is used for a different purpose and in different situations.

Systematic sampling is classified under the 'mixed' category as it has the properties of both probability and non-probability sampling designs.

The last section of the chapter described determinants of and procedures for calculating sample size. Although it might be slightly more difficult for the beginner, it was included to make you aware of the determinants involved as questions relating to this area are so commonly asked.

Step V

Writing a research proposal

13

Writing a research proposal

The research proposal

A research proposal is an overall plan, scheme, structure and strategy designed to obtain answers to the research questions or problems that constitute your research project. A research proposal should outline the various tasks you plan to undertake to fulfil your research objectives, test hypotheses or obtain answers to your research questions. It should also state your reasons for undertaking the study. Broadly, a research proposal's main function is *to detail the operational plan for obtaining answers to your research questions. In doing so it ensures and reassures the reader of the validity of the methodology for obtaining answers to your research questions accurately and objectively.*

In order to achieve this function, a research proposal must tell you, your research supervisor and reviewers the following information about your study:

* *what* you are proposing to do;
* *how* you plan to proceed; and
* *why* you selected the proposed strategy.

Therefore it should contain the following information about your study:

* a statement of the *objectives* of the study;
* a list of *hypotheses*, if you are testing any;
* the *study design* you are proposing to use;
* the *setting* for your study;
* the research *instrument(s)* you are planning to use;
* information on *sample size* and *sampling design*;
* information on *data processing* procedures;
* an outline of the proposed *chapters* for the report;
* the study's *problems* and *limitations*;
* a proposed *time-frame*.

A research proposal should communicate the purpose and plan of the research in such a way that it:

* enables a researcher to return to the proposal for his/her own guidance in decision making at different stages of the research process; and
* convinces your research supervisor or a reviewer that your proposed methodology is meritorious, valid, appropriate and workable in terms of obtaining answers to your research questions or objectives.

Universities and other institutions may have differing requirements regarding the style and content of a research proposal. Requirements may also vary within an institution, from discipline to discipline or from supervisor to supervisor. (The guidelines set out in this chapter therefore provide a framework within which a research proposal should be written.)

Your proposal should follow the suggested guidelines and be written in an academic style. It must contain appropriate references in the body of the text and a bibliography at the end. Your survey of the relevant literature should cover major publications on the topic. The *theoretical frame* for your study must emerge from this literature review and must have its grounding in empirical evidence. As a rule, the literature review includes:

- a conceptual framework, and theoretical and empirical information about the main issues under study; and
- some of the major research findings relating to your topic, research questions raised in the literature, and gaps identified by previous researchers.

A literature review also raises issues relating to methodology. For example, it may examine how other studies operationalised the major variables of relevance to your study and may include a critique of methodology relevant to your study. The critiques of methods and procedures should be included under their respective headings. For example, a critique of the sampling design you adopt should be included under 'sampling' or a critique to the study design should be discussed under 'study design'.

Note that the suggested outline does not contain a section entitled 'survey of the literature' or 'literature review'. This is because references to literature should be integrated with your arguments conceptually rather than chronologically. Issues to do with research methodology and problems pertinent to the various aspects of research procedures should be discussed under their respective headings. For example, issues pertaining to the study design under 'study design', issues relating to sampling under 'sampling', and literature pertaining to the research instrument under the 'measurement procedure'.

In suggesting this format it is assumed that you are acquainted reasonably well with research methodology and an academic style of writing. That is, you know how to write a set of objectives or construct a hypothesis, you are familiar with the various study designs, and you can construct a research instrument or cite a reference.

The pages that follow outline a framework for a research proposal. The contents under each heading may vary markedly from discipline to discipline and according to the academic level of the student (BA Hons, MA, PhD).

Each section of the proposed outline for a research proposal is divided into two parts:

1 a suggested title for the section and an outline of its contents; and
2 examples outlining contents for the section. Three examples of research projects, each taken from a different discipline, are used as illustration.

The preamble/introduction

The proposal should start with an introduction to include some of the information listed below. Remember that some of the contents suggested in this section may not be relevant to certain studies, so use your discretion in selecting only what is pertinent to your study. In writing this section, the literature review (see Chapter 3 on reviewing the literature) is of central importance as it serves two main functions:

1 It acquaints you with the available literature in the area of your study, thereby broadening your knowledge base.
2 It provides you with information on methods and procedures other people have used in similar situations and tells you what works and what does not.

The type, extent, and quality of a literature review are mostly dependent upon the academic level for which you are writing the proposal. The contents of this section may also vary greatly according to the subject area under study.

Start with a very broad perspective of the main subject area, before gradually narrowing the focus to the central problem under investigation. In doing so, cover the following aspects of your study area:

- an overview of the main area under study;
- a historical perspective (development, growth, etc.) pertinent to the study area;
- philosophical or ideological issues relating to the topic;
- trends in terms of prevalence, if appropriate;
- major theories, if any;
- the main issues, problems and advances in the subject area under study;
- important theoretical and practical issues relating to the central problem under study; and
- the main findings relating to the core issue(s).

Three examples of possible topics for the introduction/preamble for a research proposal follow.

Example A

Suppose that you are conducting a study to investigate the impact of immigration on the family. The preamble/introduction should include a brief description of the following:

- The origins of migratory movements in the world.
- General theories developed to explain migratory behaviour.
- The reasons for migration.
- Current trends in migration (national and state).
- The impact of immigration on family roles and relationships (e.g., on husband and wife, on children and parents, on parental expectations of children etc.).
- Occupational mobility.
- etc.

Example B

Suppose your research project is to conduct a study of the attitudes of foster carers towards foster payment in ... name of the place/state/ country. The preamble/introduction would include the following:

- The origins of foster placement, the philosophy of foster care, a historical overview of foster care and changes over the years.
- Reasons for foster care and changes over time.
- The origins of foster placement in ... (the country in which you are conducting your study).
- The effects of foster placement on children and parents.

- Policies with respect to foster care in ... (the region).
- The origins of foster care in ... (the region).
- Policies with respect to foster care in ... (the region).
- Administrative procedures for foster care in ... (the region).
- The training of foster parents in ... (the region)
- The role and responsibility of foster parents.
- etc.

Example C

Suppose that you plan to study the relationship between academic achievement and social environment. The preamble or introduction would include the following:

- The role of education in our society.
- Major changes in the philosophy of education over time.
- Factors affecting attitudes towards education.
- The development of education in ... (country).
- Trends in education participation rates in ... (country) with particular reference to the region in which the study is being carried out.
- Changing educational values.
- Trends in education in ... (country).
- etc.

The problem

Having provided a broad introduction to the area under study, now focus on issues relating to its central theme, identifying some of the gaps in the existing body of knowledge. Identify some of the main unanswered questions. Here some of the main research questions that you would like to answer through your study should also be raised, and a rationale for each should be provided. Knowledge gained from other studies and the literature about the issues you are proposing to investigate should be an integral part of this section. Specifically, this section should:

- identify the issues that are the basis of your study;
- specify the various aspects of/perspectives on these issues;
- identify the main gaps in the existing body of knowledge;
- raise some of the main research questions that you want to answer through your study;
- identify what knowledge is available concerning your questions, specifying the differences of opinion in the literature regarding these questions if differences exist; and
- develop a rationale for your study with particular reference to how your study will fill the identified gaps.

The following examples outline the topics that you should include in the section entitled 'the problem'.

Example A

- What settlement process does a family go through after immigration?
- What adjustments do immigrants have to make?
- What types of change can occur in family members' attitudes? (Theory of acculturation etc.).
- What is the possible impact of settlement on family roles and relationships?
- In terms of impact, what specific questions do you want to answer through the study? What does the literature say about these questions? What are the different viewpoints on these issues? What are your own ideas about these questions?
- What do you think will be the relevance of the findings of your study to the existing body of knowledge and to your profession?
- How will the findings add to the body of knowledge and be useful to professionals in your field?
- etc.

Example B

- What are the broad issues, debates, arguments and counter arguments regarding foster care payment?
- What are the attitudes of foster parents to the amount, mode and form of payment and what does the literature say about these issues?
- What are the different viewpoints/perspectives regarding payment for foster care?
- What main questions will your study answer?
- How will your findings help in policy formulation and program development?
- etc.

Example C

- What theories have been developed to explain the relationship between academic achievement and social environment?
- What is the relationship between educational achievement and social environment: what theoretical model will be the basis of your study?
- What do previous theories and research have to say regarding the components of the theoretical model and academic achievement, for example, the relationship between academic achievement and:
  —the self-esteem and aspirations/motivation of a student;
  —peer group influence;
  —parental involvement and its relationship with their socio-economic status;
  —the motivation, competence and interest in the students of teachers;
  —employment prospects;
  —etc.

The objectives of the study

In this section include a statement of both your study's main and sub-objectives (see Chapter 4). Your main objective indicates the central thrust of your study whereas the sub-objectives identify the specific issues you propose to examine.

The objectives of the study should be clearly stated and specific in nature. Each sub-objective should delineate only one issue. Use action-oriented verbs such as 'to determine', 'to find out', 'to ascertain' in formulating sub-objectives, which should be numerically listed. If the objective is to test a hypothesis, you must follow the convention of hypothesis formulation in wording the specific objectives.

Example A

Main objective:
  To ascertain the impact of immigration on the family.

Sub-objectives:

1 To determine the impact of immigration on husband/wife roles as perceived by immigrants.
2 To find out the impact of immigration on marital relations.
3 To ascertain perceived changes in parental expectations of children's academic and professional achievement.
4 To determine perceived changes of attitude towards marriage in the study population.

Example B

Main objective:
  To determine the opinion of foster carers about the form and extent of foster payment they feel they should receive for taking care of a foster child.

Sub-objectives:

1 To determine the form and mode of payment for taking care of a foster child.
2 To identify the factors that foster parents believe should be the basis for determining the rate of payment for fostering a child.
3 To determine the relationship, if any, between the socio-economic-demographic characteristics of foster parents and their views on payment.

Example C

Main objective:
  To examine the relationship between academic achievement and social environment.

Sub-objectives:

1 To find out the relationship, if any, between self-esteem and a student's academic achievement at school.

2 To ascertain the association between parental involvement in a student's studies and his/her academic achievement at school.
3 To examine the links between a student's peer group and academic achievement.
4 To explore the relationship between academic achievement and the attitude of a student towards teachers.

The hypotheses to be tested

A hypothesis is a statement of your assumptions about the prevalence of a phenomenon or about a relationship between two variables that you plan to test within the framework of the study (see Chapter 6). If you are going to test hypotheses, list them in this section.

When formulating a hypothesis you have an obligation to draw conclusions about it in the text of the report. Hypotheses have a particular style of formulation. You must be acquainted with the correct way of wording them. In a study you may have as many hypotheses as you want to test. However, it is *not* essential to have a hypothesis in order to undertake a study—you can conduct a perfectly satisfactory study without formulating a hypothesis.

Example A

H_1 = In most cases there will be a change in husband/wife roles after immigration.
H_2 = In a majority of cases there will be a change in parents' expectations of their children.
H_i = etc.

Example B

H_1 = Most people become foster parents because of their love of children.
H_2 = A majority of foster parents would like to be trained to care for foster children.
H_i = etc.

Example C

H_1 = A student's self-esteem and academic achievement at school are positively correlated.
H_2 = The greater the parental involvement in a student's studies, the higher the academic achievement.
H_3 = A student's attitude towards teachers is positively correlated with his/her academic achievement.
H_i = etc.

The study design

Describe the study design (for details see Chapter 8) you plan to use to answer your research questions. (For example, say whether it is a 'cross-sectional', 'before-and-after', 'experimental' or 'non-experimental' design.) Identify the strengths and weaknesses of your study design.

Include details about the various logistical procedures you intend to follow while executing the study design. One characteristic of a good study design is that it explains the details with such clarity that, if someone else wants to follow the proposed procedure, he/she will be able to do exactly as you would have done. Your study design should include information about the following:

- Who makes up the study population?
- Can each element of the study population be identified? If yes, how?
- Will a sample or the total population be studied?
- How will you get in touch with the selected sample?
- How will the sample's consent to participate in the study be sought?
- How will the data be collected (e.g., by interview, questionnaire or by observation)?
- In the case of a mailed questionnaire, to what address should the questionnaire be returned?
- Are you planning to send a reminder?
- How will confidentiality be preserved?
- How and where can respondents contact you if they have queries?

Example A

The study is primarily designed to find out from a cross-section of immigrants from ...., ... and .... (names of the countries) the perceived impact of immigration on family roles. Initial contact with the ethnic associations for these countries will be made through the elected office bearers to obtain a list of members. Five immigrants will be selected from the list at random, and will be contacted by phone to explain the purpose of the study and its relevance, and to seek their agreement to participate in the study. Those who give their consent will be interviewed at their home or any other convenient place. To select a further sample a snowball sampling technique will be used until the desired sample size is obtained.

Example B

The study design is cross-sectional in nature, being designed to find out from a cross-section of foster parents their opinions about foster payment. All foster parents currently registered with the Department .... (name of the office) constitute the study population. From the existing records of this department it seems that there are 457 foster parents in .... (name of the region). As it is impossible for the researcher, within the constraints of time and money, to collect information from all the foster parents, it is proposed to select a sample of 50 per cent of the study population with the proposed sampling strategy. The questionnaire, with a supporting letter from the department, will be sent with a prepaid envelope. The respondents will be requested to return the questionnaire by .... (date). The letter from the researcher attached to the questionnaire will explain the objectives and relevance of the study, assure the respondents of anonymity, and give them the option of not participating in the study if they do not wish to. A contact number will be provided in case a respondent has any questions. In the case of a low response rate (less than 25 per cent), a reminder will be sent to respondents.

Example C

It is proposed that the study will be carried out in two government high schools in the metropolitan area. The principals of the schools most accessible to the researcher will be contacted to explain the purpose of the study and the help needed from the school, and to seek their permission for the students to participate in the study. As the constraints of time and resources do not permit the researcher to select more than two schools, negotiations with other schools will cease when two schools agree to participate in the study.

It is proposed to select year 9 students as the academic achievement of students in years 8 and 10 could be affected by factors unique to them. Year 8 students may be experiencing anxiety as a result of having just made the transition to a new system. The motivation of students in year 10 could be affected by their being at the stage in their education where they must decide if they will continue on at school.

In order to control the variance attributable to the gender of a student it is proposed to select only male students.

Once the principal of a school agrees to allow the study to be carried out, the researcher will brief the teacher in charge about the study and its relevance, and will arrange a date and time for administering the questionnaire.

When the students are assembled ready to participate in the study, the researcher will explain its purpose and relevance, and then distribute the questionnaire. The researcher will remain in the class to answer any questions the students might have.

The setting

Briefly describe the organisation, agency or community in which you will conduct your study. If the study is about a group of people, highlight some of the salient characteristics of the group (e.g., its history, size, composition, structure) and draw attention to any available relevant information.

If your research concerns an agency, office or organisation, include the following in your description:

- the main services provided by the agency, office or organisation;
- its administrative structure;
- the type of clients served; and
- information about the issues that are central to your research.

If you are studying a community, briefly describe some of the main characteristics, such as:

- the size of the community;
- a brief social profile of the community (i.e., the composition of the various groups within it); and
- issues of relevance to the central theme of your study.

Note that due to the nature of the content, it would be difficult to provide examples.

Measurement procedures

This section should contain a discussion of your instrument (see Chapters 9 and 10) and the details of how you plan to operationalise your *major* variables (Chapter 5).

To start with, justify your choice of research tool, highlighting its strengths and pointing out its weaknesses. Then outline the major segments of your research tool and their relevance to the main objectives of the study. If you are using a standard instrument, briefly discuss the availability of evidence on its reliability and validity. If you adapt or modify it in any way, describe and explain the changes you have made.

You should also discuss how you are going to operationalise the major concepts. For example, if measuring effectiveness, specify how it will be measured. If you plan to measure the self-esteem of a group of people, mention the main indicators of self-esteem and the procedures for its measurement (e.g., the Likert or Thurstone scale, or any other procedure).

Ideally you should attach a copy of the research instrument to your proposal. Note that due to the nature of the content, it would be difficult to provide examples

Sampling

Under this section of the proposal include the following (consult Chapter 12 on sampling):

- the size of the sampling population (if known), and from where and how this information will be obtained;
- the size of the sample you are planning to select, and your reasons for choosing this size; and
- an explanation of the sampling design you are planning to use in the selection of the sample (simple random sampling, stratified random sampling, quota sampling etc.).

Example A

Because a lack of information as to the exact location of migrant families makes it difficult to use a probability sampling design, it is proposed that the researcher will employ a snowball sampling technique. The researcher will make the initial contact with five families who have emigrated from .... (name of the country) during the last seven to ten years, who are either known to him/her or on the basis of the information obtained from the office bearers of the formal associations representing the migrant groups. From each respondent the researcher will obtain names and addresses of other immigrants who have come from the same country during the same period. The respondents thus identified will then be interviewed and asked to identify other respondents for the researcher. This process will continue until the researcher has interviewed 70 respondents.

Example B

Because of the constraints of time and resources it is proposed to select 50 per cent of the foster parents currently registered (457) with the department using the Systematic Random sampling technique. Every other foster parent registered with the department will be selected, thus 229 individuals will constitute the sample for the study.

Example C

The selection of schools will be done primarily through Quota sampling. Schools will be selected on the basis of their geographical proximity to the researcher. The researcher will prepare a list of schools, in rank order, of accessibility. Once two schools agree to participate in the study, negotiations with other schools will cease.

All year 9 male students will constitute the study population. It is expected that the sample will not exceed 100 students.

Analysis of data

In general terms, describe the strategy you intend to use for data analysis (Chapter 15). Specify whether the data will be analysed manually or by computer. For computer analysis, identify the program and the statistical procedures you plan to perform on the data. Also identify the main variables for cross-tabulation.

Example A

Frequency distributions in terms of:

- age;
- education;
- occupation;
- number of children;
- duration of immigration;
- etc.

Cross tabulations:
  Impact of husband/wife roles

- age;
- number of children;
- education;
- occupation;
- etc.

Example B

Frequency distributions in terms of:

- age;
- income;
- education;
- occupation;
- marital status;
- duration of foster care;
- number of foster children;
- etc.

Cross tabulations:
  Attitude towards foster payment

- age;
- number of children;
- education;
- occupation;
- etc.

Statistical tests to be applied:

- Chi square;
- regression analysis;
- etc.

Example C

Frequency distributions in terms of:

- age;
- parents' occupation;
- parents' educational levels;
- students' occupational aspirations;
- parental involvement in students' studies;
- self-esteem;
- peer group influence;
- number of hours spent on studies;
- etc.

Cross tabulations:
Academic achievement

- peer group influence;
- parental involvement in students' studies;
- self-esteem;
- occupational aspirations;
- attitude towards teachers;
- etc.

The structure of the report

As clearly as possible, state how you intend to organise the final report (see Chapter 17). In organising your material for the report, the specific objectives of your study are of immense help. Plan to develop your chapters around the main themes of your study. The title of each chapter should clearly communicate the main thrust of its contents.

The first chapter, possibly entitled 'Introduction', should be an overall introduction to your study, covering most of your project proposal and pointing out deviations, if any, from the original plan.

The second chapter should provide some information about the study population itself, i.e., some of its socio-economic–demographic characteristics. The main aim of this chapter is to give readers some background on the population from which you collected the information. The second chapter, therefore, may be entitled, 'Socio-economic–demographic characteristics of the study population' or 'The study population' or any other title that communicates this theme to readers. Titles for the rest of the chapters will vary from study to study but, as mentioned, each chapter should be written around a main theme. Although the wording of chapter titles is an individual choice, each must communicate the main theme of the chapter. In developing these themes the specific objectives of the study should be kept in the forefront of your mind.

Example A

It is proposed that the report will be divided into the following chapters:

Chapter 1: Introduction
Chapter 2: The socio-economic-demographic characteristics of the study population
Chapter 3: The impact on husband/wife roles
Chapter 4: The impact on marital relations
Chapter 5: The impact on expectations of children
Chapter 6: The impact on attitudes towards marriage
Chapter 7: Summary, conclusions and recommendations

Example B

The dissertation will be divided into the following chapters:

Chapter 1: Introduction
Chapter 2: A profile of the study population
Chapter 3: Foster carers' perceptions of their role
Chapter 4: Attitudes of foster carers towards foster care payment
Chapter 5: The preferred method of payment
Chapter 6: General comments made by respondents about foster care
Chapter 7: Summary, conclusions and recommendations

Example C

The report will have the following chapters:

Chapter 1: Introduction
Chapter 2: The study population
Chapter 3: Occupational aspirations, self-esteem and academic achievement
Chapter 4: The extent of parental involvement and academic achievement
Chapter 5: Peer group influence and academic achievement
Chapter 6: Academic achievement and student attitudes towards teachers
Chapter 7: Summary, conclusions and recommendations

Problems and limitations

This section should list problems you thought you might encounter concerning, for example, the availability of data, securing permission from the agency/organisation to carry out the study, obtaining the sample, or any other aspect of the study.

You will not have unlimited resources and as this may be primarily an academic exercise, you might have to do less than an ideal job. However, it is important to be aware of—and communicate—any limitations that could affect the validity of your conclusions and generalisations.

Here, problems refer to difficulties relating to logistical details, whereas limitations designate structural problems relating to methodological aspects of the study. In your opinion the study design you chose may not be the best but you might have had to adopt it for a number of reasons. This is classified as a limitation of the study. This is also true for sampling or measurement procedures. Such limitations should be communicated to readers.

Work schedule

You must set yourself dates as you need to complete the research within a certain time-frame. List the various operational steps you need to undertake and indicate against each the date by which you aim to complete that task. Remember to keep some time towards the end as a 'cushion' in case the research process does not go as smoothly as planned. Develop a chart as shown in Table 13.1.

Appendix

As an appendix, attach your research instrument and a list of references. Included with your instrument, and preceding it, should be a list of your specific objectives, research questions and/or hypotheses. Against each question identify the variables needed to obtain answers to it, and also the question number from the instrument providing that information. This will assure your supervisor of the relevance of each question in your research instrument.

Summary

A research proposal details the operational plan for obtaining answers to research questions. It must tell your supervisor and others what you propose to do, how you plan to proceed and why the chosen strategy has been selected. It thus assures readers of the validity of the methodology used to obtain answers accurately and objectively.

The guidelines set out in this chapter provide only a framework within which a research proposal should be written and assume that you are acquainted reasonably well with research methodology and an academic style of writing. The contents of your proposal are arranged under the following headings: preamble/introduction, the problem, objectives of the study, hypotheses to be tested, study design, the setting, measurement procedures, sampling, analysis of data, structure of your report, and problems and limitations.

Table 13.1 Developing a time-frame for your study

To be completed by

(Weeks or months)

Tasks (Any tasks which you consider important)	1	2	3	4	5	6	7	8	9	10	11	12	13	14	15
Proposal writing															
Insturment construction															
Data collection															
Coding															
Data analysis															
Report/first															
Report/final															
Typing															

The 'preamble' or 'introduction' introduces the main area of the study. To start with, the literature review is broad and then it gradually narrows down to the specific problem you are investigating. The theoretical framework should be a part of this section. The next section, 'the problem', details the specific problem under study. The research questions for which you are planning to find answers are raised in this section. 'Objectives of the study' contains your main and sub-objectives. Hypotheses, if any, should be listed in the section entitled 'hypotheses to be tested'. The logistical procedures you intend to follow are detailed under 'study design'. 'The setting' consists of a description of the organisation or community in which you plan to conduct your study. The procedure for obtaining information and the measurement of major variables are explained under 'the measurement procedure' section. How you will select your sample is described under 'sampling'. The procedure for data analysis is discussed under 'data analysis'. Anticipated problems in conducting the study and limitations with its design are described under 'problems and limitations'. The way you plan to structure your report is outlined under 'structure of the report'.

As an appendix to your proposal attach a copy of the research instrument.

Step VI

Collecting data

Considering ethical issues in data collection   **Chapter 14**

Considering ethical issues in data collection

Ethics

Stakeholders in research

Ethical issues concerning research participants
• Collecting information
• Seeking consent
• Providing incentives
• Seeking sensitive information
• The possibility of causing harm to participants
• Maintaining confidentiality

Ethical issues relating to the researcher
• Avoiding bias
• Provision or deprivation of a treatment
• Using appropriate research methodology
• Correct reporting
• Using information

Ethical issues regarding the sponsoring organisation
• The use of information

Summary

Ethics

All professions are guided by a code of ethics that has evolved over the years to accommodate the changing ethos, values, needs and expectations of those who hold a stake in the professions. Some professions are more advanced than others in terms of the level of development of their code of ethics. Some have very strict guidelines, monitor conduct effectively and take appropriate steps against those who do not abide by the guidelines.

Most professions have an overall code of conduct that also governs the way they carry out research. In addition, many research bodies have evolved a code of ethics separately for research. Medicine, epidemiology, business, law, education, psychology and other social sciences have well-established codes of ethics for research.

Let us first examine what we mean by 'ethics' or 'ethical behaviour'. According to the *Collins Dictionary* (1979: 502), ethical means 'in accordance with principles of conduct that are considered correct, especially those of a given profession or group'. The key words here, 'principles of conduct' and 'considered correct', raise certain questions:

• What are these principles of conduct?
• Who determines them?
• In whose judgement must they be considered correct?

Closely related questions are:

• Are there universal principles of conduct that can be applied to all professions?
• Do these change with time?
• Should they?
• What happens when a professional does not abide by them?

The subject of ethics needs to be considered in the light of these questions.

The way each profession serves society is continuously changing in accordance with society's needs and expectations and with the technology available for the delivery of a service. The ethical codes governing the manner in which a service is delivered also need to change. What has been considered ethical in the past may not be so judged at present, and what is ethical now may not remain so in the future. Any judgement about whether a particular practice is ethical is made on the basis of the code of conduct prevalent at that point in time.

As the service and its manner of delivery differ from profession to profession, no code of conduct can be uniformly applied across all professions. Each profession has its own code of ethics, though there are commonalities. If you want guidelines on ethical conduct for a particular profession, you need to consult the code of ethics adopted by that profession or discipline.

The question 'What are these principles of conduct?', is the most important one as it addresses the issue of the contents of ethical behaviour in a profession. As the code of conduct varies from profession to profession, it is not possible to provide a universal answer to this question. However, in research, any dilemma stemmed from a moral quandary is a basis of ethical conduct. There are certain behaviours in research—such as causing harm to individuals, breaching confidentiality, using information improperly, and introducing bias—that are considered unethical in any profession.

The next question is: In whose judgement must a code of conduct be considered correct? Who decides whether a particular practice is wrong? If a procedure is carried out wrongly, what penalties should be imposed? It is the overall body of professionals or government organisations that collectively develops a professional code of conduct and forms a judgement as to whether or not it is being followed.

As mentioned, most professions have established an overall code of ethics and also a code of ethics for conducting research in their respective fields. As this book is designed for researchers in the social sciences, we will examine ethical issues in general and issues that are applicable to most social science disciplines.

Stakeholders in research

There are many stakeholders in a research activity, so it is important to look at ethical issues in relation to each one of them. The various stakeholders are:

1 the participants or subjects;
2 the researcher; and
3 the funding body.

Participants or subjects to be considered as stakeholders depend on the profession. In the fields of medicine, public health, epidemiology and nursing, these are patients and non-patients who become part of a study, information collection exercise, experiment or drug trial, and service managers and planners who contribute information for a research study.

In the social sciences, the participants or subjects include individuals, groups and communities providing information to help a researcher to gain understanding of a phenomenon, situation, issue or interaction. In social work and psychology, participants include clients as well as non-clients of an agency from whom information is collected to find out the magnitude of a problem, the needs of a community or the effectiveness of an intervention; and service providers, social workers and psychologists, when they provide information for a study. In business, consumers as well as non-consumers of a product provide information about consumption patterns and behaviour. Managers participate in research activity examining different facets of management. In education, subjects include students, teachers and perhaps the community at large who participate in educational research activities.

Similarly, in any discipline in which a research activity is undertaken, those from whom information is collected and/or those who are studied by a researcher become participants in and/or subjects of, the study.

The researcher is in the second category of stakeholders. Anyone who collects information for a specific purpose, adhering to the accepted code of conduct, is a researcher and may represent any academic discipline.

The body funding a research activity falls into the third category of stakeholders. Most research is carried out using funds provided by business organisations, service institutions—government, semi-government, or voluntary—research bodies, and/or academic institutions. The funds are given for specific purposes. The funding body may have a vested interest in the research it is sponsoring, and this could affect the way the research is conducted or the way the report is written.

Each category of stakeholders in a research activity may have different interests, perspectives, purposes, aims, and motivations that could affect the way that research activity is carried out and the way results are communicated and used. Because of this, it is important to ensure that research is not affected by the self-interest of any party and is not carried out in a way that harms any party. Accordingly, ethical conduct in research concerning issues relating to different stakeholders should be examined under separate categories.

Ethical issues concerning research participants

Collecting information

One could ask, why should a respondent give any information to a researcher? What right does a researcher have to knock at someone's door or to send out a questionnaire? Is it ethical to disturb an individual, even if you ask permission before asking questions? Why should a person give you his/her time? Your request for information may create anxiety or put pressure on the respondent. Is this ethical?

But the above questions display a naive attitude. The author believes that if this attitude had been adopted, there would have been no progress in the world. Research is required in order to improve conditions. Provided any piece of research is likely to help society directly or indirectly, it is acceptable to ask questions, if you first obtain the respondents' informed consent. Before you begin collecting information, you must consider the relevance and usefulness of the research you are undertaking and be able to convince others of this also. If you cannot justify the relevance of the research you are conducting, you are wasting your respondents' time, which is unethical.

Seeking consent

In every discipline it is considered unethical to collect information without the knowledge of participants, their informed willingness, and expressed consent. Seeking informed consent 'is probably the most common method in medical and social research.' (Bailey 1978: 384). Informed consent implies that subjects are made adequately aware of the type of information you want from them, why the information is being sought, what purpose it will be put to, how they are expected to participate in the study, and of how it will directly or indirectly affect them. It is important that the consent should also be voluntary and without pressure of any kind. Schinke and Gilchrist write:

Under standards set by the National Commission for the Protection of Human Subjects, all informed-consent procedures must meet three criteria: participants must be competent to give consent; sufficient information must be provided to allow for a reasoned decision; and consent must be voluntary and uncoerced. (1993: 83)

Competency, according to Schinke and Gilchrist, 'is concerned with the legal and mental capacities of participants to give permission' (1993: 83). For example, some very old people, those suffering from conditions that exclude them from making informed decisions, people in crisis, people who cannot speak the language in which research is being carried out, people who are dependent upon you for a service, and children, are not considered to be competent.

Providing incentives

Is it ethical to provide incentives to respondents to share information with you? Some researchers provide incentives to participants for their participation in a study feeling this to be quite proper as participants are giving their time. Others think that the offering of inducements is unethical.

In the author's experience most people do not participate in a study because of incentives, but because they realise the importance of the study. Therefore, giving a small gift after having obtained your information, as a token of appreciation, is not unethical.

Seeking sensitive information

Information sought can pose an ethical dilemma in research. Certain types of information can be regarded as sensitive or confidential by some people and thus an invasion of privacy. Asking for this information may upset or embarrass a respondent. However, if you do not ask for the information, it may not be possible to pursue your interest in the area and contribute to the existing body of knowledge.

For most people, questions on sexual behaviour, drug use and shoplifting are intrusive. Even questions on marital status, income and age may be considered to be an invasion of privacy by some. In collecting data you need to be careful about the sensitivities of your respondents.

The dilemma you face as a researcher is whether you should ask sensitive and intrusive questions. In the author's opinion it is not unethical to ask such questions provided that you tell your respondents the type of information you are going to ask clearly and frankly, and give them sufficient time to decide if they want to participate, without any major inducement.

The possibility of causing harm to participants

Is the research going to harm participants in any way? Harm includes '... not only hazardous medical experiments but also any social research that might involve such things as discomfort, anxiety, harassment, invasion of privacy, or demeaning or dehumanising procedures' (Bailey 1976: 384).

When you collect data from respondents or involve subjects in an experiment, you need to examine carefully whether their involvement is likely to harm them in any way. If it is likely to, you must make sure that the risk is minimal. Minimum risk means that the extent of harm or discomfort in the research is not greater than those ordinarily encountered in daily life. If the way information is sought creates anxiety or harassment, you need to take steps to prevent this.

Maintaining confidentiality

Sharing information about a respondent with others for purposes other than research is unethical. Sometimes you need to identify your study population to put your findings into context. In such a situation you need to make sure that at least the information provided by respondents is kept anonymous. It is unethical to identify an individual respondent. Therefore you need to ensure that after the information has been collected, its source cannot be known. In certain types of study you might need to visit respondents repeatedly, in which case you will have to identify them until the completion of your visits. If you are doing research for someone else, you need to make sure that confidentiality is maintained by this party as well.

Ethical issues relating to the researcher

Avoiding bias

Bias on the part of the researcher is unethical. Bias is different from subjectivity. Subjectivity, as mentioned earlier is related to your educational background, training and competence in research, and your philosophical perspective. Bias is a deliberate attempt either to hide what you have found in your study, or highlight something disproportionately to its true existence.

Provision or deprivation of a treatment

Both the provision and deprivation of a treatment may pose an ethical dilemma for you as a researcher. When testing an intervention or a treatment, a researcher usually adopts a control experiment design. In such studies, is it ethical to provide a study population with an intervention or treatment that has not yet been conclusively proven effective or beneficial? But if you do not test a treatment/intervention, how can you prove or disprove its effectiveness or benefits? On the other hand, you are providing an intervention that may not be effective. Is this ethical? Is it ethical to deprive the control group of a treatment even if it may prove to be only slightly effective? And beyond the issue of control groups, is it ethical to deprive people who are struggling for life, of the possible benefit, however small it may be, which may be derived from a drug that is only under trial? As a researcher you need to be aware of these ethical issues.

There are no simple answers to these dilemmas. Ensuring informed consent, 'minimum risk', and frank discussion as to the implications of participation in the study will help to resolve ethical issues.

Using appropriate research methodology

A researcher has an obligation to use appropriate methodology in conducting a study. It is unethical to use a method or procedure you know to be inappropriate (e.g., selecting a highly biased sample, using an invalid instrument, or drawing wrong conclusions).

Correct reporting

To use an appropriate methodology, but to report the findings in a way that changes or slants them to serve your own or someone else's interest, is unethical.

Using information

How will the information obtained from respondents be used by the researcher? The use of information in a way that directly or indirectly adversely affects respondents is unethical. Can information be used to adversely affect the study population? If so, how can the study population be protected? As a researcher you need to consider and resolve these issues. Sometimes it is possible to harm individuals in the process of achieving benefits for organisations. An example would be a study to examine the feasibility of restructuring an organisation. Restructuring may be beneficial to the organisation as a whole but may be harmful to some individuals. Should you ask respondents information that is likely to be used against them? If so, the information may be used against them and if you do not, the organisation may not be able to derive the benefits of restructuring. In the author's opinion, it is ethical to ask questions provided you tell respondents of the potential use of the information, including the possibility of it being used against some of them, and you let them decide if they want to participate.

Ethical issues regarding the sponsoring organisation

Restrictions imposed by the sponsoring organisation

Most research in the social sciences is carried out using funds provided by sponsoring organisations for a specific purpose. The funds may be given to develop a program or evaluate it; to examine its effectiveness and efficiency; to study the impact of a policy; to test a product; to study the behaviour of a group or community; or to study a phenomenon, issue or attitude. Sometimes there may be direct or indirect controls exercised by sponsoring organisations. They may select the methodology, prohibit the publication of 'what was found' or impose other restrictions on the research that may stand in the way of obtaining and disseminating accurate information. Both the imposition and acceptance of these controls and restrictions are unethical, as they constitute interference and could amount to the sponsoring organisation tailoring research findings to meet its vested interests.

The use of information

How is the sponsoring body going to use the information? How is this likely to affect the study population? Sometimes sponsoring organisations use research as a pretext for obtaining management's agenda. It is unethical to let your research be used as a reason for justifying management decisions.

Summary

This chapter is designed to make you aware of the ethical issues to be considered when conducting research. How you resolve them depends upon you, and the conditions under which you are working.

Being ethical means adhering to the code of conduct that has been evolved over the years for an acceptable professional practice. For most professions, ethical codes in research are an integral part of their overall ethics, though some research bodies have evolved their own codes.

Ethical issues in research can be looked at as they relate to participants, researchers, and sponsoring organisations. With regard to participants, ethical considerations concern: collecting information; seeking consent; providing incentives; seeking sensitive information; the possibility of causing harm to participants; and maintaining confidentiality. With regard to the researcher, areas of ethical concern include: introducing bias; providing and depriving individuals of treatment; using unacceptable research methodology; inaccurate reporting; and the use of information. Ethical considerations in relation to sponsoring organisations concern restrictions imposed on research designs and the possible use of findings.

Step VII

Processing data

15

Processing data

Editing data

Coding data
- Developing a code book
- Pre-testing a code book
- Coding the data
- Verifying the coded data

Developing a frame of analysis
- Frequency distributions
- Cross tabulations
- Constructing the main concepts
- Statistical procedures

Analysing data

The role of computers in research

The role of statistics is research

Summary

If you were actually undertaking a research study, you would by now have either extracted or collected the required information. The next step is what to do with this information. How do you find the answers to your research questions? How do you prove or disprove your hypothesis if you had one? How do you make sense of the information collected? How should the information be analysed to achieve the objectives of your study? To answer these questions you need to go through a series of steps that constitute the core of data processing (Figure 15.1).

Irrespective of the method of data collection, the information collected is called *raw data* or simply *data*. The first step in processing your data is to ensure that the data are 'clean', i.e., free from inconsistencies and incompleteness. This process of 'cleaning' is called *editing*.

Editing data

Editing consists of scrutinising the completed research instruments to identify and minimise, as far as possible, errors, incompleteness, misclassification and gaps in the information obtained from the respondents. Sometimes even the best investigators can:

- forget to ask a question;
- forget to record a response;
- wrongly classify a response;
- write only half a response; or
- write illegibly.

In the case of a questionnaire, similar problems can crop up. These problems to a great extent can be reduced simply by:

- checking the contents for completeness; and
- checking the responses for internal consistency.

The way you check the contents for completeness depends upon the way the data has been collected. In the case of an interview, just checking the interview schedule for the above problems may improve the quality of the data. It is good practice for an interviewer to take a few moments to peruse responses for possible incompleteness and inconsistencies. In the case of a questionnaire, again, just by carefully checking the responses some of the problems may be reduced. There are several ways of minimising such problems:

- **by inference**—certain questions in a research instrument may be related to one another and it might be possible to find out the answer to one question from the answer to another. Of course you must be careful about making such inferences or you may introduce new errors into the data.
- **by recall**—if the data is collected by means of interviews, sometimes it might be possible for the interviewer to recall a respondent's answers. Again, you must be extremely careful.
- **by going back to the respondent**—if the data has been collected by means of interviews or the questionnaires contain some identifying information, it is possible to visit or phone a respondent to confirm or ascertain an answer. This is of course expensive and time consuming.

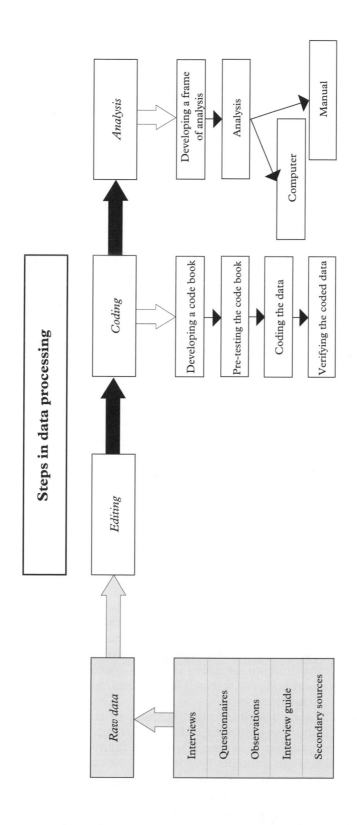

Figure 15.1 Steps in data processing

There are two ways of editing the data:

1 examine answers to one question or variable at a time; and
2 examine answers to all questions at the same time, that is, examine the responses given by a respondent.

The author prefers the second method as it provides a total picture of the responses, which also helps you to assess their internal consistency.

Coding data

Having 'cleaned' the data, the next step is to code it. The method of coding is largely dictated by two considerations:

1 the way a variable has been measured (measurement scale) in your research instrument; and
2 the way you want to communicate the findings about a variable to your readers.

For coding, the first level of distinction is whether a set of data is qualitative or quantitative in nature. For qualitative data a further distinction is whether the information is descriptive in nature (e.g., a description of a service to a community, a case history) or is generated through discrete qualitative categories. For example, the following information about a respondent is in discrete qualitative categories: income—above average, average, below average; gender—male, female; religion—Christian, Hindu, Muslim, Buddhist, etc.; or attitude towards an issue—strongly favourable, favourable, uncertain, unfavourable, strongly unfavourable. Each of these variables is measured either on a *nominal* or an *ordinal* scale. Some of them could also have been measured on a *ratio* or an *interval* scale. For example, income can be measured in $ (ratio scale), or an attitude towards an issue can be measured on an interval or a ratio scale. The way you proceed with the coding depends upon the measurement scale used in the measurement of a variable and whether a question is open-ended or closed-ended.

In addition, the type of statistical procedures that can be applied to a set of information, to a large extent, depend upon the measurement scale on which a variable was measured in the research instrument. For example, you can find out different statistical descriptors such as mean, mode and median if income is measured on a ratio scale, but not if it is measured on an ordinal or a nominal scale. It is extremely important to understand that the way you are able to analyse a set of information is dependent upon the measurement scale used in the research instrument for measuring a variable. It is therefore important to visualise—particularly at the planning stage when constructing the research instrument—the way you are going to communicate your findings.

If your aim is to describe a phenomenon, situation or program, or to write a case history, you do not need to go through the process detailed in the rest of the chapter. However, if you have many case histories and you want to analyse their contents by computer, you could use a specifically designed program such as *Ethnograph* or *Nudist*.

For analysis of data by computer, whether the data is quantitative or qualitative, it must be transferred to a form computers can interpret. Computers only understand binary language (language comprised of 0s and 1s). While it is beyond the scope of this book to explain this process, be aware that for computer analysis the data must be coded in numerical values. This process of converting information into numerical values is called *coding*.

The coding of raw data involves four steps:

1 developing a code book;
2 pre-testing the book;
3 coding the data; and
4 verifying the coded data.

Developing a code book

A code book provides a set of rules for assigning numerical values to answers obtained from respondents. Let us take an example. Figure 15.2 lists some questions taken from a questionnaire used in a survey conducted by the author in Western Australia to ascertain the impact of occupational redeployment on an individual. The questions selected should be sufficient to serve as a prototype for developing a code book, as they cover the various issues involved in the process.

To develop a code book to prepare data for computer analysis, it is important to know a little about the working of computers and the program being used. Briefly, there are three types of computer: mainframe, macro and personal. There are many statistical and other programs (software) that can be used with certain types of computer (depending upon the operating system for which the software is designed). The type of statistical procedures you can apply to your data are dependent not only upon the purpose of the analysis, the way you want to communicate your findings to the reader, and your knowledge of statistical procedures, but also on the capabilities of the software. For almost all programs, data is entered in a specified format. It is, therefore, important to know what format is required for your program.

There are two formats for data entry: 'fixed' and 'free'. In this chapter we will be using the fixed format to illustrate how to develop a code book. The fixed format stipulates that a piece of information obtained from a respondent is entered in a specific column. Each column has a number and the 'Col. no' in the code book refers to the column in which a specific type of information is to be entered. The information about an individual is thus entered in a row(s) comprised of these columns. Previously computers allowed for 80 columns per record (in each row) but nowadays one can enter the information about an individual in as many as 256 columns. If the information for an individual respondent exceeds 80 or 256 columns, you need to use the second record (or second row). As the width of a computer monitor is 80 characters, if you want to see the complete data set on your screen, you must restrict yourself to only 80 columns per record.

1 Please indicate:
a) Your current age in completed years: _____
  c) Your marital status: (Please tick)
    Currently married _____
    Living in a de facto relationship _____
    Separated _____
    Divorced _____
    Never married _____

2b If Tertiary/University, please specify the level achieved and the area of study (please specify all postgraduate qualifications)

Level of achievement	Area of study: e.g., engineering, accounting, etc.
Associate diploma	
Diploma	
Bachelor	
Graduate diploma	
Masters	
PhD	

11 What, in your opinion, are the main differences between your jobs prior to and after redeployment?

_____

_____

_____

12 We would like to know your perception of the two jobs *before* and *after* redeployment with respect to the following aspects of your job. Please rate them on a five-point scale using the following guide:

5 = extremely satisfied, 4 = very satisfied, 3 = satisfied, 2 = dissatisfied, 1 = extremely dissatisfied

Before redeployment					Areas	After redeployment				
1	2	3	4	5		1	2	3	4	5
					Job status					
					Job satisfaction					
					Motivation to work					
					Interest in the job					
					Self esteem					
					Professional competence					
					Peer interaction					
					Morale					
					Work environment					
					Social interaction					

Figure 15.2   Example of questions from a survey

For a beginner it is important to understand the structure of a code book (Figure 15.3), which is based on the responses given to the questions listed in Figure 15.2.

Col. No	Q. No	Variable name	Response pattern	Code
1	2	3	4	5
1–3	S. no	ID	Actual serial number	Code actual
4	Record no.	RNO	First record	1
			Second record	2
			Third record	3
5	1(a)	Age	20–24	1
			25–29	2
			30–34	3
			35–39	4
			40–44	5
			45–49	6
			No response	9
6	1(c)	MS	Currently married	1
			Living in a de facto relationship	2
			Separated	3
			Divorced	4
			Never married	5
			No response	9
	2(b)	TEDU	Assoc Dip.	1
			Diploma	2
			Bachelors	3
			Grad. Dip.	4
			Masters	5
			PhD	6
			Not applicable	8
			No response	9
7		TEDU1	Same as in TEDU	Code
8		TEDU2	Same as in TEDU	as in
9		TEDU3	Same as in TEDU	TEDU
		STUDY	Behavioural Sciences	1
			Business	2
			Economics/Commerce	3
			Communication	4
			Engineering	5
			Geography	6
			History	7
			Graphics	8
			Librarianship	9
			Nursing	10
			Performing Arts	11
			Secretarial	12
			Social Work	13
			Psychology	14
			Education	15
			Chartered Acct.	16

			Zoology	17
			Anthropology	18
			Social Sciences	19
			Public/Health Admin.	20
			English	21
			Audio–visual Aids Education	22
			Not Applicable	88
			No response	99
10–11	2(b)	STUDY 1	Same as in STUDY	Code
12–13		STUDY 2	Same as in STUDY	as in
				STUDY
14–15		STUDY 3	Same as in STUDY	
	11	DIFWK	Lack of job satisfaction	
			–current job	01
			–previous job	02
			Less responsibility	
			–current job	03
			–previous job	04
			Low morale	
			–current job	05
			–previous job	06
			Lack of recognition of hard work	
			–current job	07
			–previous job	08
			Skills irrelevant	
			–current job	09
			–previous job	10
			Repetitious nature	
			–current job	11
			–previous job	12
			Job more segmented	
			–current job	13
			–previous job	14
			Reduction in occup. status	15
			Greater involvement in total process	
			–current job	16
			–previous job	17
			More restricted duties	
			–current job	18
			–previous job	19
			Less flexibility	
			–current job	20
			–previous job	21
			More people contact	
			–current job	22
			–previous job	23
			Less people contact	
			–current job	24
			–previous job	25
			More responsibility	
			–current job	26
			–previous job	27

Better work environment
    –current job   28
    –previous job   29

Better work morale
    –current job   30
    –previous job   31

Working in a team
    –current job   32
    –previous job   33

Work as an individual
    –current job   34
    –previous job   35

Lack of job security
    –current job   36
    –previous job   37

Current job full–time   38

Better career prospects
    –current job   39
    –previous job   40

No commonality   41

Different working   42
conditions

Change in occup. status   43
(not specified)

High occup. level
    –current job   44
    –previous job   45

More job security in present job   46

More professional environment in
    –current job   47
    –previous job   48

Different skills to
learn in current job   49

Higher workload
    –current job   50
    –previous job   51

Less supervision in
    –current job   52
    –previous job   53

Current job more relevant to my training   54

Current job more rewarding   55

Better morale in current job   56

Greater variety of duties in
    –current job   57
    –previous job   58

Current job more
rewarding   59

Better morale in
    –current job   60

Less variety of tasks
in current job   61

			Fewer skills required in	
			−current job	62
			−previous job	63
			Change in job title	64
			Previous job very demanding	65
			Opportunity to use initiative in previous job	66
			Current job does not require initiative	67
			Different skills required in current job	68
			No career prospects	
			−current job	69
			−previous job	70
			More professional environment in current job	71
			Different skills to learn in current job	72
			Different working conditions	73
			Change in occup. status (change not specified)	74
			Change in job resp. (change not specified)	75
			Current job is more structured	76
			Now part of the team	77
			No change	78
			Irrelevant response	79
			Other	80
			Not applicable	88
			No response	99
16–17	11	DIFWK1	Same as in DIFWK	code as
18–19		DIFWK2	Same as in DIFWK	in
20–21		DIFWK3	Same as in DIFWK	DIFWK
22–23		DIFWK4		
24–25		DIFWK5		
			Extremely dissatisfied	1
			Dissatisfied	2
	12	BEAFTER	Satisfied	3
			Very satisfied	4
			Extremely satisfied	5
			Same as in BEAFTER	
26		JOBSTA	Same as in BEAFTER	Code as
27		JOBSTB	Same as in BEAFTER	in
				BEAFTER
28		JOBSATA	Same as in BEAFTER	Code as
29		JOBSATB	Same as in BEAFTER	in
				BEAFTER
			and so on	

Figure 15.3 An example of a code book

In Figure 15.3, column 1 refers to the column in which a particular piece of information is to be entered. Allocation of columns in a fixed format is extremely important as when you write a program you need to specify the column in which a particular piece of information is entered so that the computer can perform the required procedures.

Column 2 identifies the question number in the research instrument for which the information is being coded. This is primarily to identify coding with the question number in the instrument.

Column 3 refers to the name of the variable. Each variable in a program is given a unique name so that the program can carry out the requested statistical procedures. Usually there are restrictions on the way you can name a variable (e.g., the number of characters you can use to name a variable and whether you use the alphabet or numerals). You need to check your program for this. It is advisable to name a variable in such a way that you can easily recognise it from its name.

Column 4 lists the responses to the various questions. Developing a response pattern for the questions is the most important, difficult and time-consuming part of developing a code book. The degree of difficulty in developing a response pattern differs with the types of questions in your research instrument (open- or closed-ended). If a question is closed-ended, the response pattern has already been developed as part of the instrument construction and all you need to do at this stage is to assign a numerical value to each response category. In terms of analysis, this is one of the main advantages of closed-ended questions. If a closed-ended question includes 'other' as one of the response categories, to accommodate any response that you may not have listed when developing the instrument, you should analyse the responses and assign them to non-overlapping categories in the same way as you would do for open-ended questions. Add these to the already developed response categories and assign each a numerical value.

If the number of responses to a question is less than nine, you need only one column to code the responses, and if it is more than nine but less than 99, you need two columns (Column 1 in the code book). But if a question asks respondents to give more than one response, the number of columns assigned should be in accordance with the number of responses to be coded. If there are, say, eight possible responses to a particular question and a respondent is asked to give three responses, you need three columns to code the responses to the question. Let us assume there are 12 possible responses to a question. To code each response you need two columns and, therefore, to code three responses you need six columns.

The coding of open-ended questions is more difficult. Coding of open-ended questions requires the response categories to be developed first through a process called *content analysis*. One of the easier ways of analysing open-ended questions is to select a number of interview schedules/questionnaires randomly from the total completed interview schedules or questionnaires received. Select an open-ended question from one of these schedules or questionnaires and write down the response(s) on a sheet of paper. If the person has given more than one response, write them separately on the same sheet. Similarly, from the same questionnaire/schedule select another open-ended question and write down the responses given on a separate sheet. In the same way you can select other open-ended questions and write down the response(s). Remember that the responses to each question should be written on a separate sheet. Now select another questionnaire/interview schedule and go through the same process, adding response(s) given for the same question on the sheet for that question. Continue the process until you feel that the responses are being repeated and you are getting no or very few new ones.

Now, one by one, examine the responses to each question to ascertain the similarities and differences. If two or more responses are similar in meaning though not necessarily in language, try to combine them under one category. Give a name to the category that is descriptive of the responses. Remember, when you code the data you code categories, **not** responses *per se*. It is advisable to write down the different responses under each category in the code book so that, while coding, you know the type of responses you have grouped under a category. In developing these categories there are three important considerations:

1 The categories should be *mutually* exclusive. Develop non-overlapping categories. A response should not be able to be placed within two categories.
2 The categories should be *exhaustive*, that is, almost every response should be able to be placed within one of the categories. If too many responses cannot be so categorised, it is an indication of ineffective categorisation. In such a situation you should examine your categories again.
3 The use of the 'other' category, effectively a 'waste basket' for those odd responses that cannot be put into any category, must be kept to the absolute minimum because, as mentioned it reflects the failure of the classification system. This category should not include more than five per cent of the total responses and should not contain any more responses than any other category.

Column 5 lists the actual codes of the code book that you decide to assign to a response. You can assign any numerical value to any response so long as you do not repeat it for another response within the same question. Two responses to questions are repeated commonly: 'not applicable' and 'no response'. You should select a number that can be used for these responses for all or most questions. For example, responses such as 'not applicable' and 'no response' could be given a code of 8 and 9 respectively, even though the responses to a question may be limited to only 2 or 3. In other words, suppose you want to code the gender of a respondent and you have decided to code female = 1 and male = 2. For 'no response', instead of assigning a code of 3, assign a code of 9. This suggestion helps in remembering codes, which will help to increase your speed in coding.

To explain the coding process, let us take the questions listed in the example in Figure 15.2. We will take each question one by one to detail the process.

Question 1a

This is an open-ended quantitative question. In questions like this it is important to determine the range of responses—the respondent with the lowest and the respondent with the highest age. To do this, go through a number of questionnaires/interview schedules. Once the range is established, divide it into a number of categories. The categories developed are dependent upon a number of considerations such as the purpose of analysis, the way you want to communicate the findings of your study and whether the findings are going to be compared with those of another study. Let us assume that the range in the study is 23 to 49 years and assume that you develop the following categories to suit your purpose: 20–24, 25–29, 30–34, 35–39, 40–44 and 45–49. If your range is correct you should need no other categories. Let us assume that you decide to code 20–24 =1, 25–29 =2, 30–34 =3 and so on. To accommodate 'no response' you decide to assign a code of 9. Let us assume you decided to code the responses to this question in column 5 of the code sheet.

Question 1c

This is a closed-ended categorical question, i.e., the response pattern is already provided. In these situations you just need to assign a numerical value to each category. For example, you may decide to code 'currently married' = 1, 'living in a de facto relationship' = 2, 'separated' = 3, 'divorced' = 4 and 'never married' = 5. You may add 'no response' as another category and assign it with a code of 9. The response to this question is coded in column 6 of the code sheet.

Question 2b

In this question a respondent is asked to indicate the area in which he/she has achieved a tertiary qualification. As a person may have more than one qualification it is a multiple response question. In such questions both aspects of the question are to be coded. In this case, this means the level of achievement (e.g., Associate Diploma, Diploma) and the area of study (e.g., Engineering, Accounting). When coding multiple responses, decide the maximum possible number of responses to be coded. Let us assume you code a maximum number of three levels of tertiary education. (This would depend upon the maximum number of levels of achievement identified by the study population). First code the levels of achievement TEDU (TEDU: T = tertiary and EDU = education. The naming of the variable—'level of achievement'—in this manner is done for easy identification) and then the area of study, STUDY (the variable name given to the 'Area of study' = STUDY). In the above example, let us assume that you decided to code three levels of achievement. To distinguish them from each other we call the first level, TEDU1, the second, TEDU2 and the third, TEDU3, and decide to code them in columns, 7, 8, and 9 respectively. Similarly, the names given to the three areas of STUDY are STUDY1, STUDY2 and STUDY3 and we decide to code them in Columns 10–11, 12–13 and 14–15. The codes (01 to 23) assigned to different qualification are listed in the code book. If a respondent has only one qualification, the question of second and third qualification is not applicable and you need to decide a code for 'not applicable'. Assume you assigned a code of 88. 'No response' would then be assigned a code of 99 for this question.

Question 11

This is an open-ended qualitative question. To code this you need to go through the process of content analysis as explained earlier. Within the scope of this chapter it is not possible to explain the details but response categories have been listed based upon the responses given by 109 respondents to the survey on occupational redeployment in Western Australia. In coding questions like this, on the one hand you need to keep the variation in the respondents answers and on the other, you want to break them up into meaningful categories to identify the commonalities. Because this question is asking respondents to identify the differences between their jobs before and after redeployment, for easy identification, let us assume this variable was named DIFWK (DIF = difference and WK = work). Responses to this question are listed in Figure 15.4. These responses have been selected at random from the questionnaires returned.

A close examination of the above responses reveals that a number of themes are common, for example, 'learning new skills in the new job'; 'challenging tasks are missing from the new position'; 'more secure in the present job'; 'more interaction in the present job'; 'less responsibility'; 'more variety'; 'no difference'; 'more satisfying'. There are many similar themes that hold for both the before and after jobs. Therefore, we developed these themes for 'current job' and 'previous job'.

One of the main differences between qualitative and quantitative research is the way responses are used in the report. In qualitative research the responses are normally used either verbatim or are organised under certain themes and the actual responses are provided to substantiate them.

In quantitative research the responses are examined, common themes are identified, the themes are named (or categories are developed), and the responses given by respondents are classified under these themes. The data is then analysed to determine the frequency of the themes. It is also possible to analyse the themes in relation to some other characteristics such as age, education and income of the study population.

The code book lists the themes developed on the basis of responses given. As you can see, many categories may result. The author's advice is not to worry about this as categories can always be combined later if required. The reverse is impossible unless you go back to the raw data.

Let us assume you want to code up to five responses to this question and that you have decided to name these five variables as DIFWK1, DIFWK2, DIFWK3, DIFWK4 and DIFWK5. Let us also assume that you have coded them in Columns 13–14, 15–16, 17–18, 19–20 and 21–22 respectively.

Respondent 3
'Hours now FT: totally different skills required; deal with public; busier— more structured day and duties; now a part of the team instead of an independent worker.'

Respondent 20
'That I am happy and made to feel as though I am a valuable part of a team.'

Respondent 41
'This one is great, other one was lousy due to mismanagement, poor morale and feelings that dedication and hard work counted for nothing. Department of ... is well managed and morale is good and the graphic design work is fun and I am supported by my supervisors and subordinates.'

Respondent 48

'Before	After
15 hours per week	24 hours per week
Monday to Friday	Very satisfactory
On the go the whole time	Dealing with the public
No sitting	Dealing with severe psychiatric
No dealings with the public	patients can be very stressful.

Respondent 52
'No difference.'

Respondent 54
'My substantive position has been the same before and after the redeployment, but before the redeployment I was acting as Project Manager (level5) and after being redeployed I was assigned to programming duties (level e).'

Respondent 63
'This position has more day-to-day administration (it includes corporate services, finance, PR, IT, etc.')

Respondent 69
'Had to find my own job.'

Respondent 72
'The job I was doing I looked after the needs of a workshop where in this job I process files and deliver them.'

Respondent 78
'Challenging tasks are missing from the new position now that I am familiar with it. Many routine activities (that I have been glad to learn in terms of career development) but that I am becoming bored with. My previous job was much more difficult and interesting than this one.'

Respondent 79
'I am more secure in my present job and it is better paid as I work longer hours now. I only worked 6 1/2 hours as a tea attendant.'

Respondent 81
'My previous job required me to be involved in the whole area of government/community and non-government requiring assistance in relation to settlement needs of migrants. My current position does not provide job satisfaction, particularly in relation to the offenders that I currently deal with.'

Respondent 97
'Less responsibility, more specific job, restricted job.'

Respondent 105
'More variety, more flexibility, more responsibility in the present job, but less confidence, more caution and some resentment.'

Figure 15.4   Some selected responses to the open-ended question (no. 11) in Figure 15.2

Question 12

This is a very structured question asking respondents to compare on a five-point ordinal scale their level of satisfaction with various areas of their job before and after redeployment. As we are gauging the level of satisfaction before and after redeployment, respondents are expected to give two responses to each area. In this example let us assume you have used the name JOBSTA for job status after redeployment (JOB = job, ST = status and A = after redeployment) and JOBSTB for before redeployment, (JOB = job, ST = status and B = before redeployment). Similarly, for the second area, job satisfaction, you have decided that the variable name, JOBSATA (JOB = job, SAT = satisfaction and A = after) will stand for the level of job satisfaction after redeployment and JOBSATB will stand for the level before redeployment. Other variable names have been similarly assigned. In this example the variable, JOBSTA, is entered in column 23, JOBSTB in column 24 and so on.

Pre-testing the code book

Once a code book is designed, it is important to pre-test it for any problems before you code your data. A pre-test involves selecting a few questionnaires/interview schedules and actually coding the responses to ascertain any problems in coding. It is possible that you may not have provided for some responses and therefore will be unable to code them. Change your code book, if you need to, in the light of the pre-test.

Coding the data

Once your code book is finalised, the next step is to code the raw data. There are two ways of doing this:

- coding on the questionnaire/interview schedule itself, if space for coding was provided at the time of constructing the research instrument; or
- coding on separate code sheets that are available for purchase. Figure 15.8 shows the coded data on a coding sheet.

To explain the process of coding let us take the same questions that were used in developing the code book. We select three questionnaires at random from a total of 109 respondents (Figures 15.5, 15.6, 15.7). Using the code book as a guide, we code the information from these sheets on to the coding sheet (Figure 15.8). Let us examine the coding process by taking respondent 3 (Figure 15.5).

Respondent 3

The total number of respondents is more than 99 and this is the third questionnaire so 003 was given as the identification number which is coded in columns 1–3 (Figure 15.8). Because it is the first record for this respondent, 1 was coded in column 4. This respondent is 49 years of age and falls in the category 45–49, which was coded as 6. As the information on age is entered in column 5, 6 was coded in this column of the code sheet. The marital status of this person is 'divorced', hence 4 was coded in column 6. This person has a Bachelors degree in librarianship. The code chosen for a Bachelors degree is 3, which was entered in column 7. Three tertiary qualifications have been provided for, and as this person does not have any other qualifications, TEDU2 and TEDU3 are not applicable, and therefore a code of 8 is entered in columns 8 and 9. This person's Bachelors degree is in librarianship for which code 09 was assigned and entered in columns 10–11. Since there is only one qualification, STUDY2 and STUDY3 are not applicable, therefore a code of 88 was entered in columns 12–13 and 14–15. This person has given a number of responses to question no. 11 (DIFWK), which asks respondents to list the main differences between their jobs before and after redeployment. In coding such questions much caution is required. Examine the responses named DIFWK1, DIFWK2, DIFWK3, DIFWK4 and DIFWK5, to identify the codes that can be assigned. A code of 22 (now deal with public) was assigned to one of the responses, which we enter in columns 16–17. The second difference, DIFWK2, was assigned a code of 69 (totally different skill required), which is coded in columns 18–19.

1   Please indicate:
a) Your current age in completed years: ___49___
   c) Your marital status: (Please tick)
      Currently married _____
      Living in a de facto relationship _____
      Separated _____
      Divorced ___✓___
      Never married _____

2b   If Tertiary/University, please specify the level achieved and area of study. (Please specify all postgraduate qualifications).

Level of achievement	Area of study: e.g., engineering, accounting, etc.
Associate Diploma	
Diploma	
Bachelor	*Librarianship*
Graduate Diploma	
Masters	
PhD	

11 What, in your opinion, are the main differences between your jobs prior to and after redeployment?

"Hours -now F.T" , "Totally different skills required", "Now deal with public",
"Busier , more structured day and duties", "Now part of the team instead of
independent worker"

12 We would like to know your perception of the two jobs *before* and *after* redeployment with respect to the following aspects of your job. Please rate them on a five-point scale, using the following guide:

5 – extremely satisfied, 4 = very satisfied, 3 = satisfied, 2 = dissatisfied, 1 = extremely dissatisfied

Before redeployment					Areas	After redeployment				
1	2	3	4	5		1	2	3	4	5
			✓		Job status					✓
			✓		Job satisfaction					✓
			✓		Motivation to work					✓
			✓		Interest in the job					✓
			✓		Self esteem					✓
			✓		Professional competence				✓	
			✓		Peer interaction					✓
			✓		Morale				✓	
			✓		Work environment				✓	
				✓	Social interaction			✓		

Figure 15.5   Some questions from a survey—respondent 3

1   Please indicate:
a) Your current age in completed years: __45____
   c) Your marital status: (Please tick)
      Currently married __✓____
      Living in a de facto relationship _____
      Separated _____
      Divorced _____
      Never married _____

2b   If Tertiary/University, please specify the level achieved and area of study. (Please specify all postgraduate qualifications.)

Level of achievement	Area of study: e.g., engineering, accounting, etc.
Associate Diploma	
Diploma	
Bachelor	*Behavioural Sciences*
Graduate Diploma	
Masters	
PhD	

11 What, in your opinion, are the main differences between your jobs prior to and after redeployment?

_____*"Less Responsibility"*, *"More specific jobs"*_____
___*"Restricted scope".*_____

_____

12 We would like to know your perception of the two jobs *before* and *after* redeployment with respect to the following aspects of your job. Please rate them on a five-point scale using the following guide:

5 = extremely satisfied, 4 = very satisfied, 3 = satisfied, 2 = dissatisfied, 1 = extremely dissatisfied

Before redeployment					Areas	After redeployment				
1	2	3	4	5		1	2	3	4	5
			✓		Job status		✓			
			✓		Job satisfaction			✓		
			✓		Motivation to work		✓			
				✓	Interest in the job			✓		
				✓	Self esteem			✓		
				✓	Professional competence			✓		
				✓	Peer interaction				✓	
				✓	Morale		✓			
				✓	Work environment			✓		
			✓		Social interaction				✓	

Figure 15.6   Some questions from a survey—respondent 59

1   Please indicate:

a) Your current age in completed years: ___42___

    c) Your marital status: (Please tick)

        Currently married ___✓___

        Living in a de facto relationship _____

        Separated _____

        Divorced _____

        Never married _____

2b   If Tertiary/University, please specify the level achieved and area of study. (Please specify all postgraduate qualifications.)

Level of achievement	Area of study: e.g., engineering, accounting, etc.
Associate diploma	
Diploma	
Bachelor	*Social Work*
Graduate diploma	
Masters	
PhD	

11 What, in your opinion, are the main differences between your jobs prior to and after redeployment?

"My previous position required one to be involved in the whole area of Govt/ community and non-Govt. My current position does not provide job satisfaction, particularly in relation to the offenders that I currently deal with"

12 We would like to know your perception of the two jobs *before* and *after* redeployment with respect to the following aspects of your job. Please rate them on a five-point scale using the following guide:

5 = extremely satisfied, 4 = very satisfied, 3 = satisfied, 2 = dissatisfied, 1 = extremely dissatisfied

Before redeployment					Areas	After redeployment				
1	2	3	4	5		1	2	3	4	5
		✓			Job status		✓			
			✓		Job satisfaction		✓			
				✓	Motivation to work			✓		
			✓		Interest in the job		✓			
			✓		Self esteem		✓			
		✓			Professional competence		✓			
		✓			Peer interaction			✓		
			✓		Morale		✓			
			✓		Work environment		✓			
		✓			Social interaction		✓			

Figure 15.7   Some questions from a survey—respondent 81

Program

Programmer   Date

Labels: *Identification Number*, *Marital status*, *Study areas*, *Difference in work*, *Level of satisfaction*, *Record No. Age*, *Achievement level*

1	2	3	4	5	6	7	8	9	10	11	12	13	14	15	16	17	18	19	20	21	22	23	24	25	26	27	28	29	30	31	32	33	34	35	36	37	38	39	40
	0	0	3	1	6	3	8	8	0	9	8	8	8	8	2	2	6	9	7	7	7	8	3	8	5	4	5	4	5	4	5	4	5	4					
	0	5	9	1	1	3	8	8	0	1	8	8	8	8	0	3	1	8	7	7	8	8	8	8	2	4	3	4	2	4	3	5	3	5					
	0	8	1	1	1	2	8	8	1	3	8	8	8	8	1	7	0	1	8	8	8	8	8	8	2	3	2	4	3	5	2	4	2	4					

Figure 15.8 An example of coded data on a code sheet

DIFWK3 was assigned a code of 77 (current job more structure) and coded in columns 20–21. Similarly, the fourth (DIFWK4) and the fifth (DIFWK5) difference in the jobs before and after redeployment are coded as 78 (now part of the team instead of independent worker) and 38 (Hours-now full time), which are entered in columns 22–23 and 24–25 respectively. Question 12 is extremely simple to code. Each area of a job has two columns, one for before and the other for after. Job status (JOBST) is divided into two variables, JOBSTA for a respondent's level of satisfaction after redeployment and JOBSTB for his/her level before redeployment. JOBSTA is entered in column 26 and JOBSTB in column 27. For JOBSTA the code, 5, (as marked by the respondent) is entered in column 26 and the code for JOBSTB, 4, is entered in column 27. Other areas of the job before and after redeployment are similarly coded.

The other two examples are coded in the same manner. The coded data is shown in Figure 15.8. In the process of coding you might find some responses that do not fit your predetermined categories. If so, assign them a code and add these to your code book.

Verifying the coded data

Once the data is coded, select a few research instruments at random and record the responses to identify any discrepancies in coding. Continue to verify coding until you are sure that there are no discrepancies. If there are discrepancies, re-examine the coding.

Developing a frame of analysis

Although a framework of analysis needs to evolve continuously while writing your report, it is desirable to broadly develop it before analysing the data. A frame of analysis should specify:

- which variables you are planning to analyse;
- how they should be analysed;
- what cross tabulations you need to work out;
- which variables you need to combine to construct your major concepts or to develop indices (in formulating a research problem concepts are changed to variables—at this stage change them back to concepts);
- which variables are to be subjected to which statistical procedures.
  To illustrate, let us take the example from the survey used in this chapter.

Frequency distributions

Frequency distributions group respondents into the sub-categories into which variables have been divided. Unless you are not planning to use answers to some of the questions, you should have a frequency distribution for all the variables. Each variable can be specified either separately or collectively in the frame of analysis. To illustrate they are identified separately by the names used in the code book.

Frequency distribution is for the following variables:

- AGE;
- MS;
- TEDU (TEDU1, TEDU2, TEDU3—multiple responses, to be collectively analysed);
- STUDY (STUDY1, STUDY2, STUDY3—multiple responses, to be collectively analysed);
- DIFWK (DIFWK1, DIFWK2, DIFWK3 DIFWK4 DIFWK5—multiple responses, to be collectively analysed);
- JOBSTA, JOBSTB;
- JOBSATA, JOBSATB; and
- MOTIVA, MOTIVB.
- etc.

Cross-tabulations

Cross-tabulations analyse two variables, usually independent and dependent or attribute and dependent, to determine if there is a relationship between them. The sub-categories of both the variables are cross-tabulated to ascertain if a relationship exists between them. Usually, the absolute number of respondents, and the row and column percentages, give you a reasonably good idea as to the possible association.

In the study we cited as an example in this chapter, one of the main variables to be explained is the level of satisfaction with the 'before' and 'after' jobs after redeployment. We developed two indices of satisfaction:

1 satisfaction with the job before redeployment (SATINDB); and
2 satisfaction with the job after redeployment (SATINDA).

Differences in the level of satisfaction can be affected by a number of personal attributes such as the age, education, training and marital status of the respondents. Cross-tabulations help to identify which attributes affect the levels of satisfaction. Theoretically, it is possible to correlate any variables, but it is advisable to be selective or an enormous number of tables will result. Normally only those variables you think have an effect on the dependent variable should be correlated. The following cross-tabulations are an example of the basis of a frame of analysis. You can specify as many variables as you want.

SATINDA and SATINDB by:

- AGE;
- MS;
- TEDU;
- STUDY;
- DIFWK; and
- SATINDB.

These determine whether job satisfaction before and after redeployment is affected by age, marital status, education etc.

SATINDA by:

- SATINDB.

This ascertains whether there is a relationship between job satisfaction before and after redeployment.

Constructing the main concepts

There may be places in a research instrument where you look for answers through a number of questions about different aspects of the same issue, for example, the level of satisfaction with jobs before and after redeployment (SATINDB and SATINDA). In the questionnaire there were nine aspects of a job about which respondents were asked to identify their level of satisfaction before and after redeployment. The level of satisfaction may vary from aspect to aspect. Though it is important to know respondents' reactions to each aspect, it is equally important to gauge an overall index of their satisfaction. You must therefore ascertain, before you actually analyse data, how you will combine responses to different questions.

In this example the respondents indicated their level of satisfaction by selecting one of the five response categories. A satisfaction index was developed by assigning a numerical value—the greater the magnitude of the response category, the higher the numerical score—to the response given by a respondent. The numerical value corresponding to the category ticked was added to determine the satisfaction index. The satisfaction index score for a respondent varies between 9 and 45. The interpretation of the score is dependent upon the way the numerical values are assigned. In this example the higher the score, the higher is the level of satisfaction.

Statistical procedures

Regression analysis:

- SATINDA and SATINDB.

Multiple regression analysis:

- SATINDA with AGE, EDUCATION, MS.
- SATINDB with AGE, EDUCATION, MS.

ANOVA:

Similarly, it may be necessary to think about and specify the different variables to be subjected to the various statistical procedures.

Analysing data

Coded data can be analysed manually or with the help of a computer. If the number of respondents is reasonably small, there are not many variables to analyse, and you are neither familiar with a relevant computer program nor wish to learn one, you can manually analyse the data. However, manual analysis is only useful for calculating frequencies and for simple cross-tabulations. In addition, if you want to carry out statistical tests, they have to be calculated manually. However, the use of statistics depends upon your expertise and desire/need to communicate the findings in a certain way.

Be aware that manual analysis is extremely time-consuming. The easiest way to analyse data manually is to code it directly onto large graph paper in columns in the same way as you would enter it into a computer. On the graph paper you do not need to worry about the column number. Detailed headings can be used or question numbers can be written on each column to code information about the question (Figure 15.9).

To manually analyse data (frequency distributions), count various codes in a column and then decode them. For example, age from Figure 15.9, 5 = 1, 6 = 2. This shows that out of the three respondents, one was between 40–44 years of age and the other two were between 45–49. Similarly, responses for each variable can be analysed. For cross-tabulations two columns must be read simultaneously to analyse responses in relation to each other.

If you want to analyse data using a computer, you should be familiar with the appropriate program. You should know how to create a data file, how to use the procedures involved, what statistical tests to apply and how to interpret them. Obviously in this area knowledge of computers and statistics plays an important role.

ID	Age	MS	Education			Study area			Difference in work					Status		Satisfaction	
			1	2	3	1	2	3	1	2	3	4	5	Before	After	Before	After
03	6	4	3	8	8	01	88	88	22	69	77	78	38	5	4	5	4
59	6	1	3	8	8	01	88	88	03	18	77	88	88	2	4	3	4
81	5	1	2	8	8	13	88	88	17	01	88	88	88	2	3	2	4

Figure 15.9 Manual analysis using graph paper.

The role of computers in research

Knowledge of computers and the relevant programs is extremely important and ultimately saves time. Data can be analysed with the help of computers even for qualitative and descriptive information. Computers primarily help to save labour in manual data analysis and in the calculation of descriptive and inferential statistics. Computers are tools that increase your speed, handle complicated statistical and mathematical procedures, type the report, display the analysed data and present them graphically. They are designed to perform extremely complicated procedures, which otherwise could be very time-consuming, in an extremely short time.

While computers are designed to help, a good understanding of them is required to be able to benefit from them. The time spent in learning about computers is ultimately worthwhile, whether you classify yourself as a qualitative or quantitative researcher.

The role of statistics in research

The role of statistics in research is sometimes exaggerated. Statistics have a role only when you have collected the required information, adhering to the requirements of each operational step of the research process. Once data is collected you encounter two questions:

1　How do I organise this data to understand it?
2　What does it mean?

In a way, the answer to the first question forms the basis for the second. Statistics play a very important role in answering research questions.

From individual responses, particularly if there are many, it becomes extremely difficult to understand the patterns in the data, so it is important for the data to be summarised. Some simple statistical measures such as percentages, means, standard deviations and co-efficients of correlations can reduce the volume of data, making it easier to understand. In computing summary measures certain information is lost and therefore misinterpretation is possible. Hence, caution is required when interpreting data.

Statistics play a vital role in understanding the relationship between variables, particularly when there are more than two. With experience, it is easy to 'read' the relationship between two variables from a table, but not to quantify this relationship. Statistics help you to ascertain the strength of a relationship. They confirm or contradict what you read from a piece of information, and provide an indication of the strength of the relationship and the level of confidence that can be placed in findings. When there are more than two variables, statistics are also helpful in understanding the interdependence between them, and their contribution to a phenomenon or event.

Indirectly, knowledge of statistics helps you at each step of the research process. Knowledge of the problems associated with data analysis, the types of statistical test that can be applied to certain types of variable, and knowledge of the calculation of summary statistics in relation to the measurement scale used play an important role in a research endeavour. However, you can also carry out a perfectly valid study without using any statistical procedures. This depends upon the objectives of your study.

Summary

In this chapter you have learnt about processing data. Irrespective of the method of data collection, the information is called 'raw data' or simply 'data'. The processing of data includes all operations undertaken from when a set of data is collected until it is ready to be analysed either manually or by a computer. The process of data processing starts with data editing, which is basically 'cleaning' your data. The coding of data, which entails developing a code book, pre-testing it, coding *per se*, and verifying the coded data, is the next step. This chapter has discussed the process of developing a code book and provided a prototype for it. How to develop codes for open and closed-ended questions has been described in detail. The chapter has also taken you through the steps of coding data by taking an example from a survey.

Though the development of a framework of analysis continues until you have finished the report, it helps immensely in data analysis to develop this before you begin analysing data. In the frame of analysis the type of analysis to be undertaken (e.g., frequency distribution, cross-tabulation), and the statistical procedures to be applied should be specified.

Computers primarily help by saving labour. Their application in handling complicated statistical and mathematical procedures, word processing, displaying and graphic presentation of the analysed data save time and increase speed. Statistics are desirable but not essential for a study. The extent of their application depends upon the purpose of the study. Statistics primarily help you to make sense of data, 'read' it, explore relationships and interdependence between variables, ascertain the magnitude of an existing relationship or interdependence and place confidence in your findings.

16

Displaying data

Tables
- Structure
- Types of tables
- Types of percentages

Graphs
- The histogram
- The bar diagram
- The stacked bar chart
- The 100 per cent bar chart
- The frequency polygon
- The cumulative frequency polygon
- The stem-and-leaf display
- The pie chart
- The line diagram or trend curve
- The area chart
- The scattergram

Summary

Having analysed the data, the next task is to present findings effectively to readers. The main purpose of using data display techniques is to make the findings clear and easily understood. There are many ways of presenting information. The choice of a particular method should be determined primarily by your impressions/knowledge of your likely readership's familiarity with the topic and with research and statistics. If your readers are likely to be familiar with 'reading' data, you can use complicated methods of data display, otherwise it is wise to keep to simple techniques. Although there are many ways of displaying data, this chapter is limited to the more commonly used ones. There are many computer programs that can help you with this task.

Tables

Structure

Tables are the most common method of presenting analysed data. 'Tables offer a useful means of presenting large amounts of detailed information in a small space.' (*The Chicago Manual of Style* 1992: 321). It is, therefore, essential for beginners to know about their structure and types. Figure 16.1 shows the structure of a table.

A table has five parts:

1 **Title**—this normally indicates the table's number and describes the type of data it contains. It is important to give each table its own number as you will need to refer to the tables when interpreting and discussing the data. The tables should be numbered sequentially as they appear in the text. The procedure for numbering tables is a personal choice. If you are writing an article, simply identifying tables by number is sufficient. In the case of a dissertation or a report, one way to identify a table is by the chapter number followed by the sequential number of the table in the chapter—the procedure adopted in this book. The main advantage of this procedure is that if it becomes necessary to add or delete a table when revising the report, the table numbers for the chapter only, rather than for the whole report, will need to be changed.

The description accompanying the table number must clearly specify the contents of that table. In the description identify the variables about which information is contained in the table, for example, 'Respondents by age' or 'Attitudes towards uranium mining'. If a table contains information about two variables, the dependent variable should be identified first in the title. For example, Attitudes towards uranium mining [dependent variable] by gender [independent variable].

2 **Stub**—the sub-categories of a variable, listed along the Y axis (the left hand column of the table). According to *The McGraw-Hill Style Manual* (1983: 97), 'The stub, usually the first column on the left, lists the items about which information is provided in the horizontal rows to the right.' *The Chicago Manual of Style* (1992: 331) describes the stub as: '... a vertical listing of categories or individuals about which information is given in the columns of the table'.

3 **Caption or column headings**—the sub-categories of a variable, listed along the X-axis (the top of the table). In univariate tables the caption is

usually the 'number of respondents' and/or the 'percentage of respondents' (Tables 16.1 and 16.2). In bivariate tables it is the sub-categories of one of the variables displayed in the column headings (Table 16.3).

4 **Body**—the cells housing the analysed data.
5 **Supplementary notes or footnotes**—there are four types of footnote: source notes; other general notes; notes on specific parts of the table; and notes on the level of probability (*The Chicago Manual of Style:* 333). If the data is taken from another source, you have an obligation to acknowledge this. The source should be identified at the bottom of the table, and labelled by the word 'Source:' as in Figure 16.1. Similarly, other explanatory notes should be added at the bottom of a table.

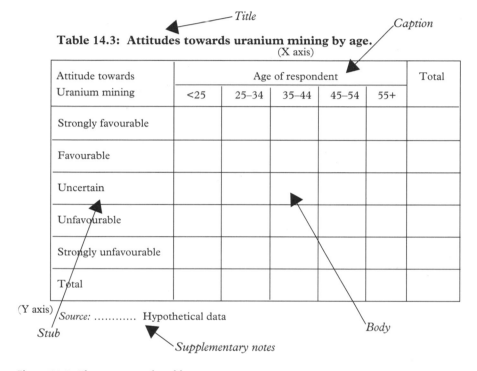

Figure 16.1 The structure of a table

Table 16.1 Respondents by age (frequency table for one population—hypothetical data)

Age	No. of respondents
<20 years	2 (2.0)
20–24	12 (12.0)
25–29	22 (22.0)
30–34	14 (14.0)
35–39	17 (17.0)
40–44	10 (10.0)
45–49	11 (11.0)
50–54	9 (9.0)
55+	3 (3.0)
Total	100 (100.0)

Note: Figures in parentheses are percentages

Table 16.2 Respondents by age (frequency table comparing two populations—hypothetical data

Age	Population A	Population B
<20	2 (2.0)	1 (0.6)
20–24	12 (12.0)	17 (10.9)
25–29	22 (22.0)	23 (14.7)
30–34	14 (14.0)	18 (11.5)
35–39	17 (17.0)	26 (16.7)
40–44	10 (10.0)	16 (10.3)
45–49	11 (11.0)	18 (11.5)
50–54	9 (9.0)	27 (17.3)
55+	3 (3.0)	10 (6.4)
No response	0 (0.0)	0 (0.0)
Total	100 (100.0)	156 (99.9*)

Note: Figures in parentheses are percentages (*rounding error)

Table 16.3 Respondents by attitude towards uranium mining and age (cross-tabulation—hypothetical data)

Attitude towards uranium mining	Age					
	<25	25–34	35–44	45–54	55+	Total
Strongly favourable	(0.0)★ 0 (0.0)@	(5.5) 2 (12.5)@	(14.8) 4 (25.0)@	(35.0) 7 (43.6)@	(100.0) 3 (18.6)@	16 (100.0)@
Favourable	(0.0)★ 0 (0.0)	(8.3) 3 (25.0)	(18.5) 5 (41.7)	(20.0) 4 (33.3)	(0.0) 0 (0.0)	12 (100.0)
Uncertain	(0.0)★ 0 (0.0)	(0.0) 0 (0.0)	(7.4) 2 (33.3)	(20.0) 4 (66.7)	(0.0) 0 (0.0)	6 (100.0)
Unfavourable	(14.3)★ 2 (20.0)	(19.4) 7 (70.0)	(3.7) 1 (10.0)	(0.0) 0 (0.0)	(0.0) 0 (0.0)	10 (100.0)
Strongly unfavourable	(85.7)★ 12 (21.4)	(66.7) 24 (42.9)	(55.6) 15 (26.8)	(25.0) 5 (8.9)	(0.0) 0 (0.0)	56 (100.00
Total	(100.0)★ 14	(100.0) 36	(100.0) 27	(100.0) 20	(100.0) 3	(100.0) 100

(★ = Column percentage; @ = Row percentage)

Types of tables

Depending upon the number of variables about which information is displayed, tables can be categorised as univariate (containing information about one variable, e.g., Tables 16.1 and 16.2), also called 'frequency tables'; bivariate (containing information about two variables, e.g., Table 16.3), also called 'cross-tabulations'; or polyvariate/multivariate (containing information about more than two variables, e.g., Table 16.4).

Table 16.4 Attitude towards uranium mining by age and gender (hypothetical data)

Attitude towards uranium mining	*Number of respondents*										*Total*		
	<25		*25–34*		*35–44*		*45–54*		*55+*				
	F	*M*	*F*	*M*	*F*	*M*	*F*	*M*	*F*	*M*	*F*	*M*	*T*
Strongly favourable	0	0	1	1	3	1	5	2	3	–	12	4	16
Favourable	0	0	1	2	3	2	3	1	0	0	7	5	12
Uncertain	0	0	0	0	1	1	2	2	0	0	3	3	6
Unfavourable	1	1	4	3	1	0	0	0	0	0	6	4	10
Strongly unfavourable	4	8	17	7	8	7	2	3	0	0	31	25	56
Total	5	9	23	13	16	11	12	8	3	0	59	41	100

Types of percentages

The ability to interpret data accurately and to communicate findings effectively are important skills for a researcher. For accurate and effective interpretation of data, you may need to calculate other measures such as percentages, cumulative percentages, or ratios. It is also sometimes important to apply other statistical procedures to data. The use of percentages is a common procedure in the interpretation of data. There are three types of percentage: 'row', 'column' and 'total'. It is important to understand the relevance, interpretation and significance of each. Let us take some examples.

Tables 16.1 and 16.2 are univariate or frequency tables. In any univariate table, percentages calculate the magnitude of each sub-category of the variable out of a constant number (100). Such a table shows what would have been the expected number of respondents in each sub-category had there been 100 respondents. Percentages in a univariate table play a more important role when two or more samples or populations are being compared (Table 16.2). As the total number of respondents in each sample or population group normally varies, percentages enable you to standardise them against a fixed number (100). This standardisation against 100 enables you to compare the magnitude of the two populations within the different sub-categories of a variable.

In a cross-tabulation such as in Table 16.3, the sub-categories of both variables are examined in relation to each other. To make this table less congested, we have collapsed the age categories shown in Table 16.1. For such tables you can calculate three different types of percentage: row, column and total.

- **Row percentage**—calculated from the total of *all* the sub-categories of one variable that are displayed along a row in different columns, in relation to only *one* sub-category of the other variable. For example, in Table 16.3 figures in parentheses marked with @ are the row percentages calculated out of the total of all age sub-categories of the variable age (16) in relation to only one sub-category of the second variable (i.e., those who hold a strongly favourable attitude towards uranium mining). In other words, one sub-category of a variable displayed on the stub by all the sub-categories of the variable displayed on the caption of a table. Out of those who hold a strongly unfavourable attitude towards uranium mining, 21.4% are under the age of 25 years, none is above the age of 55 and the majority (42.9%) are between 25–34 years of age (Table 16.3). This row percentage has thus given you the variation in terms of age among those who hold a strongly unfavourable attitude towards uranium mining. It has shown how the 56 respondents who hold a strongly unfavourable attitude towards uranium mining differ in age from one another. Similarly, you can select any other sub-category of the variable (attitude towards uranium mining) to examine its variation in relation to the other variable, age.

- **Column percentage**—in the same way, you can hold age at a constant level and examine variations in attitude. For example, suppose you want to find out differences in attitude among 25–34 year-olds towards uranium mining. The age category 25–34 (column) shows that of the 36 respondents, 24 (66.7%) hold a strongly unfavourable attitude whilst only two (5.5%) hold a strongly favourable attitude towards uranium mining. You can do the same by taking any sub-category of the variable age, to examine differences with respect to the different sub-categories of the other variable (attitudes towards uranium mining).

- **Total percentage**—this standardises the magnitude of each cell, that is, it gives the percentage of respondents who are classified in the sub-categories of one variable in relation to the sub-categories of the other variable. For example, what percentage do those who are under the age of 25 years and hold a strongly unfavourable attitude towards uranium mining, constitute of the total population?

It is possible to sort data for three variables. Table 16.4 (percentages not shown) examines respondents' attitudes in relation to their age and gender. As you add more variables to a table it becomes more complicated to read and more difficult to interpret but the procedure for interpreting it is the same.

The introduction of the third variable, *gender*, helps you to find out how the observed association between the two sub-categories of the two or more variables, age and attitude, is distributed in relation to gender. In other words, it helps you to find out how many males and females constitute a particular cell showing the association between the other two variables. For example, Table 16.4 shows that of those who have a strongly unfavourable attitude towards uranium mining, 24 (42.9%) are between 25–34 years of age. This group is comprised of 17 (70.8%) females and 7 (29.2%) males. Hence, the table shows that a greater proportion of female than male respondents between the ages of 25–34 hold a strongly unfavourable attitude towards uranium mining. Similarly, you can take any two sub-categories of age and attitude and relate these to either sub-category (male/female) of the third variable, gender.

Graphs

Statistical data not only requires careful analysis but also attractive display for easier understanding and communication. One of the choices you need to make is whether a set of information is best presented as a table, a graph or as text. The main objective of a graph is to present data in a way that is easy to understand and interpret, and interesting to look at. Your decision to use a graph should be based mainly on this consideration. 'A graph is based entirely on the tabled data and therefore can tell no story that cannot be learnt by inspecting a table. However, graphic representation often makes it easier to see the pertinent features of a set of data.' (Minium 1978: 45).

Graphs can be constructed for every type of data—quantitative and qualitative—and for any type of variable (measured on a nominal, ordinal, interval or ratio scale). There are different types of graph and your decision to use a particular type should be made on the basis of the measurement scale used. It is equally important to keep in mind the measurement scale when it comes to interpretation. It is not uncommon to find people misinterpreting a graph and drawing wrong conclusions simply because they have overlooked the measurement scale used in the measurement of a variable.

When constructing a graph of any type it is important to be acquainted with the following points:

- A graphic presentation is constructed in relation to two axes: horizontal and vertical. The horizontal axis is called the 'abscissa', or more commonly, the X axis, and the vertical axis is called the 'ordinate', or more commonly, the Y axis (Minium: 45).
- If a graph is designed to display only one variable, it is customary, but not essential, to represent the sub-categories of the variable along the X axis and the frequency or count of that sub-category along the Y axis. The point where the axes intersect, is considered as the zero point for the Y-axis. When a graph presents two variables, one is displayed on each axis and the point where they intersect is considered as the starting or zero point.
- A graph, like a table, should have a title that describes its contents. The axes should be labelled also.
- A graph should be drawn to an appropriate scale. It is important to choose a scale that enables your graph to be neither too small nor too large, and that your choice of scale for each axis results in the axes being roughly proportionate to one another. Sometimes, to fit the spread of the scale (when it is too spread out) on one or both axes, it is necessary to break the scale and alert readers by introducing a break (usually two slanting parallel lines) in the axes.
- As mentioned, the type of graph you choose depends upon the type of data you are displaying. For categorical variables you can construct only bar charts, histograms or pie charts, whereas for continuous variables in addition to the above, line or trend graphs can also be constructed. The number of variables shown in a graph are also important in determining the type of graph you can construct.

The histogram

A histogram consists of a series of rectangles drawn next to each other without any space between them, each representing the frequency of a category or sub-category (Figure 16.2). Their height is in proportion to the frequency they represent. The height of the rectangles may represent the absolute or proportional frequency or the percentage of the total. As mentioned, a histogram can be drawn for both categorical and continuous variables. When interpreting a histogram you need to take into account whether it is representing categorical or continuous variables. Figure 16.2a, b and c shows two histograms, using data from Tables 16.1 and 16.4.

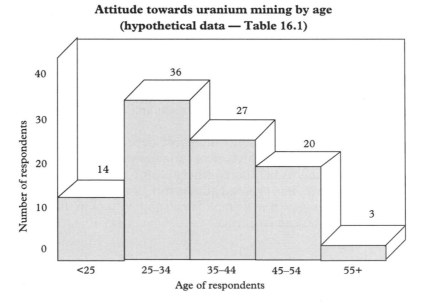

Figure 16.2a Two-dimentional histogram

Figure 16.2b Three-dimensional histogram

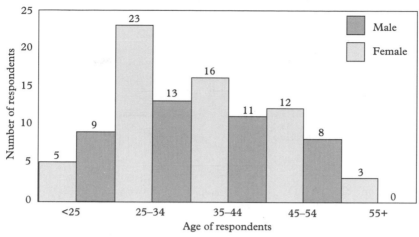

Figure 16.2c Two-dimensional histogram with two variables

The bar chart

The bar chart or diagram is used for displaying categorical data (Figure 16.3). A bar chart is identical to a histogram, except that in a bar chart the rectangles representing the various frequencies are spaced, thus indicating that the data is categorical. The bar diagram is used for variables measured on nominal or ordinal scales. The discrete categories are usually displayed along the X axis and the number or percentage of respondents, on the Y axis. However, as illustrated, it is possible to display the discrete categories along the Y axis. The bar diagram is an effective way of visually displaying the magnitude of each sub-category of a variable.

The stacked bar chart

A stacked bar chart is similar to a bar chart except that in the former, each bar shows information about two or more variables stacked onto each other vertically (Figure 16.4). The sections of a bar show the proportion of the variables they represent in relation to one another. The stacked bars can be drawn only for categorical data.

The 100 per cent bar chart

The 100 per cent bar chart is very similar to the stacked bar chart. The only difference is that in the former the sub-categories of a variable for a particular bar total 100 per cent and each bar is sliced into portions in relation to their proportion out of 100.

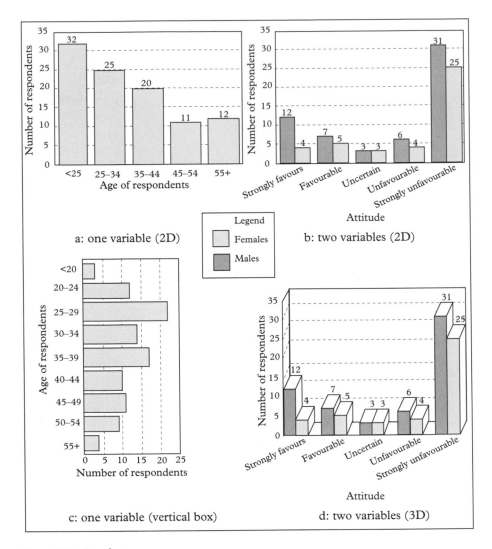

Figure 16.3   Bar charts

The frequency polygon

The frequency polygon is very similar to a histogram. A frequency polygon is drawn by joining the mid-point of each rectangle at a height commensurate with the frequency of that interval (Figure 16.6). One problem in constructing a frequency polygon is what to do with the two categories at either extreme. To bring the polygon line back to the X axis, imagine that the two extreme categories have an interval similar to the rest and assume the frequency in these categories to be zero. From the mid-point of these intervals, you extend the polygon line to meet the X axis at both ends. A polygon can be drawn using either absolute or proportionate frequencies.

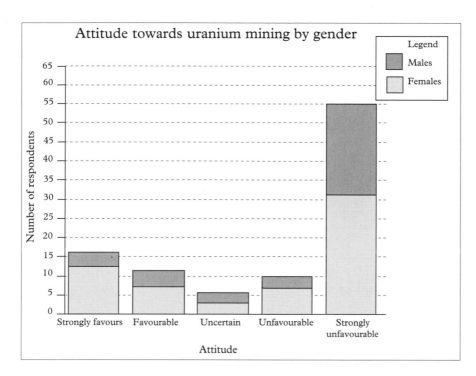

Figure 16.4 A stacked bar chart

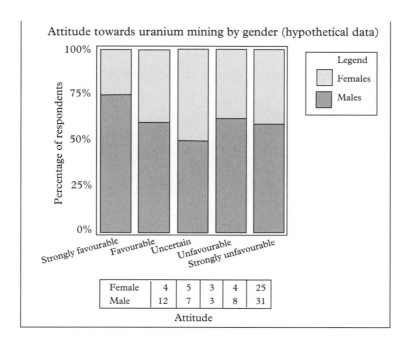

Figure 16.5 The 100 per cent chart

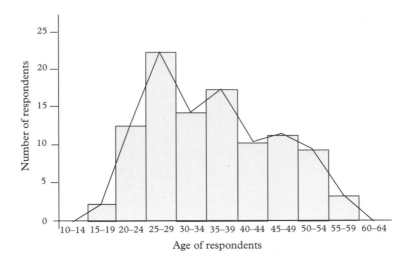

Figure 16.6   The frequency polygon

The cumulative frequency polygon

The cumulative frequency polygon or cumulative frequency curve is drawn on the basis of cumulative frequencies. The main difference between a frequency polygon and a cumulative frequency polygon is that the former is drawn by joining the mid-points of the intervals, whereas the latter is drawn by joining the end-points of the intervals because cumulative frequencies interpret data in relation to the upper limit of an interval. As a cumulative frequency distribution tells you the number of observations less than a given value and is usually based upon grouped data, to interpret a frequency distribution, the upper limit needs to be taken.

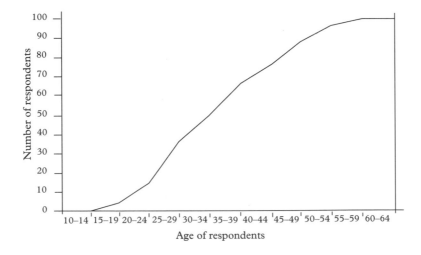

Figure 16.7   The cumulative frequency polygon

The stem-and-leaf display

The stem-and-leaf display is an effective, quick and simple way of displaying a frequency distribution (Figure 16.8). The stem-and-leaf for a frequency distribution running into two digits is plotted by displaying digits 0 to 9 on the left of the Y axis, representing the tens of a frequency. The figures representing the units of a frequency, i.e., the right-hand figure of a two digit frequency, are displayed on the right of the Y axis. Note that the stem-and-leaf display does not use grouped data but absolute frequencies. If the display is rotated 90 degrees in an anti-clockwise direction, it becomes a histogram. With this technique some of the descriptive statistics relating to frequency distribution, such as the mean, the mode and the median, can easily be ascertained, however, the procedure of their calculation is beyond the scope of this book. Stem-and-leaf displays are also possible for frequencies running into three or four digits (100s and 1000s).

1	89
2	000111222222334455555666777778889 9
3	00111222333333445555566677777889
4	1122233334445555566779
5	000113355667

Figure 16.8 The stem-and-leaf display

The pie chart

The pie chart is another way of representing data graphically (Figure 16.9), this time as a circle. There are 360 degrees in a circle, so the full circle can be used to represent 100 per cent, or the total population. The circle or pie

Figure 16.9 Two- and three-dimensional pie charts

is divided into sections in accordance with the magnitude of each sub-category, so each slice is in proportion to the size of each sub-category of a frequency distribution. The proportions may be shown either as absolute numbers or as percentages. Manually, pie charts are more difficult to draw than other graphics because of the difficulty in measuring the degrees of the pie/circle. They can be drawn for both qualitative data and variables measured on a continuous scale but grouped into categories.

The line diagram or trend curve

A set of data measured on a continuous interval or a ratio scale can be displayed using a line diagram or trend curve. A trend line can be drawn for data pertaining to both a specific time (e.g., 1975, 1976, 1977) or a period (e.g., 1965–69, 1970–74, 1975–79). If it relates to a period, the mid-point of each interval at a height commensurate with each frequency—as in the case of a histogram—is marked as a dot. These dots are then connected with straight lines to examine trends in a phenomenon. If the data pertains to exact time, a point is plotted at a height commensurate with the frequency. These points are then connected with straight lines. A line diagram is a useful way of visually conveying the changes when long-term trends in a phenomenon or situation need to be studied, or the changes in the sub-category of a variable is measured on an interval or a ratio scale (Figure 16.10). Trends plotted as a line diagram are more clearly visible than in a table. For example, a line diagram would be useful for illustrating trends in birth or death rates, and changes in population size.

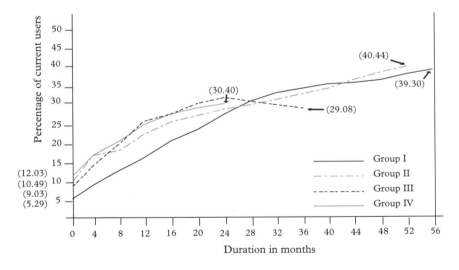

Figure 16.10　The line diagram or trend curve

The area chart

For variables measured on an interval or a ratio scale, information about the sub-categories of a variable can also be presented in the form of an area chart. It is plotted in the same way as a line diagram with the area under each line shaded to highlight the magnitude of the sub-category in relation to other sub-categories. Thus an area chart displays the area under the curve in relation to the sub-categories of a variable. For example, Figure 16.11 shows the number of male and female respondents by age.

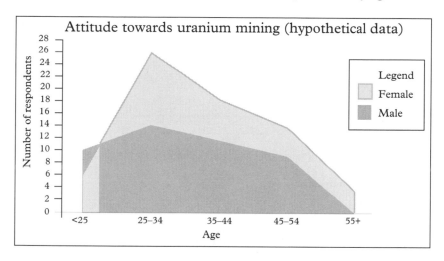

Figure 16.11   The area chart

The scattergram

When you want to show how one variable changes in relation to a change in the other variable visually, a scattergram is extremely effective.

For a scattergram, both the variables must be measured either on interval or ratio scales and the data on both the variables needs to be available in absolute values for each observation. Data for both variables are taken in pairs and displayed as dots in relation to their values on both axes. Let us take the data on age and income for ten respondents of a hypothetical study in Table 16.5. Figure 16.12 shows the relationship between age and income based upon hypothetical data. You cannot develop a scattergram for categorical variables.

Table 16.5   Age and income data

Respondent	Income	Age
A	25 500	24
B	46 000	50
C	30 500	36
D	55 000	45
E	27 000	29
F	35 000	38
G	40 000	37
H	52 000	48
I	47 000	41
J	38 000	47

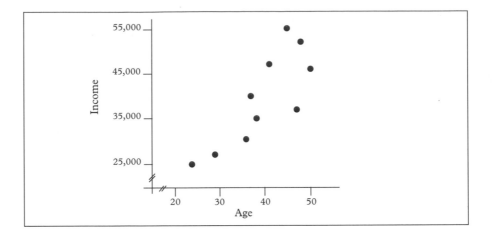

Figure 16.12   The scattergram

Summary

Research findings are usually conveyed to readers as text. However, there are times when a piece of information can be better communicated in the form of a table or graph. These do not give readers any more information but they communicate it clearly. What you use should be determined by what you think will be easiest for readers to understand. Tables have the advantage of containing a great deal of information in a small space, whilst graphs make it easy for readers to absorb information at a glance.

Ideally, a table should have five parts: title, stub, column headings or caption, body and supplementary notes or footnotes. Depending upon the number of variables about which information in a table is stored, there are three types of table: univariate (frequency), bivariate (cross-tabulation) and polyvariate.

To interpret a table, simple arithmetic procedures such as percentages, cumulative frequencies, or ratios can be used. You can also calculate simple descriptive statistical procedures such as the mean, the mode, the median, the chi-square test, the t-test, and the coefficient of correlation. If you have statistical knowledge, advanced statistics can be applied.

While there are many types of graphs, the common ones are: the histogram, the bar diagram, the stacked bar chart, the 100 per cent bar chart, the frequency polygon, the stem-and-leaf display, the pie chart, the line or trend diagram, the area chart and the scattergram. Which is used depends upon your purpose and the measurement scale used to measure the variable(s) being displayed. Some graphs are difficult to draw but several computer programs are capable of this.

Step VIII

Writing a
research report

Writing a research report   **Chapter 17**

17

Writing a research report

Research writing in general

The last step in the research process is writing the research report. Each step of the process is important for a valid study, as negligence at any stage will affect all of the study, not just that part. In a way, this last step is the most crucial as it is through the report that the findings of the study and their implications are communicated to your supervisor and readers. Most people will not be aware of the amount and quality of work that has gone into your study: while much hard work and care may have been put into every stage of the research, all readers see is the report. Therefore, the whole enterprise can be spoiled if the report is not well written. As Burns writes, 'extremely valuable and interesting practical work may be spoiled at the last minute by a student who is not able to communicate the results easily.' (1994: 229)

In addition to your understanding of research methodology, the quality of the report depends upon such things as: your written communication skills and clarity of thought, your ability to express thoughts in a logical and sequential manner and your knowledge base of the subject area. Another important determinant is your experience in research writing: the more experience you acquire, the more effective you will become in writing a research report. The use of statistical procedures will reinforce the validity of your conclusions and arguments as they enable you to establish if an observed association is due to chance or otherwise (i.e., whether a relationship is spurious or non-spurious) and indicate the strength of an association so readers can place confidence in your findings. The use of graphs to present the findings, though not essential, will make the information more easily understood by readers. Whether or not they are used depends entirely upon the purpose for which the findings are to be used.

The main difference between research and other writing is in the degree of control, rigorousness and caution required. Research writing is controlled in the sense that you need to be extremely careful about what you write, the words you choose, the way they are expressed and the validity and verifiability of the bases for the conclusions you draw. What most distinguishes research writing from other writing is the high degree of intellectual rigour required. Research writing must be absolutely accurate, clear, free of ambiguity, logical and concise. Assumptions as to the knowledge of readers about the study must be avoided. Bear in mind that you must be able to defend whatever you write should anyone challenge it. Do not use ornamental and superficial language. Even the best researchers make a number of drafts before writing up their final one, so be prepared to undertake this task. A research report should be written using the third person.

Referencing

The report should follow an academic style of referencing. There are four referencing systems from which to choose (Butcher 1992: 226) and you need to adopt the one that is acceptable to your university and academic discipline. 'The first of these is used in most general books, the second mainly in science and social science books; the third and fourth less frequently' (Butcher 1981: 167).

1 The short-title system;
2 The author-date system;
3 The reference by number system; and
4 The author-number system.

Writing a bibliography

Again, there are several well-established systems for writing a bibliography and your choice is dependent upon the preference of the discipline and university. In the social sciences some of the most commonly used ones are (*The McGraw-Hill Style Manual* 1983: 83):

• the Harvard system;
• the American Psychological Association system;
• the American Medical Association system;
• the McGraw-Hill system;
• the Modern Languages Association system; and
• the footnote system.

To learn about these systems and styles, consult the references provided at the end of this book or consult your library.

Developing an outline

Before you start writing your report, it is a good practice to develop an outline (chapterisation). This means deciding how you are going to divide your report into different chapters and planning what will be written in each one. In developing chapterisation, the sub-objectives of the study provide immense guidance. Develop the chapters around the main themes of your study. Depending upon the importance of a theme, either devote a complete chapter to it or combine it with related themes to form one chapter. The title of each chapter should be descriptive of the main theme, should communicate its main thrust, and should be clear and concise.

The first chapter of your report, possibly entitled, 'Introduction', should be a general introduction to the study, covering most of your project proposal and pointing out the deviations, if any, from the original plan. This chapter covers all the preparatory tasks undertaken prior to conducting the study, such as the literature review; the theoretical framework; the objectives of the study; study design; the sampling strategy; and the measurement procedures. An example is the study on foster care payments referred to in earlier chapters. This chapter could be written around the following sub-headings:

Chapter I   Introduction

- Introduction;
- The development of foster care;
- Foster care in Australia;
- Foster care in Western Australia;
- The department of community services;
- The out of home and community care program;
- Current trends in foster care placement in Western Australia;
- Becoming a foster carer;
- Foster care subsidies;
- Issues regarding foster care payment;
- Rationale for the study;
- Objectives of the study;
- Study design;
- Sampling;
- Measurement procedures;
- Problems and limitations; and
- Working definitions.

The second chapter should provide information about your study population. Here, the relevant social, economic and demographic characteristics of the study population should be described. This chapter serves two purposes.

1 It provides readers with some background information about the population from which you collected the information so they can relate the findings to the type of population studied.
2 It helps to identify the variance within a group, for example, you may want to examine how the level of satisfaction of the consumers of a service changes with their age, gender or education.

The second chapter, therefore, could be entitled 'Socio-economic–demographic characteristics of the study population' or just 'The study population'. This chapter could be written around the following sub-headings:

Chapter II   The study population

- Introduction;
- Respondents by age (Information obtained in response to the question on age should be presented here. Consult 'Writing about a variable' later in this chapter);
- Respondents by gender (Follow the above suggestions for the rest of the variables);
- Marital status of the study population;
- Ethnicity of respondents;
- Study population by number of children;
- Annual average income of the study population;
- Study population by type of dwelling;
- etc.

The title and contents of subsequent chapters depend upon what you have attempted to describe, explore, examine, establish or prove in your study. As the content of each project is different, these chapters will be different. As indicated earlier, the title of each chapter should reflect the main thrust of its contents.

The outline should specify the sub-sections of the chapter. These sub-sections should be developed around the different aspects of the theme being discussed in the chapter. If you plan to correlate the information obtained from one variable with another, specify the variables. Plan the sequence for discussion of the variables. In deciding this, keep in mind the linkage and logical progression between the sections. This does not mean that the proposed outline cannot be changed when writing the report—it is possible for it to be significantly changed. However, an outline, even if extremely rough, will be of immense help to you. Again, let us take the study on foster care payment as an example:

> **Chapter III   Attitudes towards the present level of payment for foster care.**
>
> - Introduction;
> - Attitudes towards adequacy of payment for foster care (Responses to questions on the adequacy of foster care payment should be presented here);
>   - adequacy by age (cross-tabulation, i.e., responses to the question on adequacy of foster care payment are examined in relation to the responses to questions on age);
>   - adequacy by marital status (cross-tabulation, i.e., responses to the question on adequacy of foster care payment are examined in relation to the responses to question on marital status);
>   - adequacy by income of the family (cross-tabulation—responses to the question on adequacy of foster-care payment are examined in relation to the responses to questions on income);
> - Aspects of foster care not covered by the payment;
> - Major costs borne by foster carers;
> - Effects of the current level of payment on the family;
> - Reasons for increasing the payment;
> - Proposed level of payment;
>   - proposed level by income of the family; and
> - Conclusions.
>
> Note: cross tabulations can be included for any variable where appropriate.

Writing about a variable

Having developed a chapter outline, the next step is to start writing. Though the way researchers organise their writing is extremely individualised, the following guidelines and format may prove helpful for beginners.

When writing about the information obtained in response to a question (variable), write as if you are providing answers to the following questions.

- Why did you think it important to study the variable? What effects, in your opinion, may this variable have on the main variable you are explaining? (*This is where you provide your own rationale for studying the variable*);
- In the case of a cross-tabulation, what relationships have other studies found between the variables you are analysing? (*This is where the literature review is integrated into the findings of the study.*)
- What did you expect to find out in terms of the relationship between the two variables? (*If you have formulated a hypothesis, state it here.*)
- What has your study found out? (*Provide the hard data from your study here, either as tables, graphs or text.*)
- What does the data show? (*Interpret the findings of your analysis.*)
- What conclusions can you draw? How do the conclusions drawn from your study compare with those from similar studies in the past? Does your study support or contradict them?
- What explanation can you provide for the findings of your study?

The above is only a suggested format for ordering your thoughts, not a list of sub-headings. You may wish to change the suggested order to make the reading more interesting. Below is an example of writing about a variable, 'Adequacy of payment for foster care' from Chapter 4.

- Why did you think it important to find out if foster care payments are adequate? What effects, in your opinion, could the adequacy or otherwise of payment for foster care have on the quality of foster care?
- What have other studies in your literature review said about the adequacy of foster care payments?
- What did you expect to find out from your study population in terms of their feelings about the adequacy of foster care payment? If you formulated a hypothesis, you should specify that here. For example, Hi = Most foster parents would consider the current level of foster care payments to be adequate.
- What did you find out about the adequacy of foster care payment? What proportion of the study population said it was adequate? What proportion said it was inadequate? Provide a table or graph showing the distribution of respondents by their response to the question regarding the adequacy of foster care payment.
- What does your data show about the adequacy of foster care payment? What are the main findings of your study? How do these findings compare with other studies you reviewed in your literature review? Does your study support or contradict them?
- What conclusions can you draw about the adequacy of the amount of payment for foster care?
- What explanation can you provide for the observed findings? Why do you think those who said that foster payments are either adequate or inadequate feel that way?

In the suggested format in writing about information obtained from questions, notice that the literature review is integrated with the findings and conclusions. The extent of the integration of literature with findings mostly depends upon the level at which you are writing your dissertation (Honours, Masters or PhD). The higher the level, the more extensive the literature review needs to be and the more careful and confident you need to be about your conclusions.

The suggested format is organised around the main themes of the study. There are other formats. Some researchers write everything under one heading, 'The findings'. This format is appropriate for a research paper, because it is short, but not for a research report or dissertation. Other writers follow the same order as in the research instrument, for example, findings are discussed under each question. The reader needs to continuously refer to the instrument for each question. This format does not explain the content at the beginning and should not be followed.

Summary

In a way, writing your report is the most crucial step in the research process as it communicates the findings to your research supervisor and readers. A badly written report can spoil all the hard work you have put into your research study.

Styles of research writing vary but all research reports must be written clearly and concisely. Furthermore, scientific writing requires intellectual rigour and there are certain obligations in terms of accuracy and objectivity. Reports can be written in different formats and this chapter has suggested one that research students have found to be helpful.

There are different ways of referencing and of writing a bibliography. You need to select the system that is acceptable to your discipline and university.

Before you start writing the research report, develop an outline of the different chapters and their contents. The chapters should be written around the main themes of the study, for which your sub-objectives are of immense help. When providing specific information about a variable, the write-up should integrate the rationale for studying the variable; the literature review; the hypothesis, if any; findings; conclusions drawn; and possible explanations for the findings.

The suggested format can be described as *thematic writing*—writing organised around the significant themes of your study. Within a theme the information is provided in an integrated manner following a logical progression of thought.

Appendix

Developing a research project—a set of exercises for beginners

Application is the essence of knowledge. However, there always remains a gap between theoretical knowledge and its application. It is only with practice that this gap can be narrowed. A beginner attempting to apply theorctical knowledge needs direction and guidance. This set of exercises has been developed with this belief. They are based upon the operational steps in the research process and can be applied to the development of any research project—or, more correctly, a research project can be developed while working through these exercises.

The main aim of these exercises is to provide a broad framework for developing the operational steps. For each operational step, there is at least one exercise. Within each exercise, questions are provided to stimulate awareness of issues relevant to the steps, to help you to think through procedures and to provide a framework for the development of an outline your study.

Answers to these questions and awareness of the issues that the exercises outline will put you in a position to complete the framework suggested for writing a research proposal (Chapter 13), and these will constitute the core of your research proposal.

It is important for a beginner to work through these exercises with considerable thought and care.

Exercise 1: Formulating a research problem

Selecting a research problem is one of the most important aspects of social research. Thinking through a research problem with care can prevent a tremendous wastage of human and financial resources. A research problem should be clearly stated and specific in nature. The feasibility of the study in terms of the availability of technical expertise, finances and time, and in terms of its relevance, should be considered thoroughly at the problem-formulation stage. In studies that attempt to establish a causal relationship or an association, the accuracy of the measurement of independent (cause) and dependent (effect) variables is of crucial importance and, hence, should be given serious consideration. If you have already selected a problem, you need not go through this process.

Start by identifying a broad area you are interested in. For example: a health, education or treatment program; migration, patient care, community health, community needs, foster care; or the relationship between unemployment and street crime. Chapter 4 of this book will help you to work through this exercise.

Step I Select a broad area of study that interests you from within your academic discipline. _____

Having selected an area, 'dissect' it in order to identify its sub-areas. For example, say your broad area of interest is migration. Some aspects or sub-areas of migration are:

- A socio-economic–demographic profile of immigrants.
- Reasons for immigration.
- Problems of immigrants.
- Services provided to immigrants.
- Attitudes of immigrants towards migration.
- Attitudes of host communities towards immigrants.
- The extent of acculturation and assimilation.
- Racial discrimination in the host country.

Perhaps you are interested in studying a public health program. Dissect it as finely as possible in order to identify the aspects that could be studied. List them as they come to you. For example:

- A socio-economic–demographic profile of the target group.
- The morbidity and mortality patterns in a community.
- The extent and nature of program utilisation.
- The effects of a program on a community.
- The effectiveness of a particular health promotion strategy.

Or your interest may be in studying delinquents. Some aspects of delinquency are:

• Delinquency as related to unemployment, broken homes or urbanisation.
• A profile of delinquents.
• Reasons for delinquency.
• Various therapeutic strategies.

Step II 'Dissect' your broad area of study into sub-areas as discretely as possible. Have a one-person brain-storming session.

1 _____

2 _____

3 _____

4 _____

5 _____

To investigate all these sub-areas is neither advisable nor feasible. Select only those sub-areas that would be possible to study within the constraints of time, finance and expertise at your disposal. One way to select your sub-area is to start with a process of elimination: delete those areas you are not very interested in. Towards the end it may become difficult but you need to keep eliminating until you have selected a sub-area that can be managed within your constraints. Even one sub-area can provide you with a valid and exhaustive study.

Step III From the above sub-areas, select a sub-area or sub-areas in which you would like to conduct your study.

1 _____

2 _____

3 _____

Step IV Within each chosen sub-area, what research questions do you hope to answer? Be as specific as possible.

Sub-area	Specific research questions to be answerd
1.	1. _____
	2. _____
	3. _____
	4. _____
	5. _____

2. 1. —————————————————————————————
    2. —————————————————————————————
    3. —————————————————————————————
    4. —————————————————————————————
    5. —————————————————————————————

3. 1. —————————————————————————————
    2. —————————————————————————————
    3. —————————————————————————————
    4. —————————————————————————————
    5. —————————————————————————————

The research questions to be answered through the study become the basis of your objectives. Use action-oriented words in the formulation of objectives. The main difference between research questions and objectives is the way they are written. Questions are worded in question form and objectives are statements referring to the achievement of a task.

Your main objective should indicate the overall focus of your study and the sub-objectives, its specific aspects. Sub-objectives should be numerically listed. They should be worded clearly and unambiguously. Make sure each objective contains only one aspect of the study.

Step V On the basis of your research questions, formulate the 'main' and 'sub-objectives' of your study.

Main objective (the main focus of your study):

_____

_____

_____

Sub-objectives (specific aspects of your study):

1 _____

   _____

2 _____

   _____

3 _____

   _____

4 _____

   _____

5 _____

Step VI Carefully consider the following aspects of your study.

Task	What is involved	Time needed	Approx. cost	Technical expertise needed	Gaps in knowledge and skills
Literature review					
Instrument construction					
Data collection					
Data analysis					
Draft report					
Final report					

Now you have developed the objectives of your study. Take some time to think about them. Be clear about what tasks are involved, what time is realistically needed and what skills you need to develop to conduct your study. Consider these areas carefully.

Step VII Double check:

- Are you really interested in the study?
  Yes ☐ No ☐ Uncertain ☐

- Do you agree with the objectives of the study?
  Yes ☐ No ☐ Uncertain ☐

- Are you certain you want to pursue the study?
  Yes ☐ No ☐ Uncertain ☐

- Do you have adequate resources?
  Yes ☐ No ☐ Uncertain ☐

- Do you have access to an appropriate study population?
  Yes ☐ No ☐ Uncertain ☐

If your answer to any of these questions is either 'no' or 'uncertain', re-examine the aspect carefully and make the appropriate changes.

What, in your opinion, is the relevance of this study to theory and practice? How will your study contribute to the existing body of knowledge, help the practitioners in your profession and assist in program development and policy formulation?

Relevance to theory: —————————————————

——————————————————————————

——————————————————————————

——————————————————————————

Relevance to practice: —————————————————

——————————————————————————

——————————————————————————

Exercise 2: Identifying variables

In the process of formulating a research problem, knowledge about variables plays an important role. Concepts are highly subjective as their understanding varies from person to person, and as such, they may not be measurable. Any concept, perception or imagination that can be measured on any one of the four measurement scales (nominal, ordinal, internal or ratio), is called a variable. It is important for concepts used in a study to be operationalised in measurable terms so that the extent of variation in a study population's understanding of them is reduced, if not eliminated.

Think how you will operationalise any concepts used in the objectives, research questions or hypotheses formulated: what are their indicators and how will they be measured?

The following table suggests how you might operationalise the concept of 'effectiveness', in relation to a health education program on AIDS. It lists the indicators of effectiveness, sets out the variables that measure the indicators, and describes the unit of measurement for the variables.

Concept	*Indicator*	*Variable (s)*	*Unit of Measurement*
Effectiveness	*Awareness* of AIDS	Extent of change in:	Change in the *proportion* of the population, before and after the health education program, with respect to:
	Knowledge about AIDS	Awareness Knowledge Practice	Awareness of, and knowledge about different aspects of AIDs.
	Use of contraceptives (*practice*)		Use of contraceptives for safe sex.

This exercise is designed to help you operationalise the major concepts used in your study. Refer to Chapter 5 for a discussion of variables.

Step I   Operationalise your concepts.

Objectives/research questions/hypotheses	Major concepts	Indicators	Variables	Unit of measurement

It is essential to develop a working or operational definition of your study population. For example, who would you consider to be a patient, an immigrant, a youth, a psychologist, a teacher, a delinquent or a Christian? Working definitions play a crucial role in avoiding ambiguities in the selection of a sample and help you to narrow your study population.

Step II Operationally define your study population.

_____

_____

_____

_____

Exercise 3: Constructing hypotheses

As discussed, some believe that one must have a hypothesis to undertake an investigation, however in the author's opinion, hypotheses, although they bring clarity, specificity and focus to a research problem, are not essential for a study. You can conduct a valid investigation without constructing a single formal hypothesis. On the other hand, you can construct as many hypotheses as you think appropriate. In epidemiological studies, to narrow the field of investigation, one must construct a hypothesis as to the probable cause of the condition to be investigated.

A hypothesis is a hunch, assumption, suspicion, assertion or idea about a phenomenon, relationship or situation, which you intend to investigate in order to find out if you are right. If it proves to be right, your assumption was correct, hence, you prove that your hypothesis was true, otherwise you conclude it to be false.

Disproving a hypothesis is as important as, or more important than, proving it. As a hypothesis is usually constructed on the basis of what is commonly believed to be right, your disproving it might lead to something new that has been ignored by previous researchers.

A hypothesis should be conceptually simple, clear and specific, capable of verification and of being expressed operationally.

There is a specific way of writing a hypothesis, with which you need to be familiar (refer to Chapter 6).

Step I   Construct your hypothesis or hypotheses for each sub-objective/ research question.

Objectives/research questions	Hypotheses to be tested
	1.
	2.
	3.
	1.
	2.
	3.
	1.
	2.
	3.

Exercise 4: Conceptualising a study design

All the previous exercises have been developed to help you decide *what* you want to find out *about*. The next step is to decide *how* to investigate. This includes deciding on a plan, procedures and methods. The details of your plan, procedures and methods become the core of your study design.

A study design describes the design *per se* and details the logistical procedures required to obtain information from the study population. It provides you with an overall plan for undertaking your study.

The issues raised in this exercise will help you to conceptualise your study design. Chapter 8 details the various types of study design.

Step I   Answer the following questions about your study.

1   Describe the study design that you propose to adopt to conduct your study. (Is it a cross-sectional, longitudinal, experimental or comparative study?)

2   Why did you select this design?

3   What, in your opinion, are the strengths of this design?

4   What are the limitations of this design?

5   Who constitutes your study population?

6   Will you be able to identify each respondent?

Yes ☐   No ☐

6a   If yes, how will they be identified?

_____

_____

_____

6b   If no, how do you plan to get in touch with them?

_____

_____

_____

_____

7 Do you plan to select a sample?

Yes ☐   No ☐

7a   In either case, explain the reasons for your decision.

_____

_____

_____

8 How will you collect data from your respondents (e.g., interview, questionnaire)?

_____

_____

8a   Why did you select this method of data collection?

_____

_____

8b   What, in your opinion, are its strengths and weaknesses?

Strengths:

_____

_____

Weaknesses:

_____

_____

8c   If you are interviewing, where will the interviews be held?

_____

8d   If you are using mailed questionnaires:
      i   From where will you obtain the addresses of potential respondents?

_____

_____

ii Are you planning to enclose a self-addressed stamped envelope with the questionnaires?

Yes ☐ No ☐

iii In the case of a low response rate, will you send a reminder?

Yes ☐ No ☐

iv If there are queries, how should respondents get in touch with you?

_____

_____

Step II On the basis of the above information, describe your study design (for further guidance, consult Chapter 8).

_____

_____

_____

_____

_____

_____

_____

_____

_____

_____

_____

_____

Exercise 5: Developing a research instrument

The construction of a research instrument is the first practical step in operationalising your study. It is the most important aspect of your research as it constitutes the input; the output, the findings and conclusions, are entirely dependent upon it. Items in an instrument are questions asked of respondents. Responses become the raw data that are processed. The famous saying about computers 'garbage in garbage out', also applies to research. To a large extent, the validity of the findings depend upon the quality of the raw data which, in turn, depends upon the research instrument you have used. If the latter is valid and reliable, the findings should also be valid and reliable.

The quality of a research instrument largely depends upon your experience in research. It is important for a beginner to follow the suggested steps outlined in Chapter 9.

The wording of your questions should be simple and without ambiguities. Do *not* ask leading questions or questions based upon presumptions. Double- barrelled questions should also be avoided.

The pre-test of a research instrument is an integral part of instrument construction. As a rule, the pre-test should not be carried out on your sample but on a similar population.

Step I Formulate questions by examining your sub-objectives/ research questions/hypotheses; by specifying what information you require to address them; by identifying the required variables; and by formulating questions to obtain the required information.

Step II Write down these questions on a piece of paper, giving particular attention to the following:

- the wording of questions;
- the order of questions; and
- the relevance of each question.

Specific objectives/ research questions/ hypotheses	Specifically what information do you require?	Identify the required variables	Formulate questions

Step III If you are developing a questionnaire, incorporate interactive statements at appropriate places.

Step IV After developing the first draft of your research instrument answer the questions yourself, that is, interview yourself. If you are unable to answer a question, re-examine it.

Step V Once you are satisfied with the instrument, select a few respondents from a population similar to the one you are going to study and pre-test it. The purpose of the pre-test/field-test is not to obtain information but to uncover problems with the instrument. If the instrument is an interview schedule, interview the pre-test respondents to find out if they understand the questions. If a question is not understood, find out what the respondent did not understand. If the same problem is identified by others, change the wording. If your instrument is a questionnaire, ask the pre-test respondents to go through the questions with the aim of identifying any questions that are difficult to understand. It may be necessary to change the wording of questions with which pre-test respondents have difficulties

Step VI When you are sure that the instrument is free from ambiguities and other problems, finalise it.

Step VII Having developed the instrument, take a piece of paper and draw two columns. In one column write each sub-objective, research question and hypothesis separately, and in the other, write the question number(s) that provide information for these objectives, research questions or hypotheses. In other words, make each question match the objective for which it provides information. If a question cannot be linked to a specific objective, research question or hypothesis, examine why it was included.

Step VIII Prepare the final draft of your research instrument.

Step IX If you plan to use a computer for data analysis, you may provide space on the instrument for coding the data.

Exercise 6: Selecting a sample

The accuracy of your research results also depends upon the way in which you select your sample. The basic objective of any sampling design is to minimise, within the limitation of cost, any difference between the values obtained from your sample and those prevalent in the population.

The underlying premise in sampling is that if a relatively small number of units is scientifically selected, it can provide, with a sufficiently high degree of probability, a true reflection of the sampling population that is being studied.

Sampling theory is guided by two principles:

the avoidance of bias in the selection of a sample; and
the attainment of maximum precision for a given outlay of resources.

You can select a probability or a non-probability sample. Both have advantages and disadvantages and both are appropriate for certain situations. But whatever sampling design you choose, make sure you take steps to avoid introducing bias.

For details on sampling designs, refer to Chapter 12.

Step I   Answer the following about your sampling design.

1 What is the total size of your study population?

☐ _____   ☐ Unknown

2 Do you want to select a sample?

Yes ☐   No ☐

2a If yes, indicate your sample size? _____

3 How will you select your sample?

_____

_____

_____

4 Why did you select this design? (What are its strengths?)

_____

_____

_____

5 In your opinion, what are the limitations of this design?

_____

_____

_____

_____

Step II On the basis of the answers to the above questions, write about your sampling design as described in Chapter 13, writing a research proposal.

_____

_____

_____

_____

_____

_____

_____

Exercise 7: Data analysis and developing a frame of analysis

In general terms describe the strategy you plan to use for data analysis. Specify whether the data will be analysed manually or by computer. For computer analysis you need to identify the program you plan to use.

You should also specify the type of analysis you plan to carry out, that is, frequency distributions, cross-tabulations, regression analysis or analysis of variance. It is also important to plan which variables will be subjected to which type of statistical procedure.

If you have used certain concepts in your study, how will these concepts be operationalised? For example, if you were measuring the effectiveness of a health program, how would the responses to the various questions be combined to ascertain effectiveness? Keep in mind that when you actually carry out data analysis, you may develop new ideas on how to improve the analysis of data. Refer to Chapter 15 for details.

Step I   Think through the following issues:

1   If you are planning to use a computer for data analysis, what software will you use?

_____

2   Which variables will you subject to frequency distribution analysis?

_____

_____

_____

_____

3   Which variables will be cross-tabulated?

_____

_____

_____

_____

_____

4 Which variables will be subjected to which statistical procedures (e.g., regression analysis, ANOVA, factor analysis)?

_____

_____

_____

_____

5 How do you plan to construct the major variables (e.g., satisfaction index, effectiveness)?

_____

_____

_____

_____

Exercise 8: Developing an outline of your chapters

Although each operational step is important, in a way, writing the report is the most crucial as it tells others about the outcome of your study: it is the outcome of the hard work you have put into your study and is the only thing visible to readers. Hence you could lose even the most valuable work if your report is not well written.

The quality of your report depends upon many things: your writing skills, the clarity of your thoughts and their logical expression, your knowledge of the subject, and your experience in research writing.

Developing an outline for the structure of the report is extremely useful. As a beginner it is important that you think through carefully the contents of your report, organise them around the main themes of your study, and ensure that the various aspects of a theme are well integrated and follow a logical progression.

This exercise is designed to help you to organise your thoughts with respect to writing your research report. You should, as far as possible, attempt to place the various aspects of your report into chapter headings, even if these are very tentative. However, for this exercise just develop headings for your chapters. When you actually start writing the contents of each chapter can be developed and adjusted in greater detail. Consult Chapter 17 for more details.

1 What are the main themes of your study?

_____

_____

_____

_____

_____

_____

2 Develop chapter headings under which the above themes will be organised in writing your report.

_____

_____

_____

_____

_____

_____

References

Ackroyd, Stephen and John Hughes, 1992, *Data Collection in Context*, New York, Longman.

Alwin, Duane F. (ed.), 1978, *Survey Design and Analysis—Current Issues*, London, New York.

Babbie, Earl, 1989, *The Practice of Social Research*, California, Wadesworth Publishing Company.

Babbie, Earl, 1990, *Survey Research Methods* (2nd ed.), California, Wadesworth Publishing Company.

Bailey, Kenneth D., 1978, *Methods of Social Research*, (3rd ed.) New York, The Free Press.

Barton, Ruth, 1988, *Understanding Social Statistics—An Introduction to Descriptive Statistics*, Editorial/Publication Unit, Division of Arts, Education and Social Sciences, Curtin University of Technology.

Black, James A. and Dean J. Champion, 1976, *Methods and Issues in Social Research*, New York, John Wiley and Sons, Inc.

Bradburn, M. Norman and Seymour Sudman, 1979, *Improving Interview Method and Questionnaire Design*, London, Jossey-Bass Publishers.

Brinberg, David and Joseph E. McGreth, 1985, *Validity and the Research Process*, Beverly Hills, Sage Publications.

Bulmer, Martin (ed.), 1977, *Sociological Research Methods—An Introduction*, London, The MacMillian Press Ltd.

Burns, Robert B., 1994, *Introduction to Research Methods* (2nd ed.), Melbourne, Longman Cheshire.

Butcher, Judith, 1981, *Copy-Editing, The Cambridge Handbook for Editors, Authors and Publishers*, (3rd ed.), Cambridge, Cambridge University Press.

The Chicago Manual of Style, (14th ed.), 1993, Chicago and London, The University of Chicago Press.

Cohen, Morris R. and Ernest Nagel, 1966, *An Introduction to Logic and Scientific Methods*, London, Routledge and Kegan Paul Ltd.

Collins Dictionary of the English Language, 1979, Sydney, Collins.

Cozby, C. Paul, 1985, *Methods in Behavioral Research*, London, Mayfield Publication Company.

de Vas, D.A., 1985, *Survey in Social Research*, Sydney, Allen and Unwin.

Dixon, Beverly and Gary Bouma, 1984, *The Research Process*, Melbourne, Oxford University Press.

Duncan, Otis Dudley, 1984, *Notes on Social Measurement—Historical and Critical*, New York, Russell Sage Foundation.

Festinger, Leon and Daniel Katz (eds), 1966, *Research Methods in Behavioral Sciences*, New York, Holt, Rinehart and Winston.

Grinnell, Richard Jr. (ed.), 1988, *Social Work Research and Evaluation*, Illinois, F. E. Peacock Publishers.

Grinnell, Richard Jr. (ed.) 1993, *Social Work, Research and Evaluation*, (4th ed.), Illinois, F.E. Peacock Publishers.

Hakim, Catherine, 1987, *Research Design—Strategies and Choices in the Design of Social Research*, London, Allen and Unwin.

Hawe, Penelope, Deirdre Degeling and Jane Hall, 1992, *Evaluating Health Promotion*, Sydney, Maclennan+petty.

Hessler, Richard M., 1992, *Social Research Methods*, New York, West Publishing Company.

Kerlinger, Fred N., 1973, *Foundations of Behavioural Research*, (2nd ed.), Holt, Rinehard and Winston, Inc., New York.

Kerlinger, Fred N., 1979, *Behavioral Research—A Conceptual Approach*, Sydney, Holt, Rinehart and Winston.

Kerlinger, Fred N., 1986, *Foundations of Behavioral Research*, (3rd ed.) New York, Holt, Rinehart and Winston.

Leary, Mark R., 1991, *Introduction to Behavioral Research Methods*, California, Wadesworth Publication Company.

Longyear, Marie (ed.), 1983, *The McGraw Hill Style Manual*, A Concise Guide for Writers and Editors, McGraw Hill.

Lundberg, George A., 1942, *Social Research—A Study in Methods of Gathering Data* (2nd ed.), New York, Longmans, Green and Co.

Martin, David W., 1985, *Doing Psychological Experiments*, (2nd ed.), Monterey California, Brooks/Cole Publishing Company.

Minium, Edward W., 1978, *Statistical Reasoning in Psychology and Education*, (2nd ed.), New York, John Wiley and Sons.

Moser, C.A. and G. Kalton, 1989, *Survey Methods in Social Investigation*, England, Gower.

Nachmias, David and Clara Nachmias, 1987, *Research Methods in Social Sciences*, New York, St. Martin's Press.

Poincaré, 1952, *Science and Hypothesis*, New York, Dover Publications.

Powers, Gerald T., Thomas M. Meenaghan and Beverley G. Twoomey, 1985, *Practice Focused Research: Integrating Human Practice and Research*, Englewood Cliffs, NJ, Prentice Hall.

Rohlf, F. James and Robert R. Sokal, 1969, *Statistical Tables*, San Francisco, W.H. Freeman and Company.

Schinke, Steven P. and Gilchrist, Lewayne, 1993, 'Arrics in Research' in R.M. Grinnell (ed.) *Social Work, Research and Evaluation* (4th ed.), Illinois, F.E. Peacock Publishers.

Selltiz, Jahoda, Deutsch and Cook, 1964, *Research Methods In Social Relations*, (revised), New York, Holt, Rinehart and Winston.

Siegel, Sidney, 1956, *Nonparametric Statistics for the Behavioral Sciences*, Sydney, McGraw-Hill Book Company Inc.

Simon, Julian L., 1969, *Basic Research Methods in Social Sciences—The Art of Empirical Investigation*, New York, Random House.

Smith, Herman W., 1991, *Strategies of Social Research* (3rd ed.), Holt, Rinehart and Winston.

Steven, S.S., 1951, 'Mathematics, Measurement, and Psychophysics' in *Handbook of Experimental Psychology*, S. S. Steven (ed.), New York, Wiley.

Thyer, Bruce A., 'Single-systems Research Design' in R.M. Grinnell (ed.), *Social Work, Research and Evaluation*, (4th ed.), Illinois, F.E. Peacock Publishers.

Yegidis, Bonnie and Robert Weinback, 1991, *Research Methods for Social Workers*, New York, Longman.

Young, Pauline V., 1966, *Scientific Social Survey Research*, (4th ed.), Englewood Cliffs, Prentice Hall Inc.

Index